THE FABRIC OF CHARACTER

The Fabric of Character

ARISTOTLE'S THEORY OF VIRTUE

Nancy Sherman

CLARENDON PRESS · OXFORD
1989

Oxford University Press, Walton Street, Oxford OX2 6DP
Oxford New York Toronto
Delhi Bombay Calcutta Madras Karachi
Petaling Jaya Singapore Hong Kong Tokyo
Nairobi Dar es Salaam Cape Town
Melbourne Auckland
and associated companies in
Berlin Ibadan

Oxford is a trade mark of Oxford University Press

Published in the United States by
Oxford University Press, New York

© Nancy Sherman 1989

British Library Cataloguing in Publication Data
Sherman, Nancy
The fabric of character: Aristotle's
theory of virtue.
1. Ethics. Theories of Aristotle, 384–322
B.C.
I. Title
170'.92'4
ISBN 0-19-824451-7

Library of Congress Cataloging in Publication Data
Sherman, Nancy, 1951–
The fabric of character: Aristotle's theory
of virtue / Nancy Sherman.
Includes index.
1. Aristotle—Ethics. 2. Virtue—History.
3. Character—History.
I. Title.
B491.V57S52 1989   171'.3—dc19
88-29109 CIP
ISBN 0-19-824451-7

Set by Oxford Text System
Printed in Great Britain
at the University Printing House, Oxford
by David Stanford
Printer to the University

For Marshall

PREFACE

ARISTOTLE'S ethical theory has enjoyed a resurgence of interest of late. The ancient idea that ethical theory is about how to lead a good life, and that such a life will express the emotions as well as reason, has found a sympathetic ear in many. I am among these, and the aim of this work is to capture the way in which the sentiments and practical reason together constitute character. The work, in some sense, began life as a thesis submitted for my Ph.D. at Harvard in 1982. At the time, I was struck by the fact that discussions of Aristotle's theory of virtues often side-stepped an account of their acquisition, Two notable exceptions were articles by Burnyeat and Sorabji,[1] but on the whole the idea of moral habituation as a kind of non-cognitive practice was unquestioningly accepted. The aim of the thesis was to debunk this view, both as an interpretation of Aristotle and as a plausible theory in its own right. Little of the thesis survives in this present book, but the motivating idea, to demonstrate that character is inseparable from the operations of practical reason, remains.

In writing a book on Aristotle, I have felt acutely the problem of Aristotle's inherent sexism, and have struggled with the awkward issue of just how to allow women into the ranks of the decent and wise. I have not come to any ready solution, and, perhaps with some anachronism, have in the end allowed myself to use women as well as men as the subjects of my examples, moving freely between the masculine and feminine pronoun. For my own process of writing and interpretation, this seemed to be necessary and crucial for sympathetic appreciation of the theory. If not

---

[1] Myles Burnyeat, 'Aristotle on Learning to be Good', in A. O. Rorty (ed.), *Essays on Aristotle's Ethics* (University of California Press, 1980), 69–92; Richard Sorabji, 'Aristotle on the Role of Intellect in Virtue', *Proceedings of the Aristotelian Society*, 74 (1973–4), 107–29, repr. in Rorty, 201–19.

abetted by Aristotle, it seems at least within his own dictum of allowing time to be a co-partner in and co-discoverer of the details of his theory (*NE* 1098a22). Where appropriate, I have examined in some detail Aristotle's position on women, and, especially in the case of their role as moral tutors within the family, have pointed to inconsistencies in his views.

Many people have helped at different stages in the growth of this book, and to all of them I owe my gratitude. My deepest debt is to Martha Nussbaum. As a teacher and thesis supervisor at Harvard she was everything a graduate student could want, and more. Her interest never flagged, and her vigilant supervision at all stages of the thesis was incomparable. At later stages of the book, too, she was a careful critic. Indeed, it would be hard to imagine acknowledging my debt to her in any brief space. For coming to understand Aristotle's place in the larger sweep of moral philosophy, I owe deep appreciation to my second thesis supervisor, John Rawls. His writing, and his remarkable lectures in moral philosophy, have remained the foundation of my own education in that subject. His forceful defence of Kantian ethics compelled me then (and now) to take seriously the challenge Kant poses to Aristotelian theory. Many thanks are also due to Steven Strange, who read the thesis, and who offered helpful criticisms along the way.

The book began life again at Yale, and benefited from the various seminars at which its ideas were developed. To the many students whose discussions helped to shape this book, I am most grateful. I also owe thanks to my Yale colleagues for their encouragement and support of my work. John Fischer's careful reading of earlier drafts of two chapters led to substantial improvements, and conversations with Sarah Waterlow Broadie clarified my own thinking about difficult issues in Aristotle's theory. Both R. I. G. Hughes and Giovanni Ferrari read and commented on several chapters of the book, and I am thankful for their interest. To Ruth Marcus, for her steady encouragement and warmth over the past six years, I owe special thanks.

I would also like to thank Lawrence Blum, who commented extensively on one of the chapters and whose own work has helped me greatly in thinking about Aristotle. I also owe a debt to Amelie Rorty, who read several of the chapters, and to Aryeh Kosman, whose introduction to Aristotle, when I was an undergraduate, left a lasting impression.

I received extensive and extraordinarily helpful written comments on the penultimate draft of the manuscript from Norman Dahl and Richard Kraut. Kraut's detailed and astute criticisms saved me from many mistakes, and his challenges forced me to revise and clarify positions. I have tried to acknowledge his help at many places, although I am sure I have not given a full accounting. Dahl's suggestions on how to tighten the structure of the book were invaluable in writing the introduction, and offered me an external vantage-point that I very much needed. Also, his challenge to take more seriously the rationality of the vicious agent led to my rethinking various arguments at the end of Chapter 3. Though I cannot hope to have satisfied these readers fully, I am most grateful to them for taking my views seriously. I also owe thanks to the useful criticisms of an anonymous reader who read the penultimate draft.

This work was supported through various research funds. Since the work began as a thesis, I would like to thank the Charlotte Newcombe Division of the Woodrow Wilson Foundation for fellowship support when I was a graduate student, as well as Professor Zeph Stewart, then chair of the Harvard Classics Department, for supporting my work through the Teschemacher Fellowships. The writing of the book began again on a leave from Yale (1984–5) in which I received a fellowship from the National Endowment for the Humanities (NEH) and was completed during a leave (1987–8) supported by the American Council for Learned Societies and a Mellon Fellowship, awarded by the Whitney Humanities Center at Yale. I would like to thank these many groups for their generosity, as well as the Philosophy Department at Yale for allowing me time free from teaching.

There are other sorts of debts that are due, especially to those in my family. The first beginning of this book as a

Ph.D. was marked by the birth of our daughter Kala; its second beginning during my NEH year saw the birth of our son Jonathan. But, as C. S. Lewis once noted of one of his Narnia tales, 'When I began it, I had not realized that girls [and boys] grow quicker than books.' Both children have grown, and with patience, curiosity, and respect have watched this book slowly come to life. For their understanding, I am grateful. And to my husband Marshall, for his humour, his flexibility, and his unfailing encouragement in these years, I have the deepest gratitude. This book owes more than can be said to him.

Earlier versions of parts of this work have been previously published. Chapter 2 grew out of 'Character, Planning, and Choice in Aristotle', *Review of Metaphysics*, 39 (Sept. 1985), and Chapter 3 is a later version of 'Aristotle on Friendship and Shared Happiness', *Philosophy and Phenomenological Research*, 47 (June 1987).

N.S.

CONTENTS

ABBREVIATIONS

The Works of Aristotle I use are abbreviated as follows:

DA	*De Anima*
EE	*Eudemian Ethics*
MA	*De Motu Animalium*
Mem.	*On Memory and Recollection*
Meta.	*Metaphysics*
MM	*Magna Moralia*
NE	*Nicomachean Ethics*
Phys.	*Physics*
Po. An.	*Posterior Analytics*
Poet.	*Poetics*
Pol.	*Politics*
Rh.	*Rhetoric*
Top.	*Topics*

The works of Plato are abbreviated as:

Protag.	*Protagoras*
Rep.	*Republic*

Translations of the *Nicomachean Ethics* to which I refer are:

Irwin, T. H., *Nicomachean Ethics* (Hackett, 1985)

Ross, W. D., *Nicomachean Ethics* (Oxford University Press, 1915)

Urmson, J. O., *Nicomachean Ethics*, in J. Barnes (ed.), *The Complete Works of Aristotle: The Revised Oxford Translation* (Princeton University Press, 1985)

Commentaries to which I refer are:

Gauthier, R. A. and Jolif, J. Y., *Aristote: L'Éthique à Nicomaque*, 2nd edn., 4 vols. (Publications Universitaires de Louvain, 1970)

Grant, A., *The Ethics of Aristotle* (Longmans, Green, 1885)
Greenwood, L. H. G., *Aristotle: Nicomachean Ethics, Book VI* (Cambridge University Press, 1909; repr. Arno Press, 1973)
Stewart, J. A., *Notes on the Nicomachean Ethics of Aristotle*, i and ii (Oxford University Press, 1892; repr. Arno Press, 1973)

Note. References to the works of Aristotle follow the conventional system based on the pages, columns, and lines of the Bekker edition (Berlin, 1831). References to Plato are to the pagination standardized by Stephanus. Unless otherwise noted, the translations of Aristotle are my own. References throughout the text that are not otherwise identified are to the *Nicomachean Ethics*.

INTRODUCTION

I. CHARACTER

THE focus of this work is on character. For Aristotle, as for us, the term has to do with a person's enduring traits; that is, with the attitudes, sensibilities, and beliefs that affect how a person sees, acts, and indeed lives. As permanent states, these will explain not merely why someone acted this way *now*, but why someone can be *counted on* to act in certain ways. In this sense, character gives a special sort of accountability and pattern to action. Following Aristotle, I will be concerned primarily with *good* character—with the virtues that guide a good life. Not that Aristotle ignores vice: the virtues are, in all cases, relative to excesses which would lead a person, if not to moral turpitude, at least to foolishness or unsensible ways. But the description of these is in the service of showing what the good life is like—what its constituents are and what sorts of persons are likely to lead it.

As a whole, the Aristotelian virtues comprise just and decent ways of living as a social being. Included will be the generosity of benefactor, the bravery of citizen, the goodwill and attentiveness of friends, the temperance of a non-lascivious life. But human perfection, on this view, ranges further, to excellences whose objects are less clearly the weal and woe of others, such as a healthy sense of humour and a wit that bites without malice or anger. In the common vernacular nowadays, the excellences of character cover a gamut that is more than merely moral. Good character—literally, what pertains to ethics—is thus more robust than a notion of goodwill or benevolence, common to many moral theories. The full constellation will also include the excellence of a divine-like contemplative activity, and the best sort of happiness will find a place for the pursuit of pure leisure, whose aim and purpose has little to do with social improvement or welfare. Human perfection thus pushes outwards at both limits to include both the more earthly and the more divine.

But even when we restrict ourselves to the so-called 'moral' virtues (e.g. temperance, generosity, and courage), their ultimate basis is considerably broader than that of many alternative conceptions of moral virtue. Emotions as well as reason ground the moral response, and these emotions include the wide sentiments of altruism as much as particular attachments to specific others. The claim is not the familiar one argued by some that sentiments and attachments enable us to fulfil the moral requirements determined by a more impartial reason. That would be far too Kantian. Rather, it is that emotions themselves are modes of moral response that determine what is morally relevant and, in some cases, what is required. To act rightly is to act rightly in affect and conduct. It is to be emotionally engaged, and not merely to have the affect as accompaniment or instrument. It is to reason and see in a way that brings to bear the lessons of the heart as much as the lessons of a calmer intellect. An action motivated by the right principle but lacking in the right gesture or feeling falls short of the mean; it does not express virtue. Indeed, for Aristotle, to act for the right reasons, as the person of practical wisdom does, is to act from the sort of wisdom that itself includes the vision and sensitivity of the emotions. Moral choice issues from that wisdom without necessarily presupposing the reflections of an impartial agent. Emotions and attachments need not be stripped or, more weakly, justified from a higher-order perspective, where one asks how others, similarly circumstanced, would respond.

This point is not new. The impartial standpoint characteristic of modern moral theory (Kantianism and consequentialism alike) is not one rooted in ancient moral theory. And apart from the hedonistic theory found at the end of the *Protagoras*, procedural methods of assessing correct choice are not particularly emphasized.[1] This is not

---

[1] Aristotle's criticism of this view (as it figures in the Socratic account of *akrasia*—weakness of will) is at *NE* VII. 3; on this see David Wiggins, 'Weakness of Will, Commensurability, and the Objects of Deliberation and Desire', in

to deny that impartialism will have its place. In Aristotle's account, the *phronimos* or person of practical wisdom will need to correct for biases and preferences that interfere with the deliberation at hand; but recognition of this never leads to the identification of the impartial point of view with the point of view of ethical assessment in general.[2]

Aristotle's account can thus be seen as shedding some light on the current debate between impartialist and particularist moral theories. With the particularist, he will argue that the point of view of moral assessment does not require a higher-order perspective of impartiality. It is not merely that the detail of situations is often lost in the retreat to coarser-grained principles. It is that our judgement of particular cases and our knowledge of how to 'compose the scene' is itself part of the moral response. Discerning the morally salient features of a situation is part of expressing virtue and part of the morally appropriate response. Pursuing the ends of virtue does not begin with making choices, but with recognizing the circumstances relevant to specific

A. O. Rorty (ed.), *Essays on Aristotle's Ethics* (University of California Press, 1980). On the same subject see Martha Nussbaum, *The Fragility of Goodness. Luck and Rational Self-Sufficiency in Greek Ethical Thought: The Tragic Poets, Plato, and Aristotle* (Cambridge University Press, 1986), ch. 10, and 'The Discernment of Perception: An Aristotelian Conception of Private and Public Rationality', in John Cleary (ed.), *Proceedings of the Boston Area Colloquium in Ancient Philosophy*, i (University Press of America, 1985), 151-201.

[2] Thus, in general, Aristotle is eager to distinguish practical reason both from the top-down, deductive methods of *epistēmē* and from the procedural methods of *technē*. *Epistēmē* or scientific understanding is a kind of knowledge which has as its subject-matter unqualified and unchanging truths; given the contingent circumstances of human action, the model will not work for ethical theory (cf. 1141a25). In contrast to *epistēmē*, the subject-matter of *technē* is what is contingently produced by our efforts; but still Aristotle insists that the reasoning characteristic of such productions (*poiēseis*) is fundamentally distinct from the reasoning characteristic of action (*praxis*; 1140b6). Productions, he continues, have ends extrinsic to the producing, while the ends of *praxeis* are immanent in *praxeis*. For problems with this latter distinction see David Charles's 'Aristotle: Ontology and Moral Reasoning', in Julia Annas (ed.),*Oxford Studies in Philosophy*, iv (Oxford University Press, 1986), 121-43. His claim is that the excessively simple distinction undermines the fact that *praxeis*, too, are done for the sake of certain end states, though end states that are internal rather than external consequences of the action, and 'which occur without any change being produced in another object' (132-43). The worth of the *praxeis* (say courageous activity) thus depends not upon achieving planned results, but upon a courageous state being exemplified. I believe this rendering of *praxis* is compatible with the notion I go on to develop of intrinsically fine action in ch. 3, sect. 7.

ends. In this sense, character is expressed in what one *sees* as much as what one *does*. Knowing how to discern the particulars, Aristotle stresses, is a mark of virtue.[3]

In a general way, then, this book will address issues that figure in contemporary moral debate. But it takes its lead from Aristotle's own views and texts. In this sense, it is an interpretative work, and the method combines argument with exegesis. The objective is to understand Aristotle's ethical theory, not to construct a theory which uses Aristotle, or other historical figures, to illustrate its particular positions. While I have no objections to the latter approach, it is not the one I have adopted here. Still, as with any interpretative work, the hope here is to make Aristotle come alive on particular issues, and to deliver his insights in a way that has relevance to questions which concern us now. In a sense this is the aim of interpretation—to show the permanent importance of a text to issues of fundamental human concern. And Aristotle himself urges us to take this role seriously: time (and future generations), he says, must be co-workers and co-discoverers in the development of his theory (1098a22).

2. THE INSEPARABILITY OF CHARACTER AND PRACTICAL REASON

The focus of the book, as I have said, is on character. But to talk about character requires one to talk about practical reason. For it is practical reason that integrates the different

---

[3] Recent discussions from within an impartialist (Kantian) point of view of the importance of ethical perception are Onora O'Neill, 'The Power of Example', *Philosophy*, 61 (1981), 4–29; O'Neill, 'How Can We Individuate Moral Problems?', *Social Policy and Conflict Resolution* (Bowling Green Studies in Applied Ethics, 6: 1984) and Barbara Herman, 'The Practice of Moral Judgment', *Journal of Philosophy*, 82 (1985), 414–36. Martha Nussbaum has explored the issue from an Aristotelian viewpoint in 'The Discernment of Perception'. A particularist conception is taken up by Lawrence Blum in 'Particularity and Responsiveness', in J. Kagan (ed.), *The Emergence of Morality in Children* (University of Chicago Press, 1986), and 'Iris Murdoch and the Domain of the Moral' *Philosophical Studies*, 50 (1986), 343–67. I argue here and in ch. 2 that the Kantian and Aristotelian accounts of ethical perception are still quite distinct.

ends of character, refining and assessing them, and ultimately issuing in all considered judgements of what is best and finest to do. The inseparability of character and practical reason is often inadequately appreciated by readers of the *Nicomachean Ethics*. The reason may be Aristotle's own classification of virtue or excellence (*aretē*) into that of character (*ēthikēs*) and intellect (*dianoētikēs*) in *NE* II. 1, and his announced plan of treating each separately. But while he offers some sort of sequential treatment, with the excellence of intellect the special focus of *NE* VI, and to some extent *NE* X. 6–8, the descriptions of the virtues of character are in all cases descriptions of character states which are at once modes of affect, choice, and perception. The definition of virtue makes this painfully clear: to have virtue is to be able to make the choices characteristic of the person of practical wisdom. 'Virtue', Aristotle says, 'is a character state concerned with choice, lying in the mean relative to us, being determined by reason and the way the person of practical wisdom would determine it' (1107a1). And he is again at pains to make the point, as he concludes his account of the practical intellect in *NE* VI: 'it is not possible to be fully good without having practical wisdom, nor practically wise without having excellence of character' (1144b31–2).

My own interpretation will follow these leads, examining different aspects of practical reason concerned with character. In particular, I shall be considering at least four aspects of practical reason, centring on moral perception, choice-making, collaboration, and finally the development of these several capacities within moral education. A brief outline of the argument that follows might be helpful preparation here.

Most accounts of Aristotle's theory of practical reason begin with the practical syllogism. We start out with some end, and then decide *how* to act. But this is misleading, both as an interpretation of Aristotle and as an accurate account of what we in fact do. The process begins further back with a perception of the circumstances and a recognition of its morally salient features. Before we can know how to act, we must acknowledge that action may be required. And this reaction to circumstances is itself part of the virtuous response. It is part of how the dispositional ends of character become occurrent. In Chapter 2, I argue that Aristotle has much to offer on this issue, though for the most part it has been overlooked in the literature.

But equally the account of deliberation is much more complex than the simple model of the practical syllogism suggests. To have character requires the integration of different ends and interests in a unified life over time. As such, choice-making will not simply be a linear process of promoting the means to single ends, but a process of promoting ends in the light of other ends, where overall fit and mutual adjustment of ends will be as important as efficiency. I shall argue in Chapter 3 for an account of deliberation along these lines. As part of this extended account of deliberation, I shall oppose the view that Aristotle's practical syllogism necessarily issues in immediate action. The conclusion, I argue, can be a present or future intention to act.

Mediating the perceptual and deliberative aspects of practical reason is a collaborative dimension, which I take up in Chapter 4. Virtuous agents conceive of their well-being as including the well-being of others. It is not simply that they benefit each other, though to do so is both morally appropriate and especially fine. It is that, in addition, they design together a common good. This expands outwards to the *polis* and to its civic friendships and contracts inwards to the more intimate friendships of one or two. In both cases, the ends of the life become shared, and similarly the resources for promoting it. Horizons are expanded by the point of view of others, and in the case of intimate relationships, motives are probed, assessed, and redefined. Not surprisingly, the family will be entrusted with the role of cultivating affiliative capacities, and I shall be exploring the origins of attachment in this chapter. *Philiai* or relations of affection and caring will characterize the child's earliest relation to the social world, and through various transformations will be preserved as an essential element of adult moral life. Attachment thus stretches backwards to childhood and forwards to maturity; there is no moment of self-sufficiency which marks full independence from others.

The process by which character is shaped is examined

more fully in Chapter 5. Contrary to the popular interpretation according to which ethical habituation is non-
rational, I argue that it includes early on the engagement of
cognitive capacities. Thus, habituation is not mindless drill,
but a cognitive shaping of desires through perception, belief,
and intention. These capacities are involved in acting *from*
character, and, to a different extent and degree, in *acquiring*
character. Thus, moral education will itself cultivate the perceptual and deliberative capacities requisite for mature character. If excellence of character is inseparable from practical
intellect, then an account of moral education must recognize
this fact. I shall argue that Aristotle provides a developmental account that does this.

In an important sense the argument of these chapters will
be cumulative, with the same topic returned to more than
once in connection with the different aspects of practical
reasoning. Thus, while discernment of ethical salience will
be an issue in the next chapter, it will also be returned to in
the chapter which follows as part of a more complete account
of how we promote our ends, and again in the final chapter
in the description of how emotions are reformed. The arguments of later chapters will fill in and supplement what has
been said in earlier chapters and vice versa.

3. A PRACTICAL THEORY

Aristotle's ethical theory is ultimately practical. It includes
educational method within its purview, and conceives of
friendship, and the family, as serving important educative
goals. But, on Aristotle's view, to engage in ethical inquiry
is itself a practical matter. The intended audience of his
lectures are those who already care about virtue (1095b4–6),
and the end is to deepen their commitment (and ability) to
lead a good life. Aristotle reminds us of this as he concludes
the *Nicomachean Ethics*:

Since we have now said enough in outline about happiness and the
virtues, and also about friendship and pleasure, should we thus
think that our decision to examine these matters has achieved its

end? On the contrary, as it surely is said, the end of practical theory is not to study and know each thing, but rather to act on that knowledge. Hence it is not enough to know about virtue, but we must also try to possess and exercise it, or become good in any other way. (1179a33–b4)

As suggested, the inquiry itself is meant to deepen one's commitment to the good life. It is a clarification that will guide action. By and large, the inquiry proceeds by dialectical argument, beginning with the accepted beliefs (*ta endoxa*) of the many and wise, working through the difficulties and puzzles (*hai aporiai*), and arriving at first principles that are essentially a refined and systematized version of some subset of *ta endoxa*.[4] Together they form a system of claims about the necessary features of the good towards which human beings must ultimately aim.

It would not be amiss at this point to summarize briefly the early findings as they emerge in the first book of the *Nicomachean Ethics*. The argument, as it appears there, is generally recognized as one of the best examples of the dialectic at work.[5] The account will include: *formal* features of

---

[4] On the dialectical process see G. E. L. Owen's '*Tithenai ta phainomena*' in S. Mansion (ed.), *Aristote et les problèmes de méthode* (Papers of the Second Symposium Aristotelicum, Publications Universitaires de Louvain, 1961) repr. in Martha Nussbaum (ed.), *Logic, Science, and Dialectic* (Cornell University Press, 1986) as well as more recent discussions: Martha Nussbaum, 'Saving Aristotle's Appearances' in Malcolm Schofield and Martha Nussbaum (eds.), *Language and Logos: Studies in Ancient Greek Presented to G. E. L. Owen* (Cambridge University Press, 1982)—revised version of this essay appears as ch. 8 of Nussbaum's *Fragility of Goodness*; Jonathan Barnes, 'Aristotle and the Methods of Ethics', *Revue internationale de philosophie*, 34 (1980), 490–511; T. H. Irwin, 'First Principles in Aristotle's Ethics', *Midwest Studies in Philosophy*, 3 (University of Minnesota Press, 1978), 252–72; Henry Richardson, 'Rational Deliberation of Ends', Ph.D. thesis (Harvard University, 1986). That the dialectical method need not in the end vindicate common-sense morality is argued persuasively by Barnes. In this vein he shows that the *endoxa* may be easy or hard to unearth, revealed implicitly or explicitly in language or action, the views of many or of a more restricted élite. On the relation of the Rawlsian notion of reflective equilibrium to what Rawls himself takes to be its essentially Aristotelian origins (John Rawls, *A Theory of Justice* (Harvard University Press, 1971), 51 n., cf. 46–53), see ch. 4 of Richardson's discussion.

[5] That the book reports the *beliefs* of the 'many and wise' is explicit from the outset in its pronouncement that 'every craft and method, and equally every action and choice, *is thought* [*dokei*] to aim at some good'. Cognates of the term *dokein* are repeated at pivotal moves in the argument. Other celebrated examples of dialectic are the discussion in *NE* VII of *akrasia*, and the discussion at IX. 9 of the place of friendship in the self-sufficient life.

the good, e.g. that it must be unqualifiedly complete, in the sense that other things are chosen for it but never it for anything else (it is thus the best or chief good); that it must be self-sufficient, in the sense that the end is choice-worthy and lacking in nothing (required for an essentially human life). It will also include *substantive* features which meet these criteria. While it is agreed by most that *eudaimonia* or happiness satisfies the formal criteria (1097b22), the identity, Aristotle asserts, is essentially empty (1095a20) since happiness means different things to different people. The remaining task of the *Nicomachean Ethics*, indeed its primary theoretical task, is therefore to specify that content—to say in what way happiness is realized through certain recognized intrinsic and external goods, e.g. virtue or excellence (*aretē*), reason, pleasure, and honour, on the one hand (1097b1), and good fortune, wealth, skills, and friends on the other.[6] As part of that task it will be established early on that it is not mere possession of excellence (*aretē*), but excellent *activity* (*energeia kat' aretēn*), that will characterize the most complete good (1098a7, 1098a16, 1099a1), that the best and most complete excellent activity (1099a16, 1102a5) will involve primarily the excellences of character *and* intellect (1103a15), and that complete excellent activity will be to some extent dependent upon external factors (1099a32). These, in outline, are the early findings. The fuller project requires a specification of the several virtues and an account of their internal unity and their relation to the operations of practical reason, pleasure, and desire.

But the overall project of specifying the constituents of the highest good also goes on at the individual level. The choices the virtuous agent makes require refinements of more vaguely grasped ends, as well as their assessment in terms of overall fit within a coherent conception of good living. A grasp of the relationship of specific virtues to each other, an understanding of their more qualified and unqualified forms, and an appreciation of the external goods

---

[6] Virtue, reason (theoretical and practical), honour, and pleasure are intrinsic or complete goods in the sense that they would be chosen even if nothing else resulted from them—though each is not the most complete good, since each is also chosen for the sake of (i.e. as a component of) happiness.

and circumstances requisite for achieving specific virtuous
ends are all aspects of the deliberative mode. They are part
of exercising practical reason in implementing a good life.
To choose as a character does is to pursue rationally ends
that aim at some structure and pattern.

What I want to suggest, then, is that Aristotle's theory is
the more abstract and programmatic end of the same process
by which we, as practical agents, deliberate and arrive at
some conception of good living. Some version of this position has been argued by T. H. Irwin and more recently and
extensively by Henry Richardson.[7] As I shall defend the
claim, the exercise of practical reason in its various aspects
(i.e. perceptual, deliberative, and collaborative) will be ways
in which the virtuous agent proceeds, at a determinate level,
to construct a conception of good living. Ultimately, through
an agent's construal of her environment, through her choice
of friends, through her selection of how and in what way to
act on her commitments, she weaves a life that expresses her
character and aims at her conception of happiness. Specific
ends are revised in the light of other ends and new information. The overall end is shaped through the process. In
the reflective life, this process will easily reverse directions
moving to a more general level in order to untangle conflicts
between specific claims, or more simply to understand the
foundations and connections of one's specific ends. From
such a perspective, one may come to some understanding of

---

[7] See Irwin, 'First Principles', and 'Aristotle's Methods of Ethics', in D. J.
O'Meara (ed.), *Studies in Aristotle* (Catholic University Press, 1981), and Richardson, 'Rational Deliberation of Ends'. The claim that the theoretical enterprise is
essentially deliberative is disputed by John M. Cooper in *Reason and Human Good
in Aristotle* (Harvard University Press, 1975), 59–71. His view is that the deliberative process works towards an ultimate, fixed end in a way that the dialectical
process does not. That end, set by the virtuous person through moral intuition,
can be established independently by dialectical reasoning. I have argued that the
process of dialectically arriving at such an end is continuous with the process of
determinately constructing, through deliberative choice, a conception of the good
life. This seems to be required to make sense of Aristotle's claim that a practical
ascent to first principles (*archai*; 1095b1–8) must have practical import for how one
lives. To arrive at the *telos* for a human, he insists, is just to set a practical mark
(*skopos*) at which to aim. For we cannot order the goods in our lives unless we have
such a target: '. . . everyone able to live according to choice must set down some
target [*skopon*] of good living . . . (since not to arrange one's life with regard to
some end is a sign of great foolishness) . . .' (*EE* 1214b8).

the proper place of fame or money in a life, or of the value to be placed on family and friends. Equally, one may gain insight about how a responsible civic life can be combined with the serenity of contemplation. The reflection will draw upon one's own convictions, but also upon those embedded in the culture and in the views of the intellectually most respected. It is this perspective, of course, that is most akin to the one Aristotle himself assumes in the theoretical inquiry. But my point now is that it is part of the deliberative mode. We often move to it when we ruminate about the ramifications of specific actions: it is the cost of particular actions that makes us question the value of the ends they promote, and the suffering of actual damages that puts into perspective the place of the lost value in the overall plan of things. In this sense, the move from particular deliberations to the reflective mode is continuous and a part of the same complex process of determining what is good in life. The practically wise individual is thus in a certain way a theoretician, capable of a reasoned conception of happiness achieved through the dialectical skills of the ethicist. To a certain extent he must be able to collect and distil the meaning of *ta endoxa* and assess through argumentation and analysis which views are best justified. And, conversely, the Aristotelian ethicist must be practically wise. For the theory ultimately requires familiarity with the particular circumstances of human life;[8] it is based upon experience, and it is about individuatable particulars, even if the account it gives is not detailed or precise enough to determine choice (1094b22–7, cf. 1107a28–32). As theory, it remains inexact, awaiting the more determinate operations of practical reason in its perceptual and decision-making roles.

Ethical theory, then, is practical in so far as it is part of a greater project of setting a goal which guides actions. As Aristotle urges, the purpose of his inquiry is to give us a

---

[8] On Aristotle's conception of 'the particulars' see Irwin's helpful notes in his translation of the *Nicomachean Ethics* (Hackett, 1985), 418–19. In general I have found his translation and notes of enormous benefit, and have been guided by them at many points. Cooper's notion of 'perceiving the particulars' as including 'the capacity to recognize things of all the relevant specific types' (43) is in essential agreement with my above point; cf. Cooper, *Reason and Human Good*, 30–43.

'knowledge [*gnōsis*] of the good that will have great influence on our lives. And like archers who have some target [*skopon*] to aim at, with this knowledge we shall be more likely to hit upon what is right' (1094a22-4).[9] The *Eudemian Ethics*, too, reiterates that to establish an end (*telos*) is just to set a practical mark (*skopos*) for fine living (1214b8). In the chapters which follow we shall be exploring the various aspects of practical reason involved in fine living.

[9] Aristotle goes on to say that this knowledge is the concern of political inquiry (*politikē*). As Irwin notes ('First Principles', 258), political inquiry (*politikē*) in *NE* VI. 8 is a kind of practical reason concerning the affairs of the city (*hē peri polin phronēsis*, 1141b23-5); since the two are the same state of mind (*hexis*), and practical reason is deliberative, the suggestion again is that the inquiry will be deliberative: it will be a figuring out of how to live. L. H. G. Greenwood is helpful in sorting out the narrower and wider uses of *phronēsis* and *politikē* in this chapter; see his commentary on the *Nicomachean Ethics*, Book VI (Cambridge University Press, 1909; repr. Arno Press, 1973), 60-4. Note that I understand *politikē* to be deliberative not merely in the narrow, popular sense, which Aristotle himself takes to be too restrictive at 1141b28-9.

2

DISCERNING THE PARTICULARS

IN this chapter I wish to consider the way in which practical reason involves a discrimination (*krisis*) of the particular circumstances relevant to action and assessment. My concern is thus with practical reason as a kind of perception, as a way of judging or construing the case prior to deciding how to act. The chapter will divide as follows: I shall begin by arguing that Aristotle's remarks about equity within the law are relevant to the issue, for his concern in discussing equity is to show how any account of the law must be supplemented by an account of the tailoring of law to fit the exigencies of the case. I then continue the discussion of ethical perception by considering what Aristotle might regard as lacking in the Kantian account of moral choice. From here I turn to Aristotle's substantive discussion of the perceptual aspect of practical reason. I consider both its affective and its cognitive components, and finally take up some possibly troubling consequences of Aristotle's requirement that practical reason involve a familiarity with the particulars.

I. EQUITY WITHIN THE LAW

Aristotle's most sustained discussion of rules is in his instructive, though largely ignored, remarks about law in *NE* V and *Rh.* I. 13. While he acknowledges there the necessary and legitimate place of rules, he none the less steadily cautions against their intrinsic defects and the dangers of over-rigorous applications. In this section I want to examine the account, focusing on the special role of equity or fair-mindedness (*epieikeia*). In outlining the requirements of equity, we learn something about the more general requirements of a sensitive and fair reading of the circumstances constitutive of the ethical response.

Any Athenian of Aristotle's day could have attested to the importance of written law in Athenian life.[1] There were standard procedures for revising the law and for supplementing it in a way consistent with the rest of the law, as well as penalties for violating consistency. There were different courts for different types of actions, different types of penalties for different offences, restrictions on who could prosecute in different cases. Equally, there were distinctions between private and public cases, the latter generally involving offences affecting the community as a whole. Most of this was a matter of public knowledge, the law's proscriptions and prescriptions posted at the courts under whose jurisdiction the cases would rest. A walk to the courts and a perusal of the laws would provide details of the relevant procedures.[2] In practice, a large number of Athenians would have been familiar with these details of law, given the extensive amount of time they spent either on juries or in litigation. (This is the butt of Aristophanes' quip in the *Clouds* in which Strepsiades, pointing to a map, says, 'What, this can't be Athens. There are no jurors sitting!')[3]

On Aristotle's own account, the aim of legal proceduralism is to establish impartiality through the exercise of an impersonal reason. This is made clear in the following striking remarks from the *Politics*:

He who bids law to rule seems to bid God and intelligence [*nous*] alone to rule, but he who bids man to rule puts forward a wild beast. For appetite is like a wild beast, and spiritedness perverts even the best of men. Accordingly, law is intelligence without desire. (*Pol.* 1287a28–32)

Though Aristotle adopts the Platonic metaphor for the soul, here, as always, he qualifies it, arguing not that law is subordinate to a transcendent intelligence, but that law itself *is*

---

[1] And equally any modern reader of Aristotle's *Athenaion Politea*.

[2] For a most useful discussion of these issues, see D. M. MacDowell, *The Law in Classical Athens* (Thames and Hudson, 1978).

[3] Again in the *Birds*: 'What country are you from?' 'From the country of the fine ships.' 'You're not jurors, are you?'

intelligence; it has its own rationality or *logos* (*NE* 1134a29–b2).⁴ Accordingly, the impersonality of reason does not fix law as external or rigid, but rather establishes it as an expression of ongoing and active reason. What is final is not the deliverances of written law, but rather the 'best judgements' of those who, guided by experience and the law, can improve upon it (*Pol.* 1287a25–7). On Aristotle's view, then, the benefits of proceduralism never obscure the fact of written law's uneasy fit to the particular case. This emerges as the central focus of Aristotle's discussion:

In those cases, then, in which it is necessary to speak universally [*katholou*], but not possible to do so correctly, the law takes the usual case [*epi to pleon*], though it is not ignorant of the possibility of error. And it is none the less correct; for the error is not in the law nor in the legislator but in the nature of the thing, since the matter of practical affairs is of this kind from the start. (*NE* 1137b14 ff.)

Law is thus inevitably general. But it is limited as a result. What it says in a general (*katholou*) and relatively unqualified (*haplōs*)⁵ way (*NE* 1137b25) is always subject to further stipulation.⁶ To speak legally (*nomikōs*) is to speak of general types (*tous tupous*), leaving aside for further consideration a more precise treatment of individual cases (*kath' hekaston akribologian, Pol.* 1341b30–2).

Within the judicial process, this more precise treatment is

---

⁴ This point is made by Ernest Weinrib in his insightful account of the significance of Aristotle's view for contemporary legal debate: Weinrib, 'The Intelligibility of the Rule of Law', in Allan C. Hutchinson and Patrick J. Monahan (eds.), *The Rule of Law: Ideal or Ideology?* (Carswell Legal Publications, 1987). See also his 'Liberty and Community in the Theory of Private Law' (forthcoming).

⁵ The term *haplōs* is ambiguous. It may mean 'unconditional', 'true not merely in relation to certain circumstances, but generally', as in what is good for a human being as such; or, alternatively, 'not yet precise' and thus 'subject to further restrictions'. It is clear from my above remarks and from the passage itself that law is unqualified in the second sense. Cf. T. H. Irwin's notes to his translation of the *Nicomachean Ethics* (Hackett, 1985), 428.

⁶ Even so political considerations may require restrictions on when the law is to be revised or repealed: 'It is clear that some mistakes of the legislators and rulers should be passed over, where the improvement would be small, and where it would be a bad idea to accustom individuals to dissolve too easily the laws; for in making the changes, the people will not be as much benefited as harmed by becoming accustomed to distrust their rulers . . . For the law has no power to compel obedience apart from the force of custom' (*Pol.* 1269a15–22).

the special claim of equity (*epieikeia*).⁷ Its aim is not to make
the law more comprehensive or exhaustive, but to tailor its
judgements to the requirements of the case: 'And this is the
nature of what is equitable: it is a rectification of law in so far
as the universality of law makes it deficient' (*NE* 1137b26-7).
It thus reveals the spirit of the law, rather than its letter, and
as such is an antidote to legal rigorism. To the degree that it
provides a more exacting treatment, Aristotle regards equity
as a superior form of justice: 'it is better than the error
resulting from the rule being stated unconditionally'
(1137b24-5, 1137b9). Aristotle elaborates in the *Rhetoric*:

The second kind [of unwritten law]⁸ makes up for the defects of a
community's written code of law. This is what we call equity;
people regard it as just; it is in fact the sort of justice which goes
beyond the written law. Its existence partly is and partly is not
intended by legislators; not intended, where they have noticed no
defect in the law; intended, where they find themselves unable to
define things exactly [*diorisai*], and are obliged to legislate as if
that held good always which in fact only holds good usually [*epi to
polu*]; or where it is not easy to be complete owing to the endless
possible cases [*di' apeirian*] presented, such as the kinds and sizes
of weapons that may be used to inflict wounds—a lifetime would
be too short to enumerate [*diarithmounta*] all of these. If, then, the
law is imprecise and yet legislation is necessary, then law must be
expressed widely without restriction [*haplōs*]. (*Rh.* 1374a25-35; cf.
NE 1137b20-8; *Pol.* 1269a8-12)

Aristotle cites several overlapping reasons for the existence
of equity as a supplement to statutory law.

1. The law is essentially incomplete; no enumeration

---

⁷ The term 'equitable' is also used by Aristotle in a less technical way as a
synonym for decent or good, and is thus descriptive of the virtuous agent; see *NE*
1126b21, 1128b21, 1132a3 ff., 1169a3, 1169a16.

⁸ Equally interesting is the first type of unwritten law which Aristotle discusses
in this passage. It concerns what we might call supererogatory acts, or, as Aristotle
describes them, acts that are excessively virtuous (or vicious), and that in a certain
sense go beyond the requirements of law. The list of such excessively virtuous acts
(e.g. gratitude to benefactors, willingness to help friends) is significant, in that these
seem to be included simply as virtues in the *Nicomachean Ethics*. The one exception
is in the account of magnanimity (IV. 3), where gratitude does not count as superlative virtue, but quite the opposite, as a sign of defect. On magnanimity, see my
'Common Sense and Uncommon Virtue', in *Midwest Studies in Philosophy*, 13
(University of Notre Dame Press, 1988).

(*diarithmounta*), no matter how imaginative or far-sighted, could possibly be comprehensive. So, for example, the legislator cannot begin to cover all the kinds of weapons that could conceivably be used in murder, nor to cite the circumstances and details of all conceivable murder cases. The notorious case in the *Euthyphro*, of leaving a man bound in a ditch so that death results, undoubtedly falls under homicide law, but is almost certainly not explicitly mentioned in the law.[9]

2. In judging the applicability of law to a given case, the legislative intention of the law must be determined: equity thus considers 'what the legislator would have said himself, had he been present, and what he would have prescribed, had he known, in his legislation' (*NE* 1137b23).[10] In some cases, this may be a matter of qualifying existing law, i.e. stipulating that the law holds in conditions *A*, *B*, and *C*, but not *D* and *E*. As such, it makes the law more conditional.

---

[9] Documents concerning the laws of slander illustrate the point with some humour. In the speech against Theomnestos (Lysias 10), the speaker brings a charge of slander against Theomnestos for saying that he had killed his own father in the time of the Thirty:

> Perhaps he will say . . . that it is not one of the forbidden words if one says someone has killed his father, because the law does not forbid that, but prohibits calling him a murderer. But surely, men of the jury, you should go not by the words but their sense, and you all know that those who have killed people are murderers and those who are murderers have killed people. It would have been a long business for the law-maker to write out all the words which have the same meaning; by mentioning one he indicates them all. You would not, I suppose, Theomnestos, demand legal satisfaction from someone who called you a father-beater or a mother-beater and yet, if someone said that you hit your female parent or your male parent, think he should go unpunished because he had not said any of the forbidden words. I should like you to tell me this, since you are an expert on this subject and have made a practical and theoretical study of it: if someone said you had flung away your shield (when the law says: 'if anyone alleges that he has thrown it away, he is to be liable to penalty'), would you refrain from bringing a case against him and be content to have flung away your shield, saying that it did not matter to you, because flinging is not the same as throwing? (Lysias 10. 6–9, as quoted by MacDowell, *The Law in Classical Athens*, 127).

From this speech, it is clear that the law listed certain expressions which were forbidden, including saying that a man was a murderer. The argument of the speaker is that the intention of the law is to ban not just these expressions, but any statement having the same meaning.

[10] Cf. *Rh.* 1374b11–13. It should be clear that I use the term legislative intention without implying by it any of the connotations it carries in contemporary debates on legal theory, in particular, the sense of a narrow reading of the law.

3. In other cases, however, equitably interpreting the law may require going beyond the legislative intention, correcting for a defect, which, as Aristotle suggests above, the legislator did not (or perhaps could not have) anticipate(d) (*Rh.* 1374a29). In the latter case, the revision may be forced by empirical evidence not available at the time the law was written.

4. Where no existing (or revised) law adequately applies to a case, equity requires the issuing of a decree (*psēphisma*). Literally a voting (by pebbles), the decree was an established method used by the assembly and courts for adjudicating in particular cases. While a decree had to be consistent with existing law, unlike a statute or revised law it in no way established a more general policy:

This is also the reason why not everything is guided by law, for about some matters it is impossible to lay down a law, and so a decree is needed. For the standard is indefinite where the subject-matter is itself indefinite, just like the lead ruler used in Lesbian building which does not remain rigid but adapts to the shape of the stone; similarly, a decree is adapted to fit the circumstances. (*NE* 1137b28)

The decree is indefinite (*aoristos*), then, not in the sense that it imprecisely determines the requirements of the situation (for it does determine them precisely), but in the sense that it does not determine or define a rule for other cases: 'A decree concerns actions about particulars' (*NE* 1141b28); 'unlike a statute of law it is not possible to be universal' (*Pol.* 1292a37; cf. *NE* 1134b24-5, 1094b11-27).

The effect of equity in counteracting legal rigorism is perhaps clearest in the setting of punishments. It is associated with considerateness (*suggnōmē*) and a disposition to show forgiveness, leniency, or pardon (all possible renderings of *suggnōmē*) (*NE* 1143a19-24, *Rh.* 1374b4-10, *NE* 1135b16-1136a9; cf. *NE* 1110a24). More fundamentally, and not necessarily coincident with leniency, is a concern to restore action to its original context and motives, on the assumption that abstraction from these distorts assessments of culpability:

Equity bids us . . . to consider not so much the action of the accused but the choice, and not this or that part of the account but the whole story; and to consider not what sort of a person an agent is now, but what sort of person he has been or is usually. (*Rh.* 1374b13-16)

The point is clear: determining responsibility depends upon a more rather than less complete rendering of the circumstances of action; this is an aspect of sympathetic judgement (*suggnōmē*). Compulsion, duress, ignorance of particulars, unforeseeable consequences all may conspire to limit ascriptions of responsibility. And the presence of these conditions is often grasped only upon a complete account of what happened. The familiar cases of mixed actions discussed in *NE* III. 1 come to mind. A fuller consideration of circumstances and motives may reveal, for example, that an agent, while making a voluntary choice with foreseen ill consequences, is none the less not fully culpable, for the choice was made under duress, 'under conditions of a sort that overstrain human nature and no one would endure' (1110b25). Here pardon (*suggnōmē*) is appropriate. In other cases, praise will be due to the agent who willingly endures what is shameful in order to avoid a more terrible outcome (1110a20-1). My abetting in a crime in order to avoid the sure death of my family must be distinguished from a similar action in which there are no such threats: 'such acts are voluntary, though perhaps, considered in an unqualified [*haplōs*] way, apart from these conditions, they are involuntary; for no one would choose any action of this sort for itself' (1110a18). Equally, attention to circumstances will require accidents (*atuchēma*) to be distinguished from errors of judgement (*hamartēma*) in so far as the latter may be cases of negligent ignorance, the former due to ill consequences an agent could not reasonably have been expected to foresee.[11]

---

[11] Cf. 1135a25, 1136a5-10. It is worth noting that the above two cases of error, as discussed in *Rh.* I. 13 and *NE* V. 6, significantly modify the more limited account of *NE* III. 2 in which actions due to ignorance are regarded as simply involuntary. Here it is clear that certain forms of ignorance of particulars (viz. misjudgement) do not constitute a defence and thus do not fully absolve the agent from responsibility. Even accidents may not fully absolve from responsibility, though they may considerably diminish it, and correlatively affect the degree of blame or punishment. Both these cases are distinguished from malicious acts in which the agent is held fully liable for his deliberate choice. Ignorance is involved here, too, but it is an

The additional requirement that equity attend to the pattern of actions of an agent—'to what sort of person he has been or is usually'—should come as no surprise. Civic law, Aristotle tells us, ultimately derives from the considerations of virtue as a whole (*apo tēs holēs aretēs*), and has to do with living that is productive of it (*poiētika tēs holēs aretēs*; 1130b22–6). In this way, it forms a continuing part of the education of character begun in earlier years at home (1179b31–1180a32).[12] This emphasis suggests that even where rules and proceduralism have predominance, the notion of merely lawful actions, of actions that are right or juridical but not virtuous, does not hold a comparably important place.[13]

But in practice determining character and motive may be no easy matter,[14] and the trial less well suited to these sorts of

---

accountable ignorance of the universals, or ends of good living (1110b32). Cf. *Rh.* 1374b4–10, *NE* 1135b12–1136a9. These three cases must be distinguished in turn from injuries due to passion (cf. *NE* V. 8). These acts, unlike those due to error and misfortune, are voluntary (cf. 1111a25 ff.), though neither malicious nor deliberative (*ek prohaireseōs*).

[12] 'For the majority of lawful acts are those acts prescribed [*prostattomena*] from the point of view of virtue in general. For the law prescribes [*prostattei*] living in accordance with each virtue and prohibits [*kōluei*] living in accordance with each vice' (1130b22–4; cf. 1129b20–5). What is required is an education (*peri paideian*) concerned with the virtues requisite for the common good (1130b26).

[13] Cf. 1136a9–25 for the distinction between merely lawful acts and acts that flow from character.

[14] *Hubris* provides a case in point. Laws against *hubris* were not regarded as duplicating procedures for assault and abuse: 'If one hits, one does not in all cases commit *hubris*, but only if it is for a purpose, such as dishonouring the man or enjoying oneself' (*Rh.* 1374a13–15; cf. 1378b23–5). But to prove that *hubris* was operant rather than some other brand of hostility might require a psychological judgement on the part of a juror insufficiently grounded in the evidence: 'There are many things which the hitter might do, some of which the victim might not even be able to report to someone else, in his stance, his look, his voice . . .' (*Demosthenes* 21. 72; quoted in MacDowell, *The Law in Classical Athens*, 131). MacDowell invites us to consider, in contrast, the clear evidence of Konon's *hubris* in the following testimony in which Ariston describes how he and his friend were set upon by Konon and several other men one evening:

> When we came up to them, one of them, whom I did not know, fell upon Phanostratos and held him down, while this man Konon and his son and Andromenes's son fell upon me. First they pulled off my cloak, and then they tripped me up and pushed me into the mud, and they put me in such a state, by jumping on me and treating me with *hubris*, that my lip was cut and my eyes closed. They left me in such a bad condition that I could not stand up or speak. And while I was lying there I heard them saying a lot of dreadful things. Most of them were scurrilous, and some I should not like to repeat in front of

judgements than more informal judicial processes. Aristotle recognizes this, and suggests arbitration as one such method which in certain instances (e.g. violation of contracts, and the like) may be preferable to litigation:

And an interest in equity requires us to resolve a dispute more by discussion than by deed; and to prefer arbitration [*diaitan*] over litigation [*dikēn*]—for an arbitrator goes by the equity of the case, a juror by the strict law (*tōn nomōn*); and it is for this reason that arbitration was invented—in order to give fuller weight to the considerations of equity. (*Rh.* 1374b18-22)

In the background is the notion that litigation, as it is discussed in *NE* V. 4, involves the opposition of parties with relatively fixed claims, and the consequent correction of injuries through a restoration to an original parity. Corrective justice thus assumes that the parties are treated by the court as equal, 'For it makes no difference whether a good person has robbed a bad person or a bad person a good one, nor whether it is a good or bad man that has committed adultery; the law looks only at the different amounts of damage in the injury' (1132a3-24), and that the wrongful act has brought equal gain to the wrongdoer and loss to the victim. Accordingly, restoration considers not the agent, but the act, and the cancellation of its damage.[15]

From the point of view of equity, it is easy to see how this process would appear inadequate. Circumstances and motives may throw into question not only the voluntary nature of an injurious action, but equally the reasonableness of demanding that a transgressor, given his resources and means, pay the full penalty. This explains Aristotle's remark at 1138a1-3 that the equitable or decent person, 'having the law on his side', none the less chooses to take 'less than his share'. Not a stickler for justice (an *akribodikaios*—literally, one who is *precise* as to his rights), he is willing to compromise the damages and forgo the full restitution demanded

you. But the thing which shows Konon's *hubris*, and indicates that he was the ring-leader, I will tell you: he crowed in imitation of cocks that have won fights, and the others suggested he should beat his sides with his elbows like wings. (Demosthenes 54. 8-9; quoted in MacDowell, 132)

[15] Cf. M. M. Mackenzie's discussion of the relation between culpability and responsibility in *Plato on Punishment* (University of California Press, 1981), 18-20.

by strict corrective justice. The fair-minded person is
suggnōmonikos—willing to make allowances.

But equally the actual process of arbitration illustrates the
general concerns of equity. It is clear from the contrast with
litigation that Aristotle has in mind a process of settlement
involving reconciliation rather than adversarial opposition,
and open discussion (*logos*) rather than settled deed (*ergon*)
(1374b19). More explicit remarks in *Pol.* II (1268b7 ff.)
confirm this.[16] There Aristotle tells us that arbitration,
unlike litigation, involves the conferral and dialogue of
jurors (*koinologountai allēlois*, 1268b7), who deliberate with
each other before voting. The result is a qualified verdict (*to
krinein axioun diairounta*) that renegotiates the plantiff's
original demands (1268b13-17). The underlying idea is that
discussion of the testimony may in principle encourage a
more comprehensive account of the defendant's actions and
liability. Filling in the details is again essential to equity.[17]

I have explored Aristotle's views about equity in order
to indicate that even in areas where general principles and
procedures must be formulated and made publicly access-
ible, their applicability depends upon a full and complex
reading of the case, and in turn upon an interpretation of the
legislative intention in such a case. In this vein Aristotle
argues that equity is intended by the legislator himself to be
part of the process of putting the law into practice (*Rh.*
1374a30).

2. AN ALTERNATIVE LEGISLATIVE MODEL

I now wish to consider another type of legislative model
which may help to put into perspective Aristotle's position.
On this model, an action is judged permissible if the intention of the action can be made into a principle or law that

---

[16] Note, on the whole, however, the *Politics* passage is less approving of arbitration than the *Rhetoric* account.

[17] This has interesting implications for Carol Gilligan's 'Remapping the Moral
Domain' in Ian Watt (ed.), *Reconstructing Individualism* (Stanford University Press,
1986), in which she argues for a moral point of view which aims for reconciliation
and a transformation of the initial starting points of a problem.

others similarly circumstanced could follow. The emphasis here is not squarely on the generality of the proposal (though it is presumed there will be essential and reiterable features), but on its acceptability to others who might find themselves in that position. Generalizing (or universalizing) would thus provide a test of the particular proposed intention, with the starting point at the particular decision, rather than at some rule. Thus, the process is not so much a matter of applying a body of law, from the top down (as in the application of statutory law), but of making law, from the bottom up. This procedure is at the heart of what I take to be the Kantian project of legislating the moral law in a Realm of Ends. The basic intuition is that in acting morally I guard against making an exception for myself, against allowing myself special exemptions.[18] I do this by estimating what would happen if I conceived of my action as undertaken by everyone, or if I tried actually to bring it about in these universalized conditions.[19] My proposed action is determined to be unacceptable only if it is incompatible with its universalized form. Its acceptability thus rests on its rationality.[20]

There have been many interpretations of Aristotle in a Kantian mould, and the Kantian influence has inevitably shaped the translation and meaning of key words. In particular, it has shaped the meaning of *orthos logos*, literally correct or right reason (or reasoning), but under a Kantian gloss rendered 'right rule', 'rational principle'.[21] Equally, it has influenced the notion of *to deon*, literally what one ought

---

[18] Cf. Immanual Kant, *Groundwork of the Metaphysic of Morals*, tr. H. J. Paton (Harper and Row, 1956), ch. 2. I follow the general line of interpretation proposed by Barbara Herman in 'The Practice of Moral Judgment', *Journal of Philosophy*, 82 (1985), and Onora O'Neill in *Acting on Principle* (Columbia University Press, 1975).

[19] Cf. Kant, *Critique of Practical Reason*, tr. L. W. Beck (Bobbs-Merrill, 1956), ch. 2, the section 'Of the typic of pure practical judgment'.

[20] I am referring here to the tests of acceptability Kant outlines in the *Groundwork*: the contradiction in conception test and the contradiction in will test, (91).

[21] Thus, W. D. Ross, in the Oxford translation of *Nicomachean Ethics* (Oxford University Press, 1915), standardly translates *orthos logos* as 'right rule'. J. O. Urmson has corrected this in the new revised Oxford translation of *The Complete Works of Aristotle*, ed. Jonathan Barnes (Princeton University Press, 1985), and renders *orthos logos* 'right reason'.

to do, but within this tradition, moral obligation.[22] More recently, the flow has also been in the reverse direction, with Aristotle's theory becoming increasingly congenial to neo-Kantian theorists.[23] Non-rigoristic interpretations of the Categorical Imperative, discussions of the role of emotions in the theory, and in general a revival of interest in *The Doctrine of Virtue* can all be seen as part of that trend. But while the dialogue has been and remains fruitful, it nevertheless remains a serious mistake to align the two projects too closely.

In particular—to consider a small part of such a dialogue—even the above reading of Kant (which I endorse), with its emphasis on law generated from the bottom up, doesn't really find a proper home in Aristotelian ethics. The guiding Kantian notion in constructing principles—namely that of checking against attempts to give special dispensation to oneself—is simply not a force in Aristotle's theory. This does not mean that motives of self-interest, reputation, or pleasure are viewed dispassionately by Aristotle. They are indeed seen as threats to virtue and preoccupations with them constitute false conceptions of

---

[22] Cf. the *commentaire* of R. A. Gauthier and J. Y. Jolif, *Aristote: L'Éthique à Nicomaque*, 2nd edn., ii. 2 (Publications Universitaires de Louvain, 1970), 568–75. Gauthier defends the view: 'Il est donc hors de doute que l'impératif qu'est la règle n'imprime pas une régulation, mais exprime une *obligation* [emphasis in original] proprement dite: si la règle en tant qu'impératif fait de l'acte qu'elle impère un devoir, c'est parce qu'elle énonce l'obligation morale' (573). More recently, Irwin has argued for a conception of the moral in Aristotle's ethics which emphasizes the notion of moral obligation. His view is a response to Bernard Williams's claim in M. Finley (ed.), *The Legacy of Greece*, (Oxford University Press, 1981), 251, and *Ethics and the Limits of Philosopy* (Harvard University Press, 1985), 6, that there is no conception of the moral in ancient ethics. While it would be misleading to regard Irwin's view as peculiarly Kantian, none the less he finds certain Kantian characterizations of morality present in Aristotle, such as the inescapability of obligations and the impossibility of ultimate conflict between them. His more basic claim, that a moral conception can be found in Aristotle's account of altruism, seems to offer too weak a notion of morality to satisfy Williams. See T. H. Irwin, 'Aristotle's Conception of Morality', and my commentary in John Cleary (ed.), *Proceedings of the Boston Area Colloquium in Ancient Philosophy*, i (University Press of America, 1985), 115–50.

[23] Indeed Onora O'Neill argues ('Kant After Virtue', *Inquiry* 26 (1985), 387–405) that Kant's conception of practical reasoning comfortably supplements and enhances the sort of Aristotelian picture Alisdaire McIntyre presents in *After Virtue* (University of Notre Dame Press, 1981). It is not Kant but a misreading of Kant, she claims, that has made him the target rather than the ally of the McIntyre view.

happiness (*NE* I. 5). So one finds in the ethical writings, as we have already begun to see, arguments against misplaced partiality, as well as demands for balancing friendship against the claims of other goods and ends (1134a33 ff., 1164b25–1165a4). Similarly, a notion of practical reason as narrowly concerned with one's own affairs is repeatedly criticized as antithetical to the pursuits of a human being whose nature is essentially social and whose virtue is thus a kind of justice (1129b25 ff., 1142a6). But there is no canonical procedure for catching these evasions, no procedural method of reflecting on practice, comparable to the method of the Categorical Imperative. The *orthos logos* of Aristotle's *phronimos*, that is, the reasoning by which one hits the mean (*to meson*) in action and feeling, is not constrained by an implicit method which theory lays bare.[24] It is thus misrendered by W. D. Ross as 'right principle or rule', if implied by this is either a general rule we apply or a procedure we bring to bear for constructing principles. Rather, the *orthos logos* remains always much closer to the particulars: a way of 'improvising' and 'conjecturing' (*stochazomai*) given experience and what is now at hand (1141b13; cf. 1142a33 ff., 1109a24). (Thus, *stochazomai* means both to aim and shoot at a target and to proceed by informed guessing and conjecture).

The absence of such a method reflects in general Aristotle's scepticism about the use of *technē* in ethical decision-making, and in particular (we might say by way of reconstruction) the worry that most procedures for generating or testing via principles leave out of the account the process by which we formulate the intentions to be tested. And this process depends upon what we perceive as relevant in the case, how we individuate or describe the situation.[25] If we misdescribe circumstances or fail to notice relevant

---

[24] Cf. Kant, *Groundwork*, 71.

[25] How a Kantian might incorporate such an account is taken up by Barbara Herman in 'The Practice of Moral Judgment', while Onora O'Neill considers similar issues in 'The Power of Example', *Philosophy*, 61 (1981), 4–29. Though a notion of moral perception might be found in Kant, the notion is clearly not given the same weight as it has in Aristotelian theory. Indeed, I would argue that the *Groundwork* minimizes the point, emphasizing instead the requirements of the testing procedure.

features, then the test will be testing intentions, but intentions that are inadequately responsive to what may in fact be the demands of the situation. The question is again the fit of a decision to present circumstances. And reflection which begins with the decision or intention rather than with the construal of the situation to which the intention is a response begins too far down the line.

Universalization may overlook the fit of the intention to interior circumstances as well as to exterior ones. That is, the formulated intention (and the intention one tests) may not adequately reflect one's sincere intentions or motives. Or if they are honest and sincere, they may none the less be the product of a more deep-rooted, albeit honest, deception regarding why one acted or what the circumstances were in which one acted. So, for instance, I may sincerely believe that I am acting out of respect for another, when in fact I have so acted for the sake of my reputation or honour or even out of a priggish sense of myself as virtuous. Again, I may fail to act, not for the reasons I have told myself (e.g. that I am inappropriately placed to help, etc.), but because, in fact, I undervalue another's needs or do not regard the action as sufficiently beneficial to myself. In these cases it is not sufficient to test the intentions. What is required in addition is an exploration of the alleged motives and ends which they embody. The issue is one of self-knowledge, and this cannot be canonized by a procedure.

The problem of transparency is profoundly acknowledged by Kant himself. One must try to fathom the depths of the heart, even though one can never hope fully to understand its secrets.[26] But what I have been suggesting is that an emphasis on testing intentions will not itself give us sufficient insight into how self-knowledge is to be achieved. If we begin with the idea of testing maxims, rather than with an account of how those maxims are sincerely generated, then the test may lack adequate content. It may not necessarily test the right thing. In addition, the Kantian belief that the passions are often unresponsive to reason seems to prohibit certain sorts of self-reflection and inquiry.

[26] On the depths of the heart, see Kant *The Doctrine of Virtue*, tr. Mary Gregor (University of Pennsylvania Press, 1964), 107–12.

Aristotle introduces the problem of self-knowledge in *NE* II and again in the later books on friendship, especially IX. 9. In II. 4 he insists that to act from virtue is necessarily to act knowingly, for the right reasons (1105a31) where this means consciously (*eidōs*) choosing to do what is virtuous for its own sake (1105a32), i.e. because it is fine. On the Aristotelian picture, this requires bringing *to alogon* (the non-rational part of the soul) into harmony with the rational part (*to logon exon*). More specifically, the emotions which motivate us cannot be hidden from our understanding and awareness; they must be part of our conscious and endorsed reasons for action. Part of the task of habituation, as we shall see in a later chapter, is to make motives more transparent, more susceptible to reflection as well as to warranted beliefs. As such, virtue and practical wisdom require a reflective grasp (*hupolēpsis*) of the right ends, and a confidence that actions have in fact been guided by them. Being aware of what sort of person one is (1147a5, *DA* 433a18–20) and the degree to which one exhibits avowed ends is part of critically reflective choice.

Aristotle often assigns the exploration of motives to the sphere of intimate friendships of virtue.[27] Through these sorts of friendships we gain transparency before ourselves, see ourselves, as he says in the *Magna Moralia*, as if in a mirror (*katoptron*, 1213a22). We see our foibles (*ta phaula*) and expose what we keep hidden from others (*Rh.* 1384b25). This may lead to shame and moral renewal, but, more fundamentally, to a vision of ourselves that is more resolute and definite than our purely internalized view affords. The issue is not simply that our own eyes are biased but, more generally, that the project of self-knowledge requires (external) dialogue and audience. We need 'to live together with friends and share in argument and thought' in order to be fully conscious of the sorts of lives we are leading (*NE* 1170b11–12).[28] Without this intimacy, Aristotle charges, the good

---

[27] Virtue friendship is the paradigmatic form of friendship, more lasting and complete than friendship based on utility or friendship. For an excellent discussion, see John Cooper, 'Aristotle on Friendship', in A. O. Rorty (ed.), *Essays on Aristotle's Ethics*, (University of California Press, 1980).

[28] I take this to be the conclusion of the arduous argument at 1170a15–b14, and, more precisely, the conclusion of 1170b11–14.

person cannot fully appreciate even the pleasure and goodness of his life (1170b3–10). He acts in blindness about who
he really is and, indeed, lacks true practical reason. These
are arguments we shall return to in our account of the shared
life in Chapter 4.

Now a more enlightened Kantian account may come some
way towards meeting these Aristotelian criticisms. As neo-
Kantians have persuasively argued recently, *The Doctrine of
Virtue* outlines the sort of subsidiary duties that must be
cultivated by an agent who takes seriously the moral law.
These include an education in feeling and perception such
that one will notice when beneficence is appropriate, or when
there may be a breach of justice. Also included may be the
sort of personal attachments which facilitate a self-reflective
and morally responsive life.[29] But it is not clear that for the
Kantian, the response through emotions and perception is
itself a part of what is morally valued. What is valued is the
moral choice constrained by the reasoning of the Categorical
Imperative. Properly trained feelings and judgements may
support the right choices, but they are not necessarily, as a
result of that, given moral worth. Moreover, even the instrumental role of these capacities is overlooked when the
theory is understood as offering primarily a universalizability
test of intentions. On that reading far too much of what is
needed for the assessment of action is left out.

3. PERCEIVING ETHICAL SALIENCE

The continuous thread in Aristotle's response to both rig-
orous rules from the top down and legislative procedures
from the bottom up is that they side-step the issue of how
we confront the particular case. I want to take up this issue
now. In so doing I shall be considering Aristotle's account
of ethical perception and how it figures at various stages in

---

[29] For Kant's own, brief discussion of friendship, see *The Doctrine of Virtue*,
140–5. See ch. 4, sect. 1, with notes, esp. n. 7.

the account of action. I begin with some preliminary remarks before turning to the relevant texts.[30]

On Aristotle's view, an ethical theory that begins with the justification of a decision to act begins too far down the road. Preliminary to deciding *how* to act, one must acknowledge that the situation requires action. The decision must arise from a reading of the circumstances. This reading, or reaction, is informed by ethical considerations expressive of the agent's virtue. Perception is thus informed by the virtues. The agent will be responsible for how the situation appears as well as for omissions and distortions. Accordingly, much of the work of virtue will rest in knowing how to construe the case, how to describe and classify what is before one. An agent who fails to notice unequivocal features of a situation which for a given community standardly require considerations of liberality, apparently lacks that virtue. It is not that she has deliberated badly, but that there is no registered response about which to deliberate.

This is not to suggest that most circumstances, even within a cohesive community, stand in a one-to-one relation to a description or set of ethical considerations. A given circumstance may have multiple descriptions, and yield competing ethical claims to equally virtuous individuals who simply see things differently as a result of having developed the virtues differently within their lives. Thus historical circumstance and experience may shape the full complement of virtues in different ways, and disagreements may result as to what is most pressing or relevant in a case.[31] So, for example, public beneficence in the alleviation of hunger may stand out as lexically prior to one individual and colour her response to certain circumstances, while for another the more pressing issue is strengthening the borders against enemy attacks. It is not just that guns and butter have different degrees of importance to each, but that they affect what one sees as urgent and as requiring response. Equally, they affect what each takes ultimately to be adequate action.

---

[30] My thoughts in this section have been influenced by Barbara Herman's 'The Practice of Moral Judgment'. Though her account is Kantian, a similar view applies even more perspicuously, it seems to me, to Aristotle.

[31] See ch. 4, sect. 7 and n. 28.

From this it does not follow that perceptual judgements of ethical relevance must be fixed for a given individual. There is no reason to assume that such judgements are bedrock.[32] Quite to the contrary, Aristotle insists as a requirement of virtue that we be open to inquiry and a reflective grasp of our ends. This includes reflection on our ends, conceived not abstractly but embodied and clothed in concrete circumstance. Only in this way do we actively reflect on our selves and on our lives. We have already begun to see how this works. As we have said, the virtuous agent lives a life in intimate union with others similarly committed to virtue. Through collaboration on projects and through listening to and identifying with the viewpoints of others, an agent's vision becomes expanded and enlarged (cf. 1112b11, 1112b27, 1143a12–16). The agent comes to learn different ways of reading a situation and different questions to pose in order to see the picture with increased insight and clarity. How to see becomes as much a matter of inquiry (*zētēsis*) as what to do (1112b22, 1141a35–1142b2). Such inquiry and dialogue establish the means for consensus (*homonoia*; 1167a23 ff. *EE* 1241a31–3), as well as the means for isolating differences that are genuinely irresolvable. The extent and breadth of the collaborative project will become clearer in Chapter 4. But we can already begin to appreciate that a life in dialogue with others will have its effect on how we interpret and read the circumstances of ethical action.

In addition to disagreements between individuals, the same circumstance may present competing claims to one and the same individual. The virtuous individual will have all the virtues (*NE* 1145a2), and though these cannot conflict essentially or in principle, contingent conflicts may arise. That is, virtue *A* may require one to do *x*, while virtue *B* requires one to do not *x*. Though Aristotle does not satisfactorily discuss the issue of conflict within his ethical theory, his claim that happiness is dependent upon favourable external goods can be seen to include a claim about the risk

---

[32] Cf. 1113a (and *Top.* 105a3–8) on the finality of the perception of non-ethical particulars, e.g. 'this bread'. Of course, even here there may be room for doubt, especially in the individuation of artefacts which can be seen under different descriptions depending on varying functions, contexts, and audiences. But Aristotle,

contingent conflicts place in the path of happiness. His account of such conflicts in the *Poetics* as integral to tragic plots seems to be further evidence of the effect of such conflict on one's chances of happiness. Some of these conflicts, like those between individuals, might be resolvable by reconsideration of the facts of the case in conjunction with the specific requirements of each virtue. So, for example, what seemed initially an unequivocal conflict between my more parochial and my public loyalties may soften upon reexamination; in this regard, doing something for my children may be an important expression of my civic responsibility. But a reconciliation need not always follow. Acting for certain ends may require the forfeiture (at least here and now) of other deeply valued commitments. The loss may be inescapable and not without trace. Since these issues have been examined extensively by Martha Nussbaum, I defer the reader to her discussion.[33]

Perception informed by ethical considerations is the product of experience and habituation. Through such an education, the individual comes to recognize and care about the objects of ethical consideration. Human distress becomes labelled a possible moment for generosity and unwarranted harm as an occasion for anger towards the aggressor. In this way certain facts are described evaluatively and become occasions for evaluative beliefs. Such beliefs about one's situation in turn yield reasons for action which fall within the motivational structure of specific virtues. They become specific intentions to act (*prohaireseis*) upon deliberation concerning how and in what way one should respond.[34]

Ethical sensitivity will thus be in part a matter of appropriately deploying ethical concepts. One might want to

if any one, would be sensitive to this. Cf. David Wiggins, *Sameness and Substance* (Harvard University Press, 1980).

[33] Martha Nussbaum in *The Fragility of Goodness. Luck and Rational Self-Sufficiency in Greek Ethical Thought: The Tragic Poets, Plato, and Aristotle* (Cambridge University Press, 1986), esp. chs. 11 and 12. Also T. H. Irwin, 'Permanent Happiness: Aristotle and Solon', in Julia Annas (ed.) *Oxford Studies in Ancient Philosophy*, iii (Oxford University Press, 1985), 89-124. Aristotle's explicit discussion of the dependence of happiness upon external goods is at *NE* I. 8-11 and X. 6-8. Books VIII and IX on friendship also shed light on the role of external goods. See ch. 4, sect. 2, with notes.

[34] See *NE* III. 3. I examine the deliberative process in detail in ch. 3.

argue that possessing the different virtues will include an openness to perceiving as ethically salient previously unnoticed applications of these concepts. Within Aristotle's own cultural framework, this might involve recognizing the human suffering in infancticide, or the injustice of women's and slaves' subordinate position within the social hierarchy. This point presses the difficult question of relativism, and of what an individual in a particular cultural climate can reasonably be expected to respond to given the prevailing values. I don't wish to address this problem here, except by noting that the fully enumerated list of Aristotelian virtues already reflects the political and historical realities of a specific age.

We have been considering the notion of ethical perception in a general way so far. I now want to turn to an analysis of various texts for a more precise account of the notion.

At *NE* 1114b1 ff. Aristotle asserts that the ends of action correspond to character, 'for we ourselves are somehow part causes [*sunaitioi*] of our states of character, and in being persons of a certain kind we posit the end to be so and so . . .' (1114b24). But he also asserts that how an end appears also corresponds to character:

Someone might say that everyone aims at the apparent good, but does not control its appearance; but the end appears to each person in a way that corresponds to his character. For if each person is somehow responsible for his own state of character, he will also be himself somehow responsible for its [viz. the end's] appearance [*phantasias*]. (1114b1–3; cf. 1114b17)[35]

This passage raises the difficult question, which I defer to the next chapter, of the extent to which we can choose character.[36] What I wish to focus on now is the more restricted

---

[35] For an exhaustive study of Aristotle's notion of *phantasia*, I refer the reader to Essay 5 of Martha Nussbaum, *Aristotle's De Motu Animalium* (Princeton University Press, 1978). Although Aristotle uses the term technically, it is a close relative of *phainetai* ('it appears'), and typically refers to the way an object of desire 'appears to' a subject. It is thus importantly related to the use of *phainai* in *to phainomenon agathon*—what is apparently good to an agent.

[36] In the meantime, note that Aristotle's ascription of responsibility is tentative: he qualifies the term *aitios* with *pōs* ('somehow') at both 1114b1 and 1114b23; and in the latter passage he softens *aitios* to *sunaitioi*—we are *part* causes or *partially* responsible for character.

point that character is reflected in the way an end or good appears to an agent. Aristotle's point is that an agent is not led blindly by certain ends, but controls them to the extent to which he controls his own character. What appears to him as ultimately good and as worth pursuing is a matter of his interests and dispositions. But I believe Aristotle's point can be extended to include a claim about how an agent perceives the circumstances relevant to an end. That is, how the end of good living will appear to an agent will have to do with how that agent *sees* the salient features of circumstances. The end will affect what he sees and how he composes the various scenes. To pursue an apparent good is just to construe certain moments as occasions for acting for that end.

If we think of this in terms of the practical syllogism, then responsibility for the appearance of an end includes responsibility for apprehending that now is the time for introducing a particular major premiss, that there is an occasion at hand relevant to a specific end or universal. Again, in a parallel way, we can think of this in terms of the *boulēsis* or rational wish which in a practical syllogism expresses particular ends of character and figures in the major premiss: we are responsible not merely for having certain dispositional bouletic wishes, but for these desires becoming occurrent or activated at the appropriate times.[37]

We might plausibly think that not all practical syllogisms will require this matching of bouletic desire to present circumstances. In particular, deliberations which represent future plans need not have occurrent bouletic wishes.[38] I may have, for instance, a specific end or policy (*boulēsis*) to take care of my parents in their old age and resolve now to do this at some future date. The bouletic wish, we might say, is not occurrent until I recognize that the time is right for the resolution to be enacted. Moreover, someone who argues

---

[37] The familiar distinction between dispositional and occurrent desires is applied to bouletic wishes by Alfred Mele in 'Aristotle on the Roles of Reason in Motivation and Justification', *Archiv für Geschichte der Philosophie*, 66 (1984), 124–47. His idea of an occurrent *boulēsis* as generated by the recognition of scope for some desired end (128) is essentially similar to the point I make above.

[38] Although I raise the issue of future planning here, a more detailed exploration of the notion and its relation to the practical syllogism awaits the discussion of ch. 3.

like this might acknowledge that even so I have a *present* wish for something, in the sense that I have had it and will go on having it for some time. This is to say it is dispositional. More strongly, the desire may figure in concrete bits of planning that I can do in advance of acting, e.g. ensuring that I have adequate funds, or that my house is big enough.

But I think the above line of argument is incorrect. It may be that a resolution to act (an intention) is future-indexed in the sense that enactment awaits perception of the right occasions. But the desire for some end, especially when it issues in determinate planning and resolutions, is more than merely dispositional. In such a case, it is occurrent or activated, though perhaps less by the perception of relevant circumstances than by the *anticipation* (or *phantasia*, i.e. imaginative projection) of them, e.g. my desire to care for my parents by the anticipation of their old age.[39] But even here the anticipation may arise as a result of certain perceptual signs—that they have just turned sixty, that they are nearing retirement, that they are looking older. These sorts of circumstantial signs will determine when, in fact, I act on my resolution.

There are additional texts which stress the importance of the sort of contextual perception I have been discussing. Perhaps the most celebrated passage is that which appears at the conclusion of *NE* II:

For it is not easy to define [*diorisai*] how we must be angry, and towards whom, and in what circumstances and for how long. For sometimes we praise those who are deficient and call them gentle, but sometimes we praise those who are contentious and call them brave . . . But up to what point and to what extent one can deviate before one becomes blameworthy is not easily determined by reasoning [*tōi logōi aphorisai*]. Nor is any other matter of perception. For these sorts of things are particular, and the discernment or judgement [*krisis*] rests in perception. (1109b15–23; cf. 1126b4)

This passage occurs in the context of a discussion of the mean. According to a standard formulation, action which hits the mean is directed towards the right persons, for the

---

[39] So Aristotle writes, 'the object of desire (remaining itself unmoved) originates the movement by being apprehended in thought *or imagination*' (*DA* 433b12).

right reasons, on the right occasions, and in the right manner
(e.g. 1106b21). The overwhelming sense is that virtue must
fit the case. But, as Aristotle insists above, the formula of
the mean itself seems to offer little concrete guidance.
Accordingly, attempts to find in the doctrine of the mean
a mathematical algorithm that will determine an appraisal
(or decision) seem doomed, while interpretations of it as a
principle ('always act moderately') violate the obvious truth
that many circumstances simply do not call for moderation.
Extreme anger may sometimes be just the right response.

I want to argue, nevertheless, that as a general meth-
odological point about the tailoring of action to particular
circumstances, the doctrine of the mean can have practical
force, and can lead to more individualized strategies for
accurately grasping what is relevant in a case. So Aristotle
suggests in the lines preceding the above passage that con-
scientious discernment will entail adjusting perception to
correct for biases and pleasures towards which one naturally
tends, but which are likely to distort (1109b1-12). The suggestion can be extended logically to include adjusting for
tendencies to overestimate danger, or to construe criticism
as insult, or to underestimate the self-sufficiency and
strength of others. The general notion is that determining
the mean will presuppose critical and self-reflective ways for
accurately reading the ethically relevant features of the case.
Ethical perception requires, as we saw earlier, methods by
which we can correct and expand our point of view.

The passage raises other pivotal issues. First, it needs to
be noted that Ross's translation of *krisis* in this passage—
namely as 'decision', as opposed to the rendering I have
given, 'discernment' or 'judgement'—obscures what I have
been at pains to emphasize.[40] That is, that the stage of construal and discrimination needs to be distinguished from the

---

[40] The translation of *krisis* as 'discernment' follows Martha Nussbaum in 'The
Discernment of Perception: An Aristotelian Conception of Private and Public Rationality', in John Cleary (ed.), *Proceedings of the Boston Area Colloquium on Ancient
Philosophy*, i (University Press of America, 1985). Irwin translates *krisis* as 'judgement', which I believe leaves room for the sort of point I wish to make. The
rendering 'decision' is preserved by Urmson in the revised Oxford translation. This
is of course a possible translation for *krisis*. Cognates of *krinein* are regularly used
by Aristotle to refer to critical or cognitive processes, i.e. processes which require

moment of decision (or choice) in the light of the alternatives. This bears on the next point. The passage implicitly refers to two perspectives. There is the point of view of an observer assessing another's action (i.e. praising or blaming, but equally showing understanding, approval, sympathy, or compassion—i.e. expressing reactive attitudes) and the point of view of an agent ultimately deciding how best to act. (The perspective of observer can be taken by the agent himself with regard to his own actions, and perhaps Aristotle has this in mind here; but to simplify the case, I discuss the roles as they are occupied by different individuals.)[41] Within the framework of both perspectives, the assessment/decision about action is constrained by an appreciation of the circumstances of action. That is, the kind of internal understanding essential to an agent's view of the particulars is equally central to judgements from outside of another's responsibility. Approval, condemnation, disgust, horror, and pity will not assess actions *per se*, but actions as responses to specific circumstances. This has already been brought out in our discussion of equity, where fair-minded assessment of responsibility was seen to require restoring the action to its full context, both in terms of the external circumstances and in terms of the typical pattern of behaviour of the agent (*Rh.* 1374b13-16). Such perceptual appreciation of another's circumstances will depend heavily upon imagination. At stake will be the capacity to re-enact the agent's point of view and to consider what it is like for that agent to do that action in that context.

The outside observer, then, must somehow criticize from inside. While the reactive attitudes will not themselves be exercises of practical reason (i.e. they are not first person deliberations about what to do; 1143a3-9), they are about the same things as practical reason, namely the particular circumstances of action. Moreover, the person who is wise

making distinctions and discriminations, and are contrasted with desiderative activities (see, for example, *MA* 700b20). However, since Aristotle has a more specialized term for decision (namely *prohairesis*), if this were the intended meaning one would expect him to have used that term in the passage.

[41] I have been helped here by Thomas Nagel's remarks in *The View from Nowhere* (Oxford University Press, 1986), 120-5.

with regard to his own choices is, on Aristotle's view, a fine and decent judge of other's actions too:

And it is reasonable to suppose that all these states tend towards the same point. For we assign consideration [*gnōmēn*], understanding [*sunesin*], practical reason [*phronēsis*], and *nous* to the same persons, saying that these persons have consideration and *nous*, and thus are also practically wise and understanding. For all these capacities are of the last things and are of the particulars. And indeed being a person of good understanding and of good consideration [or considerateness] consists in being able to judge [*kritikos*] those things which concern the person of practical reason. For what is equitable is the common concern of all good persons in their relations to others. (1143a25-31)[42]

Still, there is an obvious problem with the claim that wisdom with regard to my own life necessarily makes me a good judge of others' choices. Is there not the danger that I will project my own vision on to the agent's point of view? Indeed, how is knowing what the mean is 'relative to me' (1107a) helpful for knowing what the mean is relative to someone else? Aristotle does not pursue the issues further here. But presumably the same sorts of strategies that require an agent to adjust for biases in perception and choice apply to the observer intent upon fair judgement. If in judging others I tend to be exceptionally hard on those that have similar foibles to my own and, conversely, lenient towards those who excel in areas I admire but have not yet mastered, then equitable judgement, like the judgement of the mean, will require correcting for these biases. Equally, if I make too much of my own preferences and matters of taste in judging others' behaviour and so fail to distinguish between the more unequivocal requirements of a circumstance and what *I* merely would have done, then I need to be mindful

---

[42] The cognitive excellences necessary for equitable praise and blame (viz. good understanding (*eusunesia*) and fine and sympathetic consideration (*suggnōmē*)) underline the fact that the judge must take up the internal point of view of the agent. I find Irwin's translation of this passage confusing, and in general his rendering of *phronēsis* as 'intelligence' unfortunate. Translated that way, *phronēsis* sounds too much like the neutral capacity for 'cleverness' (*deinotēta*) at 1144a24. It leaves out the connotations of 'wisdom' and 'experience' which *phronēsis* surely implies. This criticism, however, does not mar my overall respect for his translation, which I have found to be, without a doubt, the best one available.

of these tendencies. As already indicated, the Aristotelian emphasis on self-knowledge within the good life (esp. *NE* IX. 9) leaves room for—indeed encourages—this sort of self-surveillance. There is a final point to notice about the above passage. The response which is being judged (in terms of its fit to the circumstances) is an emotional one: namely, whether an agent's anger is here and now appropriate. The assumption is that emotional reactions are ways of perceiving (ways of being sensitive to) particular circumstances. Through the emotions we come to recognize what is ethically salient, what for a human being counts as suffering or cruelty, what is unfair. Emotions may thus allow us to label and classify in a way that purely cognitive discrimination cannot. We shall return to this issue in the next section.

There are two additional passages which bear on the issue of ethical perception. They are fairly complex, so I will take them in turn. In *NE* VI. 9 Aristotle raises the issue by analogy:

Practical reason is obviously not scientific [*epistēmē*], for it is about the last term [the particular] [*eschatou*], as has been said. For the thing to be done is of this sort. And it is opposed to *nous*; for *nous* is about the first terms [*tōn horōn*], of which there is no account [*logos*], while practical reason is of the last thing [*tou eschatou*], which is an object not of science but of perception [*aisthēsis*]. This is not the perception of the special objects, but of the kind by which we perceive that the last figure among mathematical objects is a triangle. For perception will come to a halt here too. (1142a23–30)[43]

The passage opposes the intuitive grasp (*nous*) of first terms or most general principles (*horōn*) in deductive accounts (*epistēmai*) with the perceptual grasp of last terms (or determinate particulars) in action. The opposition, however, is

---

[43] Various points need to be noted: (*a*) Perceptual objects are not those proprietary to the different sensory modes (e.g. the objects of smell, touch, etc.; *DA* 418a), but the common sensibles. (*b*) *Nous* has been rendered in various ways by various translators: 'comprehension' (Urmson), 'understanding' (Irwin), 'inductive reason or intelligence' (Greenwood). 'Practical insight' is probably the term I would choose to characterize *nous* in its practical application. Still, I have left *nous* untranslated for want of an appropriate rendering that covers both the theoretical and the practical cases.

at best qualified, since it will turn out (in the next passage we examine), that the perception of practical circumstances through *phronēsis* is itself an exercise of *nous* in the other direction: 'For there is *nous*, not a rational account, about the first things *and* the last things' (1143a36). This apart there are various points to note. The passage repeats the claim that practical reason is not to be regarded as merely a deductive capacity. General ethical claims hold only roughly or in part; what can be said at a general level about how we ought to act is necessarily imprecise and in need of qualification to meet the particular case (1094b13). In this sense, application of ethical precepts is a very different matter from, say, application of a precept in mathematics. One needs less experience and years to recognize certain consequences of a mathematical theorem than to recognize, say, the circumstances of courageous action (1142a12-19). Given the wide array of contexts and variables, the exercise of practical reason will require considerable empirical exposure, as well as the inductive capacities to learn from such experience (1142a14-15, 1143b3-15).

Given this, the passage might be thought strange, since it after all draws an analogy between perception of ethically relevant features and perception of a mathematical figure; the geometer requires a trained eye, but one which requires comparatively less exposure and equipment. Admittedly, the analogy is inexact, but as an analogy the point it makes is reasonably clear. Aristotle has in mind a geometer, who is trying to figure out the basic compositional unit out of which a more complex geometrical figure is constructed. Perception comes to a halt (*stesetai*) at the triangle not because it is the ultimate geometrical figure (that would be a point— (*stigmē*)—not a triangle), but because it is the specific component relevant to solving this particular problem. So, if the geometer is analysing a series of connected octagons, he may see that it is composed of equilateral triangles. With this perceptual information he can go on to reconstruct correctly the more complex design.[44] He sees how to proceed.

[44] My interpretation is essentially similar to that of Troels Engberg-Pedersen, *Aristotle's Theory of Moral Insight* (Oxford University Press, 1983), 206 ff. Cf. John M. Cooper, *Reason and Human Good in Aristotle* (Harvard University Press, 1975), 33-40.

Although I have been separating the stage of construal (or perception) from the stage of reaching a decision in the light of alternative choices, the geometrical analogy suggests that the two moments may temporally coincide—that recognizing the triangle itself suffices to know how to begin to construct the figure, and so, more widely, how to act. This may sometimes be the case. To see a loved one in present and immediate danger may itself determine the action. There is no hesitation or deliberation. I just act. Many acts of courage are like this, Aristotle argues. There is no time for deliberative preparation. Instead, the act flows spontaneously from character (and vision) (1117a20–2). But while this may be true, none the less noticing a possible occasion for action and knowing exactly how to respond are conceptually separable. Noticing an occasion for courage need not result in an intention to act courageously, though to form such an intention (non-incidentally) is of course to have noticed the relevant circumstances. Thus, in so far as circumstances do not come pre-labelled as this sort of occasion or that, they must be classified by us. This process of 'seeing as' is a necessary prerequisite for action.

The passage raises the general question of where, in the process of responding and deliberating, perception enters. The short answer is that it enters at various places. I have been arguing for a certain perceptual interpretation of the major premiss, that through perception we situate and activate a general end in concrete (actual or anticipated) circumstances. However, Aristotle typically cites the minor premiss as the premiss concerned with what is particular and perceptual.[45] This is clearest in the simple example from the *De Motu*: ' "I have to drink," says appetite. "Here's drink," says sense-perception or *phantasia* or thought. At once he drinks' (*MA* 700a32–4; tr. Nussbaum). In locating the perceptual element exclusively in the minor premiss, the example seems somewhat misleading as an analogy for the ethical case. For knowing that I have to act courageously *now* involves a (logically) prior inspection of external circumstances not necessarily involved in desiring now to drink

---

[45] 1147a26. It can also be the conclusion, as my discussion of 1143a35–b5 indicates.

(not necessarily, for I may of course drink in response to seeing the cool, frothy drink placed before me).[46] Still, I am inclined to think this is not a serious problem, for Aristotle must be assuming that if a desire to bring about some end cited in the major premiss is in fact occurrent, then the necessary inspection of the particulars has been met.[47] Moreover, since, as we shall see, the minor premiss can play the role of narrowing down a more general end to circumstances, as well as of implementing antecedently fixed ends, the division of labour between major and minor premisses may be less hard and fast than standard interpretations suggest.

There are other points to note about the role of perception. In the above example from the *De Motu*, perception involves essentially an opening of my eyes, a noticing that *this* is a *that*. There is little inferential reasoning in this acknowledgement of available means.[48] In the geometrical example, by contrast, the discovery of the triangle as a means for proceeding in the construction of the complex design seems to involve a more imaginative and inferential kind of perception, inferential because the lines of the triangle are presumably not already drawn in; they have to be inferred or discovered by the geometer. Seeing the triangle is more obviously a 'figuring out' of the basic design of the complex figure. In addition to perception locating available means to ends, it enters into knowing when to implement (and make more determinate) an existing plan (to revert to our former example: 'Now is the time for me to take care of my parents'), as well as when to initiate the more distant stages of such planning ('I had better start thinking now about this eventuality and the consequences of it on other aspects of my life').

It should be clear from my remarks that I do not separate perceptual practical syllogisms from deliberative practical

---

[46] Of course, reading my appetites and other internal promptings may itself require a parallel kind of inspection.

[47] Notice that an occurrent desire may not be *kurios*—decisive or controlling— since it may be defeated by a rival desire, or by inhospitable circumstances (*MA* 701a16, *NE* 1147a30–1).

[48] Cf. *Poet.* 1448b16 ff., in which Aristotle refers to a similar process of noticing 'this is a that' as a kind of reasoning or figuring out (*sullogizesthai*); see ch. 5, sect. 4.

reasoning, as Cooper does.[49] In addition to not finding adequate warrant for the distinction in the text, I have also tried to argue that even planning that will not result in action *now* often requires the exercise of recognitional capacities similar to those involved in actually implementing a plan, (i.e. to know that now is the time to start to plan I may have to read the circumstantial signs, notice that my parents are ageing, etc.).

Finally, as we said earlier, more indirectly perceptual premisses may provide a supplementary check on our more direct perceptions. Remembering that I have these sorts of tendencies, that I am *this sort of person* (cf. *NE* 1147a5, *DA* 433a18-20), may, as we said, be part of what I am *aware* of as I critically consider what I see.

There is a final, notoriously difficult passage to which we must now turn. Since the passage has been the subject of extensive commentary, most recently by Norman Dahl,[50] I will restrict my remarks to the issues most relevant to our concerns. At 1143a35-b5, Aristotle remarks:

Nous is also concerned with the last terms [*tōn eschatōn*), and in both directions. For there is *nous*, not a rational account [*ou logos*], about the first terms [*tōn prōtōn horōn*] and the last terms or particulars [*tōn eschatōn*]. And in demonstrations there is *nous* about the unchanging and first terms while in practical reasonings [*praktikais*] *nous* is about what is last and changing, and is hence about the other premiss [*tēs heteras protaseōs*]. For these are the starting points and origins [*archai*] of the ends [*hou heneka*], since the universals emerge from the particulars [through induction, cf. 1139b28]. And of these particulars, then, we must have perception, and this is *nous*.

<hr/>

[49] See ch. 3, n. 26 for more extensive remarks about my disagreement with aspects of Cooper's account of deliberation (*Reason and Human Good*).

[50] Norman Dahl, *Practical Reason, Aristotle, and Weakness of the Will* (University of Minnesota Press, 1984), see esp. app. I, 227-36. Also, Cooper, *Reason and Human Good*, 41-5; while I agree with Cooper's understanding of *eschaton* as including *perceived* particulars as well as types whose instances *can* be perceived (or recognized), I do not agree with his sharp distinction between the deliberative stages of reasoning and the perceptual stages that is meant to correspond to that difference. Also helpful are: Richard Sorabji, 'Aristotle on the Role of Intellect in Virtue', *Proceedings of the Aristotelian Society*, 74 (1973-4), 107-29, repr. in Rorty (ed.), *Essays on Aristotle's Ethics*; Gauthier and Jolif, *Aristote: L'Éthique à Nicomagque*, ii/2, 536-7—I agree with their correction of Greenwood (69-73) in

This passage again, like the one we have just considered, contrasts theoretical *nous* of ultimate definitions with perception of what is ultimate or last (i.e. particular) in practical reasoning. However, now such perception is acknowledged to be an exercise of *nous* in the other direction. More precisely, practical *nous* is the perceptual capacity to grasp what is required as regards some more general end in these specific circumstances. Thus it yields a particular judgement or choice, such as 'I must do *x* in this sort of circumstance *as* a requirement of friendship'. And this may be an exercise of *nous* even if it turns out that the particular choice arrived at must be subject to further deliberation. In this sense, *nous*'s grasp of what is ultimate is not bedrock or unrevisable. It may prompt further reflection before one is committed to action.[51]

To have this sort of grasp, Aristotle suggests in the lines that follow (1143b8–15), depends upon experience and time of life (not literally chronological age, except in the sense in which age is meant to be a rough indicator of experience).[52] For experience gives us the eyes (*omma*) to see the particular requirements of ends correctly (1143b15).

Experience, according to Aristotle's present argument, is required for this determination; but it is also generated as a result of it. That is, it is an exercise of *nous* to know that the general end of friendship requires this sort of action now. But this determinate judgement about friendship is, as Aristotle says, the starting point (*archē*) of a wider and more comprehensive understanding of its requirements.[53] For by

insisting that practical *nous* is perception not of any concrete particulars, '*mais bien de ces réalités concrètes très particulières que sont les valeurs morales singulières*' (537).

[51] Among other difficulties, there are problems in interpreting Aristotle's term *tēs heteras protaseōs*. Though rendered by most as 'the minor premiss', I have preserved the literal translation ('the other premiss') in order to accommodate its (possible) meaning as the conclusion or final decision of a piece of deliberation, and hence as concerned with what is 'last' (*eschatou*) in practical reasoning. In so doing, I follow Dahl (*Practical Reason*, app. I).

[52] Thus, at 1095a5–8 Aristotle is explicit that immaturity may be present at any chronological age. These remarks must qualify what Aristotle means by the excellences of practical intellect having a *natural* cause at 1143b10; the idea, understood literally, is obviously foreign to his view.

[53] Note in our above passage (1143a35 ff.), starting point (*archē*) appears to have a distinct meaning from end (*tou hou heneka*). The *archai* are the *origins* of the ends of deliberation. At 1095b6 they *initiate* dialectical movement towards 'the why' (*tou*

seeing what friendship requires in this sort of case, I can go on inductively to appreciate its requirements in other relevantly similar cases. It is not that I formulate some sort of rule, but that as a result of this and past experience, I can go on to make more sensitive discriminations. Accordingly, my general understanding of the end of friendship becomes increasingly qualified and comprehensive. The various sub-ends constitutive of it are filled out, and qualified as they are related to each other, as well as to other distinct ends. This may include revision of what I saw then, through *nous*, to be choice-worthy action, or simply an understanding of its place within a more complex network of ends. In the achievement of this more comprehensive (and inductive) understanding, *nous* is engaged, for, as before, it enables us to appreciate the relevance of particular circumstances to more general ends. Thus *nous* is practical (perceptual) insight which issues in both more and less conditioned judgements about action.[54]

Finally, the inductive process must get off the ground somehow; and so in the case of the learner, Aristotle says, experience is borrowed exogenously from 'those who have experience, are older or practically wise' (1143b13). Acquiring starting-points in this way (cf. 1098b4) is not a mindless process, but one which can lead to experience only when itself viewed as an exercise in (developing) practical reason.

4. SEEING THROUGH EMOTIONS

So far we have been considering ethical perception as primarily a cognitive matter. But on Aristotle's view, attending

---

dioti). Similarly at 1098b1 ff. the *archai* (of induction) are the *starting points* (the 'thats' or 'facts'—*hoti*), which move us towards the *aitian* or cause; like *ta endoxa*, study of them is the first step in a dialectical inquiry. In other places, however, *archai* are themselves the end and explanatory cause, e.g. 1095a31-4, 1144a32. So, at 1139b27-30, *archai* are the universals which induction leads towards. Cf. *Po. An.* 81a40 ff. for general remarks on induction. The relation of inductive reasoning to dialectical reasoning is explored at length by Dahl (*Practical Reason*). For related discussion, see ch. 5, n. 32.

[54] This understanding of *nous* seems to contrast with Cooper's view in which *nous* is the grasp of ultimate first principles in ethics arrived at independently of dialectical inquiry (*Reason and Human Good*, 71). Dialectic, on his view, may give further reasons to support these principles, but it is not itself a part of the de-

to the particulars is equally a matter of emotional awareness. Often we see not dispassionately, but because of and through the emotions. So, for example, a sense of indignation makes us sensitive to those who suffer unwarranted insult or injury, just as a sense of pity and compassion opens our eyes to the pains of sudden and cruel misfortune. We thus come to have relevant points of view for discrimination as a result of having certain emotional dispositions. We notice through feeling what might otherwise go unheeded by a cool and detached intellect. To see dispassionately without engaging the emotions is often to be at peril of missing what is relevant.

As we shall see in a later chapter, the beliefs and construals which we come to form as a result of these sensitivities are themselves constitutive of the actual emotional response. On Aristotle's view, anger cannot be felt without an appropriate cognition that one has been slighted or injured, or fear without an appropriate cognition that one faces danger, etc.[55] The cognitions are essential concomitants for experiencing the emotion. As such, Aristotelian emotions are not blind feelings like itches or throbs, but intentional states directed at articulated features of an agent's environment. But whatever the constitution of emotions, the point I wish to emphasize now is that certain features are noticed rather than others, largely because of specific emotional vulnerabilities.

Still, this might establish only a ministerial role for the emotions. It might be argued that emotions assist us in noticing what is ethically salient, but lack moral worth in their own right. The Kantian argues essentially this. On that view, affective responses have no intrinsic moral worth of their own. Their cultivation is rather a derivative and instrumental duty: 'so many means to participating from moral

liberative or perceptual grasp of them. On the view I suggest above, *nous* includes a grasp of both more and less conditioned judgements about action. The most determinate grasp is informed by a comprehensive understanding of ends, which can best be described as dialectical understanding. See ch. 1, n. 7.

[55] This is clear from the discussion of emotion in the *Rhetoric*. See, for example, *Rh.* II. 2. I discuss the issue further in ch. 5, sect. 4. There is some anticipation of this in the Platonic account of the spirited or thumetic part of the tripartite soul (*Rep.* IV 436 ff.). It is described as the ally of the rational part, which through such feelings as repugnance and anger often opposes the blind urges of the appetitive part. But exactly how it works through or with reason is ultimately unclear, and awaits the developed account of intentionality Aristotle offers.

principles and from the feelings appropriate to these principles.'[56] Emotions enhance moral perception and provide a system of supportive motives which make adherence to the moral law easier.[57] Thus, if it is morality within the human sphere that is our concern, then the moral law must be experienced not only as a constraint (i.e. as a Categorical Imperative), but as a constraint whose application depends upon noticing what sorts of situations are morally relevant for humans. And this may be conveyed to us through the emotions—by visiting the sick-beds, as Kant says, so we can recognize who is in pain, and who, accordingly, requires our beneficence. But for the Kantian, while emotions are heuristic, their presence makes no essential difference to the ascription of moral worth. There is no necessary moral difference betweeen the person who has a sympathetic disposition and the person who lacks one. Though most moral motives will lack purity (i.e. will contain an admixture of emotion alongside pure practical reason), it is none the less reason, not affection, which grounds morality and which is the locus of moral praise.

The Kantian rationale for restricting the feelings is all too familiar: moral feelings are viewed as highly partial and unreliable; consequently there are circumstances to which we ought to be responsive, but are not so inclined. If it is always open to say that an agent ought or ought not to have responded with moral feelings, then there are independent

---

[56] 'Hence we have an indirect duty to cultivate the sympathetic natural (aesthetic) feelings in us and to use them as so many means to participating from moral principles and from the feelings appropriate to these principles. Thus it is our duty: . . . not to shun sick-rooms or debtors' prisons in order to avoid the painful sympathetic feelings that we cannot guard against. For this is still one of the impulses which nature has implanted in us so that we may do what the thought of duty alone would not accomplish' (Kant, *The Doctrine of Virtue*, 126). Cf.also p. 14: 'The counterpart of a metaphysic of morals, the other member of the division of practical philosophy, in general would be moral anthropology. But this would concern only the subjective conditions that hinder or help man in putting into *practice* [emphasis in text] the laws given in a metaphysic of morals. It would deal with the generation, propagation, and strengthening of moral principles (in the education of school children and of the public at large), and other such teachings and precepts based on experience. This cannot be dispensed with, but it must not precede a metaphysic of morals or be mixed with it.'

[57] Cf. Barbara Herman, 'On the Value of Acting from the Motive of Duty', *Philosophical Review*, 40 (1981), 359–81.

grounds which set moral requirements. But this picture is overly simple. To say that emotions can be blind and unreliable is to give too thin an account of them. For one can agree that sentiments have to be guided, made less blind, habituated as reliable dispositions, without claiming that this thereby invalidates their role in ethical perception.[58] It is best argued by Aristotle, if anyone, that emotions are educable, that affective capacities can be cultivated to yield dispositions that are enduring and responsive to appropriate objects and values. To see through the emotions need not presuppose, as Kant sometimes suggests, a romantic spirit free of calm and deliberate intention.

But the Aristotelian claim is really stronger. Even if without the emotion we could somehow see ethical salience, the way we see would still be defective and imperfect. That is, we might have the right (ethical) viewpoints, but lack the right modes of seeing and appreciating.[59] We would see with an inferior kind of awareness. The point is that without emotions, we do not fully register the facts or record them with the sort of resonance and importance that only emotional involvement can sustain. It is as if we could see, but only flatly and inertly, as if our perceptions were strung together in our minds but not fully understood or embraced. We would be like those who recite Empedocles without knowing what it means, or like a bad actor rehearsing lines without fully taking on the part.

Aristotle makes these sorts of claims about the akratic's knowledge (1146b30–1147a4, 1147a10–24). Like the akratic, whose failure to perceive is on Aristotle's view really a failure to be motivated by what he sees,[60] here the failure to feel is

---

[58] Larry Blum's distinction between altruistic sentiments and mere inclinations in *Friendship, Altruism and Morality* (Routledge and Kegan Paul, 1980) is instructive here.

[59] I have been helped in this paragraph and the next by Nussbaum's 'The Discernment of Perception', esp. 188–9.

[60] This is a controversial point, since Aristotle does seem to conclude his discussion of *akrasia* in *NE* VII. 3 by agreeing with Socrates that *akrasia* is, after all, an intellectual failure rather than a failure of desire. It is a failure of the minor premiss, Aristotle says, to perceive correctly the particular instance. If this is the conclusion, though, it is most surprising, since Aristotle begins his account by discrediting Socratic intellectualism as flying in the face of the facts (1145b28). In the light of this, I concur with Nussbaum that the way to understand the failure of

really a failure to record with the whole self what one sees. In a sense one lacks insight or *nous*, for one fails to situate the circumstances in the context of ongoing commitments. So, for example, when I fail to help another when I know I can and should, it may be that I *see* the other's distress, but see it without the proper acknowledgement and sympathy. I don't take it all in, or understand what the full consequences of their circumstances are for them or me. The source of the problem may not be an overly strong rival desire, but simply a phlegmatic response to the situation. Accordingly, the solution is not to quiet the passions, as Plato might have suggested through his notion of a rationally ordered soul, but to appeal to them, to be aroused by their sensitivity, to see with the heart.

The general spirit of these remarks also emerges from Aristotle's views about the sort of vision that comes with ethical maturity. As we have noted, Aristotle tells us that youth must 'attend to the undemonstrated sayings and beliefs of those who have experience and who are older and wiser, no less than to demonstrations. For these people see correctly because experience has given them the eye' (1139b10). Implicit is the notion that to see from experience is to see with the eyes of one who has *lived through* the different moments of life, who has witnessed and judged not abstractly and at a safe distance (cf. 1142a12-16), but up close, where the face and look of others can have an impact on how one reacts. The novice who has not yet encountered these moments cannot see and comprehend in the same way. The capacity for sympathy and goodwill may no doubt be there, and may be there in less diluted form than in the adult;[61] but the knowledge of towards whom and when and to what degree to express these tendencies will be absent. It is not merely that the novice cannot reliably discriminate the objects of due sympathy, etc., but that even if he could, his response would most likely lack a depth and insight which

perception is as a failure to see in a way that could motivate; see her 'Discernment of Perception', 189.

[61] *Rh.* 1389a33 ff.; cf. *NE* 1144b5 ff.

comes only from having lived and suffered.[62] The celebrated gnome of the *Oresteia—pathei mathos—*clearly has
application here. I believe it is in this stronger sense of
responding with emotion that Aristotle intends us to understand virtue as both a way of acting and a way of feeling.
Thus, on his view, ways of feeling are included with the
specific virtues and vices. Virtues are defined as states 'by
which we stand well or badly with regard to feelings'
(1105b26; cf. 1105b21–1106a13). To hit the mean is to act
in a way that is appropriate to the case, but equally to respond with the right sort of emotional sensitivity (1109a23),
to act in the manner of virtue (1107a4).

Our emotions affect how and what we see, but equally
how others see and respond to us. This is clear enough in
the case of friendship; for we do not fulfil the role of a true
friend if we fail to respond with proper feeling to another's
anguish or joy.[63] A placid and nonchalant response to my
friend's news that her father has fallen seriously ill fails to
convey the comfort one expects from a friend. Friendship
thus depends upon face to face communication which cannot
be conveyed by a third party. To the extent that I fail to
communicate appropriate affective expressions, I fall short
as a friend. But just as important, Aristotle insists, is con-
veying to others who are not our friends the proper affective
signs and gestures.[64] We must be willing to express both our
delight and enthusiasm at others' actions and our annoyance
or anger (1126b28–33). Aristotle's point again is that others
must directly feel our presence, *know* our reactions through
the direct communication of emotion and bodily response;
others must become vulnerable to us just as we have become
vulnerable to them. The issue here is not one of emotion
internally affecting *us* and our perceptions, but of it externally affecting *others* and *their* perceptions of us. At stake
is the (emotional) impact we have on others. Others may not

---

[62] Notice Aristotle's qualification of this point at *Rh.* 1389a15 ff. in which he
suggests too much experience of one's own and others' misfortunes may lead to
despair and cynicism.

[63] See *EE* 1240a36–9, 1244b18–23.

[64] This is discussed in *NE* IV. 6.

fully appreciate our response when it is pried apart from its emotional content.

We have been considering emotions as reactive responses which affect the agent as well as the observer. But within Aristotle's moral psychology, there is a level of emotion that underpins these responses. This is a sense of caring about these responses, of their mattering in the very way that virtue pursued for its own sake matters. This commitment and love is manifest in sensitivities that are not fleeting and discrete, but part of a pattern of life or character. They mark an ongoing attention to long-term ends and goods, a kind of vigilance and loyalty.

5. STRATEGIES FOR EXPANDING HORIZONS

We have seen that the effective moral agent must be exposed to a wealth of diverse circumstances. For it is not enough to have the right states of character; in addition one must have capacities for knowing when and how to exhibit them. An agent is praised not merely for possession of virtue, but for its exercise and exemplification in concrete circumstances. In this sense, virtue is a capacity to choose (1107a1) and reason correctly. Yet this requirement may present a formidable challenge. Present circumstances regarding what is just or courageous now may be so radically unlike previous circumstances that experience may fail to enable an agent to know how to go on. As such, contingencies may thwart not merely the success of action in achieving intended consequences, but the very ability to respond and choose. In this section I want to consider the sort of flexibility Aristotle demands of practical reason, and the strategies he suggests for expanding one's experience.

The virtuous person is portrayed by Aristotle as one who knows how to act and feel in ways appropriate (*hōs dei*) to the circumstances. As Irwin has put it recently, this entails not merely that efforts are well intentioned and appropriate,

but that actions are correct and successful.[65] Thus, right
reason (*orthos logos*) is correct or successful reason. The
virtuous person succeeds in making the right choices (*kator-
thein*); he hits the mean. This can be easily misconstrued.
Aristotle's point is *not* that fine action requires the achievement of causal consequences, but that it requires knowing
how to exemplify virtue here and now.[66] Thus, decisions
that are clearly right or correct may none the less lead to
unforeseeable ill consequences.[67] What the Aristotelian
agent is praised for is the decision, not the external results.

What Aristotle requires of virtue is nevertheless itself a
tall order. For contingencies may place limitations at the
moment of choice, whatever further impediments affect the
outcome. As such, externalities may impede not only one's
chances of happiness (i.e. one's chances of complete and
realized virtuous activity), but one's chances of goodness
(i.e. one's chances of responding and deciding *hōs dei*—in a
way that is appropriate now). And this is so however lucky
one may have been in acquiring virtue in the first place.
Thus we might say that there are at least three (reasonably
distinguishable) moments at which chance affects virtuous
activity: (1) At the front end, in so far as extrinsic goods
affect the acquisition of virtuous states. Thus a good family,
fine *paideia* (or education), sufficient leisure, adequate temperament, etc., are all preconditions of virtue. (2) At the
moment of response and choice, in so far as we need the
right sorts of resources and experience to set our virtue
successfully in action. (3) In the accomplishment of virtuous
actions, in so far as the complete and unimpeded exercise of
virtue is requisite for happiness. It is the second moment
that I have been, and will continue, focusing on.

[65] T. H. Irwin, 'The Unity of Aristotelian Virtue' in Julia Annas (ed.), *Oxford
Studies in Ancient Philosophy*, vi (Oxford University Press, 1988) (from the Oberlin
Colloquium of 1986).
[66] David Charles's discussion in 'Aristotle: Ontology and Moral Reasoning' (in
Julia Annas (ed.), *Oxford Studies in Philosophy*, iv (Oxford University Press, 1986))
seems to support my general view.
[67] This is the force of Aristotle's distinction between accidents which occur
through no fault of an agent, and failures of judgement which could have been
avoided (*NE* 1135a25, 1136a5-10, *Rh.* 1374b4-10). While accidents diminish one's
chances of happiness, they ought not to reflect badly on character. See Marcia
Homiak's excellent paper on the extent to which the virtuous agent minimizes the

For some actions the requisite experience will be quite ordinary and everyday, nothing very special. In other cases, more specialized expertise will be in order. So, for example, Irwin argues that the virtue of magnanimity, in so far as it is concerned with public benefaction, requires a level of prosperity and managerial skills grander than its more ordinary counterpart, generosity; it will be more like running General Motors than the corner grocery store. Yet, since the virtuous person must have all the virtues (large-scale and small-scale), he will require the more specialized sorts of expertise as well as the more ordinary. Irwin argues that the fact that virtue depends on this sort of encyclopaedic experience may diminish the overall attractiveness of Aristotle's account. Moreover, even if one were to abandon Aristotle's belief in the unity of virtues (i.e. the claim that if a person has one virtue he has them all), the demand that virtue issue in the right choices might still place an over-stringent requirement on the sort of experience virtue requires.

But various lines need to be drawn. To demand that virtue include wide and even specialized experience is of course not to demand that the practically wise person be prepared for *all* logically possible contingencies. Distinctions between what are more remote and more probable contingencies must obviously be made. To take a controversial example, a responsible choice to have an abortion in the first three months of pregnancy need not take into account the possibility of viability some day being pushed back to conception. That is a contingency we simply do not have to be prepared for at this time.[68] So too for the Athenian, the wise choice concerning allocations of public health funds did not need to take into account prospects for longevity that far exceeded the contemporary figures for average life expectancy. To be prepared for historically probable contingencies is enough.

Similarly, we might want to separate off from the notion

effect of externalities on happiness: 'The Pleasure of Virtue in Aristotle's Moral Theory', *Pacific Philosophical Quarterly*, 66 (1985), 93–110.

68 For an illuminating discussion of this issue, see Alan Zaitchik, 'Viability and the Morality of Abortion', in Joel Feinberg (ed.), *The Problem of Abortion* (Wadsworth, 1984), 58–64; repr. from *Philosophy and Public Affairs*, 10 (1981).

of experience familiarity with the sorts of circumstances that challenge even the most expert knowledge. So, for example, knowing how and in what way to help an individual who suffers contamination from a relatively unknown substance may simply await more familiarity with such cases. Collectively, there is not enough experience to know how to choose correctly. Wisdom awaits the gradual development of experience in this area. In so far as there is general ignorance about these matters, the expectations of the practically wise agent are relaxed.

These sorts of remarks are consistent with Aristotle's comments about equitable judgement in our ascription of praise and blame. To judge others we must appreciate the particular circumstances of action; as we have said, the observer's assessment, like the agent's response and choice, cannot be abstracted from these circumstances. If the circumstances baffle even the expert, then this tells us something about what it is reasonable to expect.

These sorts of cases may be distinguished in turn from those in which a character state can be more easily adapted to new circumstances. We expect the courage and skill of a general to include adapting battle techniques to new terrains and environmental conditions. Some preparedness for the most likely contingencies and efficiency in instituting changes seem to be part of the job. In other cases we may demand less, and are satisfied with a willingness and ready ability to learn new skills. The hoplite who joins the naval fleet must learn new techniques for warfare. In so far as the old methods do not easily translate into the new ones, intelligence and receptivity to new ideas become crucial. These are necessary for expanding the skills prerequisite for virtue. In yet other cases, what is most crucial is a recognition of the limits of one's experience and an acknowledgement that one may need external assistance.

This last point is pivotal if we are to acknowledge the collaborative nature of Aristotle's account of practical reason. To have practical wisdom, Aristotle writes in *NE* VI. 8, is to be interested in one's own welfare as part of the common welfare: 'one's own good cannot exist without household management or a form of government' (1142a9–

10). Practical wisdom must include political wisdom in a significant way (1141b23). This is explicit early on, in the very description in *NE* I. 7 of the criterion of self-sufficiency: the self-sufficiency of the human good is characterized not by a solitary existence, but by a life lived in social relations with others (1097b8-14). If one is to manage the ends of that life well, one will require deliberative skills that apply to community living.

This has obvious implications for the resources available for ethical perception and choice. If good living is co-operative, then the experience and expertise required for virtuous action need not reside separately in each individual, but can be borrowed from others; clearly this division of labour is part of household and political wisdom, and a part of practical wisdom in so far as it extends to include the former two.[69] In this respect, we might comment, the adult is remarkably like the child—dependent upon others who have the experience and wisdom one lacks; undemonstrated beliefs must at times be sought from others and trusted (1112b10, 1143b11-14). Unlike the child, however, the adult knows better when and how to seek such counsel, and this of course is itself the result of experience.

The idea that expert counsel counts as part of one's own resources in virtuous action is perhaps most explicit in the discussion of practical reasoning in *NE* III. 3. Certain ends are regarded as impossible, Aristotle says, when we lack available means; those that are possible, he says: 'are brought about through our own powers [*di'hēmōn*]; and in a sense this includes what our friends achieve for us, since the originating principle [*archē*] is in ourselves' (1112b27-8).

We shall go on to consider the case of friendship in Chapter 4. But for the moment it needs to be recognized that external counsel may not in all cases be a viable option. In emergencies, a direct response may be required, and required *now* of *me*. If time is of the essence, then *I* may have

---

[69] Thus political wisdom 'embraces' and 'controls' all the other more particular ends in the city; it is an 'architectonic' study (1094b1-7).

to be the one who helps, if anyone is to do so at all. While it remains an open question just when virtue requires my direct response, and at what cost, nevertheless here, if anywhere, the empirical baggage may have to hang from my shoulders, and mine alone.[70]

---

[70] A shorter version of this chapter was read at the American Philosophical Association Pacific Division Meetings in March 1987. I am grateful to Ronald Polansky for his public comments during the session.

3

THE CHOICES OF A CHARACTER

WE have been considering ethical perception as an exercise of practical reason (*phronēsis*) preliminary to choice. Ethical perception is a registering of the ethical features of a situation in response to which action may be required. But once an occasion is acknowledged as possibly requiring action, how and in what way to act, if at all, is a separate matter. Sometimes it will be a matter which requires conscious deliberation, sometimes not. But in either case, the choice is something for which an agent is held accountable. It is subject to explanation and justification. In this chapter I want to take up various rationality constraints placed upon ethical choice.

Any discussion of ethical action must of course fall within Aristotle's extensive discussion of the rationality of action. His work on the general theory of action is foundational in the history of philosophy, and unparalleled in its lasting contribution to most contemporary accounts. This has been taken up most recently in a scholarly and comprehensive way by David Charles.[1] While I shall be concerned with parts of the more general theory of action, my primary interest is the ethical account, and the special nature of moral reasoning. To the extent that I look at the general account, it will be in order to illuminate the deliberation and reflection characteristic of the good person.

We can frame the inquiry by taking up two related objections. The first, put most bluntly, is that Aristotle lacks an adequate account of moral reasoning. Thus, while there is no shortage of examples of technical deliberation, such as how a doctor deliberates to bring about healing, we have no

[1] David Charles, *Aristotle's Philosophy of Action* (Cornell University Press, 1984).

comparable examples of how a person of character deliberates to promote the ends of that character. We lack a
full account of how an agent reasons about the ends of good
living.[2] The second objection is that while Aristotle has an
account of how we reason about a decision to act now, he lacks
a more general account of intention that can accommodate
both present intention and future intention—that is, an intention now to act later.[3] The two challenges, I want to
argue, are related, though often not by the objectors. Deliberation about how best to live over the course of a life
requires a continuing interest in one's future self and a capacity to decide upon future ends that constrain the present
as well as being constrained by it. An Aristotelian conception
of the good life, with its intrinsic sense of comprehensiveness
and completeness over time,[4] requires this close knit of present and future. But if this is so, then the capacity to deliberate
about the future and to regulate the present in the light of
future plans will be particularly urgent in the living of such
a life. Deliberation about future intentions should, if anywhere, play a prominent role here. It will be a severe lim-
itation on Aristotle's view if his account of deliberation
precludes such a role for practical reason.

I want to argue that it does not, and that Aristotle has a
systematic account of deliberation about good living that
incorporates a general notion of intention, including a notion
of future intention. The account takes the notions of a character and the choices that exhibit character—*prohaireseis*—
as central. The idea is this: a character, for Aristotle, produces

---

[2] John M. Cooper raises this objection in *Reason and Human Good in Aristotle*
(Harvard, University Press, 1975) p. 1. Also, cf. Anthony Kenny, *Aristotle's
Theory of the Will* (Yale University Press, 1979), chs. 13 and 14.

[3] Cf. Donald Davidson, 'Intending', in *Essays on Action and Events* (Oxford
University Press, 1980), 96. Cooper in *Reason and Human Good*, Part I, and
Martha Nussbaum in Essay 4 of *Aristotle's De Motu Animalium* (Princeton
University Press, 1978) attempt, in quite different ways, to address this objection.
My account differs from each of these in focusing on the issue of future intention
in ethical deliberation.

[4] 1098a18. T. H. Irwin persuasively argues that happiness may require a length
of time shorter than a life, such that within a given life there can be periods of
happiness as well as its opposite ('Permanent Happiness: Aristotle and Solon' in
Julia Annas (ed.), *Oxford Studies in Ancient Philosophy*, iii (Oxford University
Press, 1985), 89-124).

plans that express an overall unity of ends in a life. Such planning is carried out by the deliberative capacities and by a capacity to make reasoned choices, or *prohaireseis*. These choices involve the assessment of actions as they cohere within some overall system of good living as well as the arrangement and revision of ends within that system. In so far as they are about long-term ends, prohairetic choices are often future indexed.[5]

1. PRESENT AND FUTURE INTENTION

I shall now consider the place of future intention and planning in Aristotle's account of moral reasoning. It may be objected that we are not even licensed to assume Aristotle has a notion of present intention. For it is well known that Aristotle claims that the conclusion of a piece of practical reasoning is an action; as he says in the *De Motu Animalium*, 'one acts swiftly and straightaway' (701a22). Most agree that this remark and similar ones are problematic, since while deliberation can result in a resolution to act, i.e. a decision or intention, it cannot equally result in an action—for actions, unlike decisions to act, are contingent upon the co-operation of a friendly world.

But I do not believe Aristotle is in fact claiming here (or elsewhere) that deliberation necessarily results in immediate action. For a start, circumstances, internal or external, may impede action. In the *De Motu* Aristotle thus adds the important caveat that an agent acts 'if nothing prevents or compels him' (701a16; cf. *NE* 1147a31), and in a related passage in the *Metaphysics* (1048a17-21), he repeats that action is necessary only so long as there are no obstacles and, moreover, the agent desires something in a decisive way

---

[5] I shall sometimes translate *prohairesis* as simply 'choice', though it should be understood that Aristotle's term has a far more restrictive meaning than our term 'choice' implies. If there is a more general notion in Aristotle it is captured by the verb *hairesthai*—to choose.

(*kuriōs oregetai*).[6] Again in *Rh*. II. 19, Aristotle says emphatically that action ensues whenever an individual has the ability and wish to do a thing, and 'nothing impedes him' or 'nothing external prevents him' (1392b21-2). In making these qualifications, Aristotle seems well aware of the distinction between intention and action, arguing that intention is translated into action only when certain favourable conditions are met. It thus does not seem at all unwarranted to ascribe to Aristotle a notion of intention.

But these passages do not speak to the issue of future intention.[7] The sort of phenomenon I have in mind is this: I can decide in June to go to a meeting in August. But my intention, having been formed, leads to no immediate action. In this case I act later, not because immediate action is now blocked by internal or external factors, but simply because I have planned from the start to go later. Indeed this is the very point of future intention: to intend now to act later.

Does Aristotle recognize this phenomenon? That he has a notion comparable to ours is quite clear from *Rh*. II. 19. In discussing there the idea of an action or event that is possible, Aristotle distinguishes intentions implicit in past actions from those implicit in present and future actions:

Questions about the past can be considered as follows: . . . That if an individual had the power and wish to do a thing [*edunatai kai ebouletai*], he has done it; for every one does do whatever he wishes to do whenever he can, there being nothing to impede him. . .And about matters concerning the future, these are clear from the same considerations: . . . That a thing will be done if there is both the power and wish to do it. . .that the thing will be done if the individual is now setting about to do it [*en hormēi*] or is going to do it later [*mellēsei*] (1392b15-20, 1393a1-5).

It seems unequivocal that in the last part of this passage Aristotle has in mind a notion of future intention—a notion

---

[6] The meaning of this last phrase is unclear, but it seems to imply that a necessary condition for action is that an agent's desire for that action should override rival desires. For further discussion of this passage, cf. Richard Sorabji, *Necessity, Cause and Blame* (Cornell University Press, 1980), 238-40, where he raises the issue of whether alternative desires can be among the obstacles that prevent action. Cf. also *NE* 1147a30-1.

[7] My formulations in this paragraph have been improved by Richard Kraut's most helpful criticisms of an earlier draft. The central example is his.

of intending now to do something later. The intention is not merely a desire to act in the future, but a commitment to act; if nothing prevents action, we can expect that the intention will be executed when the appropriate time comes: 'If a person was going to do something he has done it; for it is likely that the intention [*ton mellonta*] was carried out' (*Rh.* 1392a25). There is corroborative evidence at *DA* 433b6–10, where Aristotle notes that creatures with a 'sense of time' (*aisthēsin chronou*) can foresee (or anticipate) future pleasures (*horan to mellon*): they can resolve now to act for goods that can be realized only in the future.

Given that Aristotle recognizes this notion of future intention, we would expect this to be reflected in his account of the practical syllogism. I shall argue that it is, and that there is an extended account of planning implicit in the practical inference. But before making good that claim, we need to consider in a systematic way the general features of the practical syllogism.

2. THE PRACTICAL SYLLOGISM

The broad lines of the syllogism have been echoed in Donald Davidson's writings.[8] On Davidson's view, a reason for action consists of a desire and belief, or what Davidson calls a 'pro-attitude' and belief. For Aristotle, the case is parallel. Desire (*orexis*) and reason (*nous*) are the 'movers' of agents (*DA* 433a9, *MA* 700b19), and each is represented formally by premisses in the syllogism. The major premiss, 'the premiss of the good' (*MA* 701a25), thus expresses a desire for some object or apparent good to be realized. The minor premiss expresses a belief or perception about how to realize or further specify the end expressed in the major premiss. Since the proposed course of action must be supposed to be within the agent's power (*eph' hēmin*) (*NE* 1112a28–34), this premiss is labelled the 'premiss of the possible' (*MA*

---

[8] See Donald Davidson, *Essays on Actions and Events* (Oxford University Press, 1980).

701a25). The conclusion which follows is an action 'if nothing prevents or compels' (*MA* 701a16). As we said earlier, given this last caveat, it is not too far-fetched to say the conclusion is an intention or commitment to act.

The purpose of the practical syllogism, Aristotle argues in the *De Motu*, is to give a rational account of action comparable to the rational account of belief in the demonstrative syllogism. In the latter case, we explain beliefs on the basis of antecedent beliefs; in the former, we explain intentions on the basis of antecedent beliefs and desires:

> It looks as if almost the same thing happens as in the case of reasoning and making inferences about unchanging objects. But in that case the end is a speculative proposition (for whenever one thinks the two premisses, one thinks and puts together the conclusion), whereas here the conclusion which results from the two premisses is the action (701a8-12; tr. Nussbaum).

We need to attend to several points of explication regarding the practical syllogism before proceeding. First, we need to say more about the reference to desire in an agent's reasons for action. In an unequivocal way, Aristotle is a theorist for whom reasons for action must be desire-based. So Aristotle claims at *DA* III. 10 that motivation rests in desire, and that where there is no desire, there is no action:

> Thus there is one mover, which is the desiderative faculty [*to orektikon*]. For if there were two, reason and desire, which moved to action, they would do so according to something common to both. But in fact, reason doesn't appear to move without desire (for *boulēsis* is a kind of desire, and whenever an agent is moved according to reasoning, he is also moved according to *boulēsis*) (433a21-5 ff.).

Aristotle does not insist here or elsewhere that reasons for action must appeal to antecedently existing desires; he thus, leaves it open that considerations may give rise to a present desire just as they may appeal to one that is prior. (So, for example, I become thirsty upon seeing the frothy beer vs. I look for a beer because I am thirsty.) Equally, the desires may be non-rational or those peculiar to the rational part— rational wishes (*boulēseis*). All the same, the implication is that a reason for action will appeal to some desire or other.

As he says in the *Nicomachean Ethics*, 'thought by itself moves nothing' (*dianoia d' autē outhen kinei*, 1139a35). Motivation requires some form of desire.

But this needs to be qualified. For in a certain way, it is not an agent's desires *per se* that are among his reasons, since reasons are considerations which move one, and it is less an agent's awareness of his affective state that moves him than an awareness of the *objects* of his desires.[9] This is obvious in the case of emotions: the reason I run out of the room is not because I notice that I feel fear, but because I am aware of (or imagine) some dreaded object in the room. There is an object or intentional content to my emotion. Thus, I act because I see, imagine, or believe there to be features in the world relevant to my desire or affective state, and not typically because I am aware of the fact that I desire or am presently in such a state. Similarly, my reason for acting generously now is not because I introspectively attend to that desire and notice generous feelings welling up inside me, but because, through experience, I now recognize features in the world relevant to that dispositional desire, e.g. poverty, persons worse off than me, urgency, etc.

Now Aristotle, more than most theorists, is clear about this. His opening claim in the *Nicomachean Ethics* is that intentional action aims at some good (*agathou tinos ephiesthai*). The reason for acting thus focuses not on desire, but on the desired object—some good. In the *De Anima*, again, the mover is ultimately 'the object of desire [*to orekton*]—whether it be an actual good or apparent good' (433a28). And in the *De Motu* the object of desire is also called an object of thought, indicating that it must be conceived in a certain way if it is to be desired (700b24). To frame this in terms of the practical syllogism, the major premiss represents a desire (*orexis*) for an object that is always conceived or imagined in some specific way.[10] Thus, in a fundamental

---

[9] This point is emphasized by Stephen Darwall in *Impartial Reason* (Cornell University Press, 1983), 37. The first part of his book provides a helpful critique of the notion of a desire-based reason.

[10] 'It follows that while that which is a mover must be one in kind, namely the desiderative faculty and ultimately the object of desire, for remaining in itself unmoved it moves *by being thought or imagined* . . .' (*DA* 433b10-12; cf. 433a20, *MA* 700b23, 701a3-5). On the intentionality of Aristotle's notion of *orexis*, cf.

way, belief enters not only into the minor premiss, but in the very specification of the end desired in the major premiss.[11] Elsewhere, Aristotle puts the point in this way.[12] When we desire something it is analogous to accepting a proposition *that* something is good. And the particular mode of accepting or assenting to something as good is that under favourable conditions (e.g. no impediments, rival desires, etc.) this will lead to action, i.e. to pursuit or avoidance: 'Perception or sensation is like simple saying and thinking, and when the perceived object is pleasant or painful, the soul pursues or avoids as if it were affirming or denying it' (*DA* 431a7-14). The thought recurs in the *Nicomachean Ethics*: 'What in the case of intellect is affirming or denying, that in the case of desire is desiring or being averse . . . what the argument asserts must be exactly what the desire pursues, (1139a21-6). The claim is that desire, so to speak, accepts some proposition—that *x* is good—and accepts it in a way that , unlike mere assertion, motivates.

We might say in passing, that once we get this far, it becomes obvious why Aristotle takes perception to be such an important part of the training of desires. As we said in the last chapter, we shape desires in part by shaping beliefs about their objects, about what people take to be goods or damages. Desires may of course be recalcitrant and lag behind revised beliefs. But Aristotle's account of desire suggests that it is because something seems good to us that we desire it, and not that it is good because we desire it. If we

---

Martha Nussbaum, 'The "Common Explanation" of Animal Movement', in Paul Moraux (ed.), *Proceedings of the Ninth Symposium Aristotelicum* (Berlin, 1983), revised and expanded in *The Fragility of Goodness. Luck and Rational Self-Sufficiency in Greek Ethical Thought: The Tragic Poets, Plato, and Aristotle* (Cambridge University Press, 1986), ch. 9.

[11] In some formulations of the major premiss Aristotle obscures the role of desire, emphasizing instead the notion of a general precept. This is notably so at *DA* III. 11 and *NE* VII.3; thus, in the latter text, we have the akratic's major premiss 'Everything sweet ought to be tasted' (1147a29). Still, it is easy to appreciate that there is an implicit pro-attitude here, that the major premiss posits a desired end towards which action is directed. Moreover, the universal formulation no less than the first person statement of desired end leaves open the possibility of adding encumbrances and restrictions to the precept.

[12] I am indebted here to David Charles's formulation in *Aristotle's Philosophy of Action*, 84-96.

can change how things appear to us, then we are in a position to begin to reform our desires.

Thus it is not so much desire itself but the object of desire which bears on an Aristotelian agent's reasons for action. It might be argued, however that what Aristotle says is much weaker. When he says that where there is no desire (*orexis*) there is no action (*DA* 433a23), he may mean no more than that if action occurred, we can infer there was a motive. *Orexis* becomes a generic motive of voluntary action. It is like our inferring that an agent 'wanted' to act simply from the fact that she acted, that her action was not like a knee jerk or a twitch. On this reading, *orexis* is simply a directional pull, implying not desire or passion, but simply intentionality.[13]

Now it is true, in the *De Anima* passage in question, that Aristotle does not require any great display of anticipation or passion in order for the ascription of *orexis* to be made. *Orexis* motivates action, but not because of the alleged affective quality of *all* our motives. That would be far too restrictive a use of *orexis*, just as it would be too restrictive a use of our notion of desire. For while in some cases, the affective quality of the motive is relevant—like the anticipated satisfaction of eating a gourmet meal, or the noticeable fear that comes with approaching the battle-line— to think that all reasons had to depend upon prospects that arouse anxiety or anticipation would be absurd. Most of the time we just act routinely, with no noticeable fear or pleasure. Aristotle most certainly recognizes this as much as Hume who champions the calm desires that have the look and feel of motives of reason.[14] Having said this, it is still quite another thing to claim that *orexis* is a motive independent of *all* preference or desire. This is something

---

[13] Of related interest here, see T. H. Irwin, 'Aristotle on Reason, Desire, and Virtue', *Journal of Philosophy*, 72 (1975), 567–78; I have also found instructive Norman Dahl's discussion of Aristotle's non-Humeanism in *Practical Reason, Aristotle, and Weakness of the Will* (University of Minnesota Press, 1984), esp. 30–1. For the relevance of these issues to Kant's conception of inclination, see Thomas Hill, 'Kant's Argument for the Rationality of Moral Conduct', *Pacific Philosophical Quarterly*, 66 (1985), 3–23.

[14] David Hume, *A Treatise of Human Nature*, ed. L. A. Selby-Bigge (Oxford University Press, 1968), 417.

Aristotle would not defend. An intentional object of action is something an agent can be said to have a preference for, a pull towards (however mild, calm, or stable) in virtue of desires he empirically has. In a fundamental way, human rational agency, for Aristotle, unlike Kant, is empirically constituted.

There are further restrictions on the nature of an *orexis* that can generate voluntary action, or intention. Aristotle usually discusses this in terms of the rational wishes (*bouleseis*) that generate prohairetic intentions, but a more general point holds for all species of *orexis*.[15] A wish for what is taken to be impossible, he says, such as to be immortal, can never motivate action (*NE* 1111b22); for desires that cause action are not merely desires that something *should* happen, but desires to bring something about that is 'within one's power' (cf. 1110a14, 1111b25, *Rh.* 1392b18-20). In some cases, as with the wish of the sane adult to be immortal, the desired end will be assumed from the start to be impracticable, a mere fancy not a goal. Similarly ends, the realization of which is not logically impossible but contingently unlikely, may also be rejected from the start as unsuitable ends for deliberation: 'We don't deliberate even about all human affairs; for instance, no Spartan deliberates about the best constitution for the Scythians. For none of these things can be brought about by our own efforts ' (*NE* 1112a28-30). In sum, 'No one deliberates about impossible things or in general what is possible, which he doesn't think it is in his power to do or not do' (*EE* 1225b38). In some cases, however, the viability of a desired end may be determined only after a search for ways of implementing that end. I may desire to make truffles with wild duckling for my dinner party and reject the end only after I discover how much my culinary extravagances would cost. To think something is within one's power is consistent with ultimately rejecting it

---

[15] Together with appetite and emotion, *boulesis* comprises Aristotle's tripartite division of desire (*EE* 1223a26-7, *DA* 414b2, *MA* 700b22). Each is a kind of motive, as Aristotle summarizes in the *Rhetoric*: an action is done if an agent has the power and wish (*boulesis*) to do it; or if he has the power to do it, and is angry at the time, i.e. is moved by emotion (*thumos*); or if he has the power to do it and (appetitively) desires it, i.e. is moved by *epithumia* (1392b19-22; cf. 1393a2-3).

because deliberation has shown it to be impracticable (*NE* 1112b25-6; *EE* 1226b18-19). In this way, deliberation will often provide a test of the practicability of desires. A desire that successfully generates an intention is decisive or controlling (*kurios*). A desire that fails to do so may fail for all sorts of reasons—because of lack of skill or experience, or simply because it fails to win out over rival and conflicting desires for action. *Akrasia*, or incontinence, is one such case. Here there are competing desires implicit in competing major premisses; only one desire will eventually prevail and lead to intention. But there are other cases of conflicting desires in which, unlike *akrasia*, there is no clearly better or worse end. An action must be taken and to leave the other undone is not to be guilty of bad judgement or incontinence. Whatever choice one makes there will be a loss. The vulnerability of Aristotelian happiness to external circumstances readily suggests this.[16]

Implicit in the above remarks about the practical syllogism is a distinction between a desire to act and an intention to act.[17] Desires do not express commitment to action in the way intentions do, nor do commitments to action necessarily express desires, at least in the restrictive (but reasonably common) sense of 'consciously felt' desire discussed above. We have already talked about the second point. The first point can be made as follows (following Bratman): we are guilty of a criticizable irrationality in having inconsistent intentions in a way that we are not in having inconsistent desires. So I might desire both to lounge on the beach tomorrow afternoon and to spend that time in my office working on this book. I obviously cannot do both, though in merely desiring both there need be no criticizable inconsistency. However, if I go on to *intend* to do both, I am in a deeper sense irrational. For I cannot consistently form commitments to perform both actions.

---

[16] See Nussbaum, *The Fragility of Goodness*, chs. 11 and 12.

[17] Cf. Bruce Aune, *Reason and Action* (Reidel, 1977), ch. 2; John Searle, *Intentionality* (Cambridge University Press, 1983), 103-4; Michael Bratman, 'The Two Faces of Intention', *Philosophical Review* (1985). It is worth noting that at *EE* II. 7-8 Aristotle explicitly draws a wedge between desire and intention. But all he implies here is that some voluntary action is without a *specific kind* of desire, namely *epithumia* or appetite, not that it is without desire altogether.

The structure of the syllogism suggests that Aristotle is reasonably clear about this distinction between desire and intention: the two notions occupy different places in the syllogism, the latter much closer to action (indeed, mistaken by many readers for it). Although on some occasions Aristotle does refer to prohairetic intention as a hybrid—a deliberative desire and a desiderative belief (*NE* 1139b5, *EE* 1226b18)—his more careful explication at *EE* 1227a3-5 follows the lines of the practical syllogism: *prohairesis* is itself neither intrinsically belief nor desire, but a product derived from both through reasoning: 'It is clear that *prohairesis* is neither unqualifiedly wish nor belief, but both wish and belief when these follow as a conclusion from deliberation' (cf. *EE* 1226b9).[18] As such it is the beginning and source (*archē*) of action. Now *prohairesis*, as we shall see shortly, has considerably narrower scope than our term 'intention'. Though Aristotle lacks a less restrictive term, he recognizes, as we have shown, a more general notion of intention implicit in all voluntary action (i.e. action that is *hekōn*—willing or voluntary), and which, like *prohairesis*, as the conclusion of the practical syllogism, is neither desire nor belief, but the product of both.

Aristotle often links the concluding intention to act with a planned attempt or trial: 'if an action appears possible, we try it' (*NE* 1112b25; cf. *Rh.* 1392b31). The words 'appears' and 'possible' are crucial here. An agent can try and intend to bring about an action without firmly believing that the action will in fact be successful. Rather, the agent must merely believe that it *could* come about through one's agency, not that it necessarily will. To believe that an action is within one's power and practicable is thus consistent with having doubts about one's success in bringing it about. Depending upon the difficulty of the task at hand or the skill involved, confidence may vary. So, for example, I may try to shape

---

[18] I have been instructed here by Alfred Mele's discussion in 'Aristotle's Wish', *Journal of the History of Philosophy* 22. 2 (1984), 139-56, esp. 152-5.

my hedges into a topiary bird, and though I have little confidence that I will succeed, it nevertheless makes sense to say that I try and intend to act.[19]

Note, on this point, that a choice which expresses virtue and practical wisdom may have stronger requirements. For, as we said in the last chapter, implicit in the notion of hitting the mean is formulating an intention adequate to the situation. We may accordingly expect in the agent a sense of confidence that he has the knowledge, resources, and judgement appropriate for the occasion. This does not require, of course, the agent's confidence that the full trajectory of his action will ensue as planned or hoped for. Extrinsic impediments, well beyond an agent's reasonable foresight, care and control, may obviously crop up at various stages of the action.

3. SIMPLE PLANNING

With these features in mind, I want to turn to the account of the practical syllogism as it illustrates a conception of planning. I shall be distinguishing between a simple and a more complex model. Both leave room for future intention and planning, but to a different extent and degree, or so I shall argue. The simple model extends to what Aristotle calls cases of merely voluntary action.[20] The syllogism here represents a limited kind of practical reasoning whereby one selects means and constituent ends sufficient (and in some

---

[19] Thus Davidson's now outmoded example: I intend to make ten carbon copies of a letter, even though I have little confidence in my ability to do it flawlessly ('Intending', 92). On a similar note, Davidson, (92–5), criticizes Grice's conjecture that a conditional intention such as 'I intend to do it if I can' adds to the accuracy of our stated intention. Cf. H. P. Grice, 'Intention and Uncertainty', *Proceedings of the British Academy* 57 (1971), 203–18.

[20] For the distinction, cf. 1111b6 ff., 1112a15. Aristotle says merely voluntary action is most characteristic of the actions of children and animals, prohairetic choice of the mature, rational agent. (1111b8–10; cf. 1147b4–5). T. H. Irwin has focused on this distinction in addressing the issue of responsibility: 'Reason and Responsibility in Aristotle' in A. O. Rorty (ed.), *Essays on Aristotle's Ethics* (University of California Press, 1980). However, the force of Irwin's discussion is to minimize the interest of what I have been calling the simple model. On my view, the simple model has an important (even if limited) role in explaining planning and future intention.

cases, necessary) for the realization of an end. It is a case of limited practical reason in so far as the agent's choice does not involve, in a robust sense (to be explained), an evaluation of action in terms of what is supposed to be overall best. On the more complex model, a choice of action is regarded as on balance best after consideration of alternative actions in the light of overall ends. As such, it entails both the organization of ends and the assessment of action in light of that organization. In some cases it will further involve a reassessment of those ends, and so a refinement of one's conception of overall good living. Choices in accord with this more complex model correspond to a subclass of the voluntary, namely prohairetic or reasoned choices. It is these choices and their relation both to planning and to a firm and stable character, that will be my central concern.

Let's turn then to the simple model as illustrated by one of Aristotle's examples from the *De Motu*. The model is simple, in that it does not capture the sort of reasoning most fully expressive of the choices that stem from character. Indeed, in its most pared down form, it is meant to offer a 'common explanation' of the voluntary action of all animals (*MA* 698a4).

1. I need a covering.
2. A coat is a covering.
3. I need a coat.
4. What I need I must make.
5. I need a coat.
6. I must make a coat.
7. And the conclusion that I must make a coat is an action.
8. And he acts from a starting point.
9. If this is to be a coat, first there must be this.
10. And if this, this.
11. And he does this straightaway.

We shall be considering the way in which this case illustrates future intention and planning. But first there is a more basic principle of rationality underlying the above inference: namely, that to have an intention rationally requires willing what contributes to the realization of that intention.

If the necessary means are not available, then one drops the end. Kant captures this principle of rationality in his notion of the Hypothetical Imperative:

The proposition, 'If I fully will the effect, I also will the action required for it' is analytic; for it is one and the same thing to conceive something as an effect possible in a certain way through me and to conceive myself as acting in the same way with respect to it.[21]

Hume postulates, through an analogous, though desire-based principle, a notion of the transference of desire from end to means.[22] According to this principle, the chain of events that leads to an end is of interest to us only to the extent to which we are not indifferent to that end. Aristotle alludes to a principle of rationality similar to these when he says above, 'And if this, then this. And he does this straightaway.' In other words, if an agent intends *A*, and believes *B* is a necessary and available condition of bringing it about, then on pain of irrationality he must intend to do *B* or else drop his intention to do *A*. If he knows that he cannot do *A* unless he does *B*, then he will be incoherent if he intends *A* but not *B*. We can refer to this sort of rationality constraint as means–end coherence.

But it is misleading to view the example as just a case of means–end rationality. It has now been argued by many (including Greenwood in 1909)[23] that Aristotelian deliberation is not merely from ends to means but about ends

---

[21] Immanuel Kant, *Groundwork of the Metaphysic of Morals* , tr. H. J. Paton (Harper and Row, 1956), 85. Kant's principle is not desire-based in that agents can follow Hypothetical Imperatives in the pursuit of ends which are not necessarily empirical (e.g. in working out the means for fulfilling the obligatory ends specified in *The Doctrine of Virtue*, tr. Mary Gregor (University of Pennsylvania Press, 1964)). See Thomas Hill, 'Kant's Argument', 14. *Groundwork*, 81 n, may mistakenly suggest a more Humean reading.

[22] 'Tis from the prospect of pain or pleasure that the aversion or propensity arises towards any object. And these emotions extend themselves to the causes and effects of that object, as they are pointed out to us by reason and experience. It can never in the least concern us to know that such objects are causes, and such others effects, if both the causes and effects be indifferent to us' (Hume, *Treatise*, 414).

[23] See L. H. G. Greenwood, introductory essay to his edition of the *Nicomachean Ethics*, Book VI (Cambridge University Press, 1909; repr. Arno Press, 1973), 46-7. The non-instrumentality of Aristotelian deliberation has been noted and argued for by: D. J. Allan, 'Aristotle's Account of the Origin of Moral Principles', *Actes*

as well. We considered this somewhat in the last chapter. Aristotle's familiar Humean-sounding claim in *NE* III. 3 (1112b11) that 'we deliberate not about ends but about means' is given its Humean gloss by the standard Ross translation. But more correctly, Aristotle says, 'we deliberate not about ends, but about what contributes to ends' (*ta pros ta telē*).[24] This will include deliberation both about the constituents and specifications of an end and about the means towards an antecedently fixed end. We need look no further than the opening inference in the coat example to illustrate the point. The first task of deliberation concerns a decision not about means but about ends, and the way a specific end is to be narrowed down so as to permit determinate action. So the need for a covering is narrowed down to the need for a coat, and it is this sub-end which then motivates further reasons and actions. Aristotle's negative claim that we do not deliberate about ends can be understood most straightfowardly as saying that for a given piece of deliberation we regard certain ends as fixed, e.g. that a doctor is interested in healing is assumed in the treatment of his patients. However, that guiding end may itself be the product of previous deliberations. It may result as a choice about how best to earn a living in a way that is at once socially prestigious and humanitarian. Thus what is an end for one piece of deliberation may be a means for another deliberation hierarchically prior. Much has been written about this, and I shall leave further comment aside until a later section of this chapter.

du XIe Congres Internationale de Philosophie, 12 (1953), 120-7, repr. in J. Barnes, M. Schofield, and R. Sorabji (eds.) *Articles on Aristotle*, ii (Duckworth, 1977)— Allan provides a concise history of the debate; W. F. R. Hardie, *Aristotle's Ethical Theory* (Oxford University Press, 1968; 2nd edn. 1980), 256; Cooper, *Reason and Human Good*, 19-21; Irwin, 'Aristotle on Reason'; David Wiggins, 'Deliberation and Practical Reason', *Proceedings of the Aristotelian Society*, 74 (1973-4), repr. in Rorty (ed.), *Essays on Aristotle's Ethics*; Nussbaum, *Aristotle's De Motu*, Essay 4; Richard Sorabji, 'Aristotle on the Role of Intellect in Virtue', *Proceedings of the Aristotelian Society*, 74 (1973-4), 107-29—repr. in Rorty (ed.), *Essays on Aristotle's Ethics*; Henry Richardson, 'Rational Deliberation of Ends', Ph.D. thesis (Harvard University, 1986). For a more general discussion of similar issues, see Darwall, *Impartial Reason*, esp. ch. 3.

[24] And in the *Eudemian Ethics*: *peri de tōn eis touto teinontōn* (1226b12). The more literal rendering I offer is the way the W. D. Ross translation of the *Nicomachean Ethics* (Oxford University Press, 1915) has been revised to read by J. O.

More central to my concerns now is that Aristotle's example suggests a way in which promoting an end involves future intention. If by intending to make a coat, I must first take preliminary actions which do not themselves count as making a coat but are necessary prior first steps to it, then my intention to make a coat (at step 7) will be a future intention, realizable only as I realize more immediate intentions. It is a future intention that establishes a plan and a schedule of activities.

It might be objected that the coat case does not accommodate the notion of future intention especially well.[25] For if I must first buy material, before I make a coat, then in making the purchase I have the intention of making a coat, even though I am not now making it. Contrast this with the earlier example of deciding in June to go to a meeting in August. Here I formulate the intention, but then do nothing at all to carry it out, at least until considerably later. In a purer sense, my intention here is future. But I am not sure there is a great difference between the two cases, at least in the following respect. In the case of deciding in June to go to a meeting in August, the future intention sets an agenda of what must be done before I go, irrespective of whether I begin carrying out that agenda now or later. I thus know that, at some point or other, I will have to book a flight if I am to go. And a good planner will bear that fact in mind, if she is to take advantage of economy prices and the like. Similarly, the decision to make a coat sets an agenda of what must be done if that end is to be realized. And these steps may be taken sooner or later, depending upon all sorts of factors. Thus, what I see as the interesting point about future intention is not simply that we can decide now to act later, but that in so committing ourselves, we typically commit ourselves to more immediate plans. Indeed, the point about being a planner is not that we schedule things way in

Urmson in the revised Oxford translation of *The Complete Works of Aristotle*, ed. Jonathan Barnes (Princeton University Press, 1985). Irwin's translation—'we deliberate not about ends, but about what promotes ends' also revises the Humean gloss (*Nicomachean Ethics*, tr. T. H. Irwin (Hackett, 1985)).

25 The following objection was made to me by Richard Kraut.

advance, but that what we schedule bears on what we must do between now and then to prepare.

Still, there is an obvious restriction to the notion of planning, if, as in the coat example, the whole system of inference must end in a present intention to act 'straightaway'. What we would like Aristotle to acknowledge more explicitly, through his examples, is the basic point recognized in the *Rhetoric*, that the concluding intention of a piece of deliberation can be formulated for action that will take place now *or* later. Thus, whether the intention is to perform a particular *instance* of an action here and now, or merely a determinable *type* (to be instantiated later), in either case, there is a commitment to act.[26] A sequence of deliberation

---

[26] Cooper in *Reason and Human Good* supports something like this view (23–58). His argument rests on an interpretation of Aristotle's term (ta kath' hekasta), usually translated as the particulars. Aristotle's notion is that we come to a decision about what to do when we have grasped the particulars (1142a14, 1142a23-4, 1143b4-9, etc.), and Cooper argues that this is ambiguous between arriving at a decision to perform a *specific type* of action and arriving at a decision to realize an individual *instance* of it. He produces evidence to support the former reading as the interpretation of pivotal passages at 1141b14-23 and 1142a11-23, and I think his interpretation of these passages is plausible. But while Cooper's arguments have this merit, he mounts his case about practical reason at the cost of far too impoverished a view of the practical syllogism. In particular, he argues that the practical syllogism does not represent a piece of practical deliberation at all, but has only the more limited role of representing how we implement a decision to perform a specific kind of action previously arrived at by deliberation or spontaneously. In contrast, my own view is that the practical syllogism allows for both deliberation and implementation, and indeed I have been stressing its role in deliberation and planning.

Two important passages in the *Nichomachean Ethics* seem to tell against Cooper's interpretation. The first Cooper acknowledges as potentially damaging, but then dismisses. The passage is at 1142b22 where Aristotle speaks of false reasoning (*sullogismos*) as a case of hitting upon a desired end by the wrong means (*di' ou edei*). Aristotle's remark leaves it open as to whether one's reasons are false in the sense of non-optimal or morally impermissible (though I suspect it may be the latter, given the force of '*dei*' in this context). But however we understand it, the relevant point is that the syllogism here clearly refers to some form of reasoning about the promotion of an end. In this case, *contra* Cooper, it is not that one fails to recognize what to do once one's mind is made up to do it, but that one has not made up one's mind correctly in the first place. An important passage at *NE* VI. 12 lends further support to this aspect of the syllogism. Here it is significant that Aristotle's remarks about the practical syllogism are in the context of a discussion about practical reason (*phronēsis*) and the general ends of character: 'For the syllogisms concerning actions have a starting point, e.g. since the end is of such and such a sort and is of the best, whatever it may be (let it be for the sake of argument whatever you like). And this is not evident except to the good person' (1144a31 ff.). Aristotle argues that the practical syllogism will

thus leads to agency, not in the narrow sense of what must be done *now*, but in the broader sense of what must be done *first*. (As Aristotle says elsewhere (1112b24), what is last in deliberation is first in action.) Unfortunately, Aristotle's remarks about intending to act 'straightaway' suggest too restrictive an interpretation.

Let us consider in fuller detail the notion of future intention. It seems there are at least two good reasons for having prior or future intentions for actions.[27] The first is that we want to know what to do in advance, that is, we want to be prepared. For at the moment of action we may lack the time to decide how to proceed, or even if we have the time, we may not want to spend it considering the options. Thus, just as we stock our larder with food so we don't have to shop before each meal, so too we keep on tap certain implicit or explicit plans of action so we don't have to stop and think at each moment about what to do next. I make up my mind the night before that tomorrow morning I am going to get to work on this chapter so that come tomorrow morning I immediately know how I am going to spend my time. The plan is set and I can get on with it without further thought when the time is right.

But equally, by planning in advance I may not only be planning for the future but planning for now. That is, what I decide to do later will affect what I decide to do now. The future constrains the present, and constrains how I will act now in order to bring about some end, or at least not preclude it. The coat example makes this aspect of future intention quite clear. It sets a future goal which requires preparation

represent reasoning about the promotion of the most general ends of good living. These ends are realized not immediately through perception of available means, but by a process of planning, deliberation, and justification. As such, the syllogism here represents practical reasoning. For a view similar to Cooper's, cf. Hardie, *Aristotle's Ethical Theory*, ch. 12.

[27] I owe much to Michael Bratman's discussion of these issues in 'The Two Faces of Intention' (an earlier version of which I heard at a conference on practical reasoning held at the University of Dayton in March 1983), 'Taking Plans Seriously', *Social Theory and Practice*, 9 (1983), and 'Davidson's Theory of Intention', in Merrill Hintikka and Bruce Vermazen (eds.), *Essays on Davidson: Actions and Events* (Oxford University Press, 1985). The problems he raises in these papers stimulated and clarified many of my thoughts about related issues in Aristotle.

in the present. A future intention, then, can set an agenda of what to do between now and then. By focusing on the future, it simultaneously demands that we should not be indifferent to the present.

The fact that an agent can be concerned with the future, either directly, in the sense of being prepared in advance, or indirectly, because of its consequences for present action, indicates an important way in which Aristotle regards an agent as rationally coherent. For Aristotle, rationality requires that agents think of themselves as connected with the future (*DA* 433b8), as persisting over time, and as making decisions which motivate, whether they act upon them now or later. The fact that future plans constrain the present and force it to come into line with long term projects best indicates the force of this temporal sense of coherence. We might call this rationality constraint that of temporal coherence.

Of course future planning can only do so much work in preparing us now for the future; the rest awaits the demands of the actual situation. There is thus no way for the general to consummate fully his planned response to the enemy. The fine details of the battle plan must await the particulars of the enemy's moves, including the possibility of surprise changes. Even so, any plan is useless unless it simultaneously sets up a schedule of what we *can* do now in order to be ready for then. The general's plan will extend backwards to include careful historical and geographical research, a training of the troops and relief cadres, the securing of economic and political support, etc. In this way, action will have a trajectory which goes well back into a history of preparation. Part of the point of future intention is to set that agenda.

As I have suggested, a temporal constraint on rationality is at work in the means (constituent)–end planning characteristic of the simple model: a given end requires the setting of future intentions which in turn constrain more immediate actions. But there is another aspect of coherence over time which extends beyond this simple model. A general sort of example will help here. Imagine a plan that involves not a single end, such as making a coat (or even drawing up a battle plan), but a network of ends, such as a life with certain personal concerns, moral ends, and political ideals. Here one's actions will be constrained not merely by the isolated pursuit of separate ends over time, but by a desire to see these ends optimally co-ordinated in some coherent pattern in and through time. This integration problem emerges when one begins to consider how to live in an ordered way.

Thus, if one, as a rational agent, is to be more than bundle of disparate streams of interests, then part of planning will involve the coherence of ends side by side (synchronously) over time (diachronously) and the promotion of actions in the light of that pattern of ends.[28] Aristotle's notion of character depends upon this further sort of coherence, as we shall see. The general point is that one's character is integrated and stable to the extent to which one can form systematically related intentions that realize one's general ends. We might call this further sort of rationality constraint on action character coherence. It obviously includes the temporal coherence of the simple model of rational choice, but goes beyond it. It goes beyond it in looking to a broader range of an agent's ends as providing reasons for a decision to promote or abandon a particular end.

We have said that we make plans in order to be prepared for the future, and equally so as to know what to do now. We can now add that we make plans in order to maximize the possibility of co-ordinating our various ends. Such plans involve realizing not just a single end but a complex network of ends. On a mundane level, they are the plans that organize the activities of a day. On a grander scale, they are the plans that reveal a life and character.

Now regrettably, Aristotle's examples of deliberation do not adequately reveal the complexity of acting from character. When he talks about deliberation *per se*, he tends to focus on simple linear examples, where ends are isolated from each other. But if, as I have argued at an earlier stage, we see the deliberative and dialectical aspects of his account as of a piece, then we can gain some insight into the more

---

[28] Cf. Darwall, *Impartial Reason*, ch. 9, for a related discussion.

complex deliberative process by considering Aristotle's own project of specifying the contents of a good life. When we turn to this for the moment, it becomes clear that happiness is not a bundle of discrete goods. Rather, once the positive specification is under way, the task is to show that certain received goods, such as the virtues, the exercise of practical and theoretical reason, the external goods, pleasure, and a social life (1098b23-6), can be interpreted in a systematic and mutually supporting way. To put it most briefly and sketchily, happiness will require activity, and will accord a central place to the activities that best exemplify human excellence or virtue. Such activities will, in turn, require adequate external goods and will yield pleasure in so far as they are supported by the right external conditions. As ways of acting and judging in the world, the virtues will exercise, in an exemplary way, rational capacities. Moreover, the virtues will be directed at a social conception of good, and reason itself will be understood as having a social and political dimension. To lead a self-sufficient life will itself come to have the substantive meaning of leading a life that is social. These remarks are obviously programmatic, and oversimplify the contribution of the different sort of goods to the complete and self-sufficient life. External goods will play a more complex role,[29] as will contemplation, as we shall see. But they make plain enough the general way Aristotle wants to weave together the various received components of the good life into some more cohesive fabric.

Now a similar concern for a well-arranged life characterizes the individual pursuit of happiness. At a more determinate level, the rational agent deliberates about how to realize ends in a way that best enriches—or at times merely does not preclude—other valued ends. Displaying generosity cannot result in ignoring one's own needs, just as public munificence cannot overlook the more local needs of family. The pleasures of companionship cannot squeeze out the enjoyment of one's own company. Even a political life may

---

[29] E.g. Aristotle might be interpreted as claiming that external goods will not only be instrumental goods, but intrinsic goods, valued independently of their capacity to enable virtuous activity. This is the view of Irwin ('Permanent Happiness') and Nussbaum (*The Fragility of Goodness*).

need to find some time for contemplation. A delicate balance is constantly sought in how we choose to express what we care about. There is a mindfulness, typically, of the diversity of factors that impinge on a choice. In this sense, deliberation is non-linear. We shall go on to discuss character coherence. But before doing so I wish to restate that the simple model of merely voluntary action may itself include a kind of deliberation and assessment. Admittedly, this will not be so in the case of extremely young children and animals; in these cases, the simple syllogism will typically represent an intention arrived at immediately by perception or imagination.[30] But in the case of other merely voluntary agents, e.g. natural slaves and women, efficient planning and calculation will be required as part of the exercise of their respective functions.[31] My present point is that this sort of reasoning still falls short of a more robust capacity that manifests character.[32]

It is worth commenting that the akratic is capable of this more robust reasoning, but is akratic precisely to the extent to which he disregards the full impact of the assessments which issue.[33]   In contrast, the natural slave can act irrationally in the sense of non-optimally, but not akratically. He lacks the commitment to ends and capacity for designing a life around them essential to acting from character, and by implication essential to acting from weakness of character.

[30] That is, without any thinking or inquiry required (*MA* 701a35; cf. *DA* 433b28 ff.) on the distinction between *phantasia aisthētikē* and *phantasia logistikē*. Aristotle is not implying that the desires of these agents, capable of only the most restricted kind of voluntary choices, are without cognitive or intentional content. The accounts of voluntary movement at *MA* 6-11 and *DA* III. 9-11, as well as of emotion at *Rh.* II. 1 and 2, systematically argue against such a claim.

[31] *Pol.* 1254b22 ff., 1260a12-30, 1260b30 ff. On women and slaves, see W. W. Fortenbaugh's important piece, 'Aristotle on Slaves and Women', in *Articles on Aristotle*, ii. 135-9.

[32] That there is non-prohairetic deliberation was pointed out by Elizabeth Anscombe in 'Thought and Action in Aristotle', in R. Bambrough (ed.), *New Essays in Plato and Aristotle* (Routledge and Kegan Paul, 1965), repr. in *Articles on Aristotle*, ii. It is explicit at 1142b18: 'The akratic and bad person, if he is clever, will reach as a result of reasoning what he sets before himself, so that he will have deliberated correctly, though he secures for himself a great evil.'

[33] For the claim that the akratic does not abide by his *prohairesis* see *NE* 1148a9, 1150b30, 1151a6; cf. 1147b4. At *EE* 1223b8 Aristotle says he goes against his *boulēsis*. This formulation seems to make better sense, since a *boulēsis* does not entail commitment to action (or intention) in the way a *prohairesis* does.

(Similarly, for example, the person who decides that for the sake of her health she should not indulge excessively in sweets but nevertheless does is akratic because she goes against her overall judgement of what is best for a temperate way of life. But she is not akratic, according to Aristotle, when once having decided to eat sweets, she then procures them in a way she knows to be, as the result of deliberation, non-optimal. In the latter case, though she is acting irrationally, it is not because she is acting against a *prohairesis*, and this is so even if she has a general policy to act optimally.)

Finally, we should note that the distinction between the simple and complex models of reasoning is compatible with a developmental model which explains how a merely voluntary agent, such as the male child, gradually comes to be a prohairetic agent in possession of character and the deliberative and perceptual capacities requisite for its exercise. For, unlike the natural slave and woman, the cognitive capacities of a young boy are not permanently defective, but merely immature. I take up such an account in Chapter 5 when I turn to Aristotle's remarks on habituation.

4. THE MORE COMPLEX PLANS OF A CHARACTER

Character coherence is fundamentally related to Aristotle's notion of *prohairesis* or reasoned choice. For prohairetic choices, Aristotle says, reveal character even more than action does. It is now time to inquire what Aristotle means by *prohairesis*, and to consider the sort of deliberation it entails.

Briefly, prohairetic choices are a subclass of merely voluntary decisions (or intentions). A prohairetic choice for Aristotle is supported by reasons for supposing an action A best on balance in the light of *overall* ends of character. A merely voluntary choice does not require this sort of inclusive assessment. As such, it lacks the special sort of deliberative preference characteristic of *prohairesis*.

The etymology of Aristotle's technical word *prohairesis* underlines the notion of preference. Literally, it means 'choosing over' or 'choosing before', i.e. preferring, and Aristotle exploits this meaning. So at *EE* 1226b7–16 Aristotle says: '*Prohairesis* is a taking, but not taking simply, but taking one thing over another . . . deliberating about what is better or worse.'[34] The deliberation and assessment require at the very least the evaluation of alternatives to a given end, and probably more, as I have already indicated. *Prohairesis* is thus distinguished from weaker notions of preference. For we sometimes do speak of preferring one thing over another even in those circumstances when the preference is not grounded in any real consideration or evaluation of the alternatives. So a two-year old when presented with a choice of two sets of clothing to wear for the day may emphatically choose one over the other, but for no particular reason that she can cite. We might say she 'prefers' one to the other (and *she* most likely will insist upon it), but the preference lacks reasons that support or recommend her choice. Even the preferences which are ranked in utility calculations do not seem to require deliberative assessments. They are the inclinations felt most strongly, not necessarily those best supported.

The notion of a prohairetic choice, as a choice of action judged on balance best in the light of overall ends, is closely related to another Aristotelian notion we have already looked at, *boulēsis*. Typically rendered as wish, and sometimes as rational wish or rational (or deliberative) desire, *boulēsis* is said by Aristotle (without much explanation) to set ends, and *prohairesis* to promote them (1111b27–30, 1113b3–5). From this division of labour I understand him to suggest something like the following: a prohairetic choice assesses an action relative to ends given by *boulēsis*, but ordered by *prohairesis*. Thus, bouletic capacities posit ends, prohairetic capacities arrange them and decide upon actions in light of that arrangement. While there can be no prohairetic choice without an occurrent bouletic wish, as we indicated in the last chapter, there can be an occurrent bouletic wish without a prohairetic choice, or at least without a prohairetic choice that promotes *that* wish (*EE* 1226b16).

---

[34] Consider the parallel remark at *NE* 1112a15: '*Prohairesis* appears to be voluntary choice, but not all voluntary choice is prohairetic . . . for *prohairesis* is with reason and thought. And even the name indicates that it is what is chosen before other things.'

Given the effect of *prohairesis* on bouletic desires, these desires will, in the ideal agent, come to reflect an ordered sense of character. They will be the ends 'thought to be good' within an overall conception of good living. We might think of them as stable and integrated policies within a reflective life.[35] Along with prohairetic capacities, bouletic capacities are taken to be the distinctive mark of full practical reason. We should wonder at this point why a desiderative capacity, such as *boulēsis*, is for Aristotle so crucially connected to rational capacities. Perhaps it is because a bouletic wish cognitively specifies an end (but then all desires, on Aristotle's account, do this), or because it generates a choice (but then what is of interest falls on the prohairetic choice-making capacities rather than on the bouletic powers). I shall leave this puzzle or *aporia* unexplored for the moment, marking it as a problem to be returned to later.

One consequence of the above connection of *prohairesis* and *boulēsis* is that a *prohairesis* cannot promote the ends of lower desires, such as appetite or emotion, unless these ends themselves fall under a more general conception of good living definitive of some character. In other words, although appetites and emotions can initiate actions by positing a practical good or end, the choice-making involved will be narrowly prudential (merely voluntary), except in those cases in which the ends are viewed as part of a more comprehensive conception of how to live well. The contrast Aristotle draws between the indulgent and the akratic person illustrates the point. Whereas the indulgent person seems to make prohairetic choices in sating his appetites, the akratic person, in acting appetitively, does not.[36] For in the first case the choices are guided by an apparent unifying plan of good living—'always satisfy the present pleasure' (1146b24)—while in the second, the choices are in direct conflict with what the agent takes to be the best policy overall. Indeed, they violate the ends of character.

---

[35] So rational wishes are for what is 'noble and pleasant' as they appear 'to each character' (*kath' hekastēn hexin*) (*NE* 1113a31). See *EE* 1223b8, 1223b33; cf. *Pol.* 1253a14.

[36] I reconsider the case of the indulgent person, the *akolastos*, in the next section, and in particular his ability to make prohairetic choices.

In several places, Aristotle stipulates that prohairetic choices must issue from an actual process of deliberation (*bouleusis*) (1113a5, *EE* 1226b12).[37] But it would be unnecessarily restrictive to require that all *prohaireseis* be generated this way. For there are, of course, choices expressive of character that do not require rumination, but are chosen on the spot just because of character, and what one must do as a result of character. To have to deliberate might even, in certain cases, be regarded as a criticism of character. Any theory of moral habituation, such as Aristotle's own, must be designed with this sort of consideration in mind. As Aristotle himself suggests, character must be able to supply reliable and stable motives (*NE* 1105a35) so that one can perceive and choose correctly whether or not one has the leisure to deliberate antecedently or now (1117a19–22). In the light of this, it seems most reasonable to conceive of *prohairesis* as a choice *subject* to rational justification, though not necessarily proceeding from *prior* deliberation.[38] Indeed, the capacity to subject one's choice to *post facto* scrutiny and assessment is sufficient, and in some cases a more revealing sign of character than excessive pre-act deliberation. That the practically wise are committed to this sort of reflection is evidence, we shall see, of the special character of their practical reason.

In a celebrated passage at *NE* III. 3, Aristotle offers two general criteria for justifying a prohairetic choice. In a given piece of deliberation,

we deliberate not about ends, but about the things that promote the ends. For neither the doctor deliberates if he should heal, nor the orator if he should persuade, nor the politician if he should produce good order, nor does anyone else deliberate about his end. But positing the end, they consider how and through what means it will be achieved. And if it seems that it can be achieved by several

---

[37] An individual 'deliberates about those things which lead to an end, about whether this thing promotes it or whether that does . . . since nobody chooses [*prohaireitai*] without having first prepared and deliberated as to whether it would be better or worse to act thus . . . it is clear that *prohairesis* is deliberative desire of those things within our power to bring about' (*EE* 1226b12 ff.). Notice that Aristotle is non-commital at *NE* 1112a15.

[38] I am essentially in agreement with Cooper here; cf. his remarks and helpful note in *Reason and Human Good*, 6–9.

means, they consider further by which one it is *most easily* [*raista*] and *best* [*kallista*] realized. And if it is achieved by only one means, they consider *how* it is achieved by that means, and how *that* means is itself achieved, until they come to the first cause which is last to be discovered . . . And if they come upon an impossibility, they give up the search, e.g. if they need money and this cannot be secured; but if a thing appears possible, then they try to do it. (1112b11 ff.)

We have already said something to dispel the Humean-sounding claim that introduces this passage. As I said earlier, to posit an end without deliberation can mean simply to hold the end fixed for the purposes of this piece of deliberation, without entailing that it must be fixed in principle. Also worth noting is that according to the above passage, the piece of deliberation does not conclude with an intention to act *now* (as in the *De Motu*) but less restrictively, with what must (eventually) be done *first* in action. The path is thus open, here, for a notion of future intention. But my present focus is not on these points. Rather, I wish to focus on Aristotle's claim that if there are alternative ways and means to realize an end, we must choose that course of action that is easiest (or, we might gloss, most efficient) and best.[39] Here Aristotle offers principles of assessment noticeably absent in the more pared down model of the *De Motu*. The principles signal an awareness, obscured in the earlier model, of the apparently non-deductive and non-linear character of many cases of practical reason. Means and constituent ends seldom embody necessary conditions; there is usually, though not always, more than one way of achieving a goal. As such, actions are often under-determined by their reasons. Deciding upon which non-necessary means or constituents of ends to pursue requires invoking further criteria, of efficiency, and of 'bestness'.

But is this all Aristotle means by prohairetic reasoning? Surely some principle of efficiency must already be implicit in merely voluntary action, if the account is to apply, as Aristotle intends it to, to certain non-prohairetic agents, notably women and slaves. On his own view, as I have said,

---

[39] There may be warrant to translate *kallista* here as 'most finely', as Irwin, for example, does in his translation. See n. 71 below.

such agents require limited reasoning simply to carry out their respective functions. They can presumably weigh alternative means relative to an end, and reject an end if means prove impractical.

What we would like Aristotle to go on to discuss is the assessment of an end on the basis of other ends. The step is a natural one: if it is rational to abandon an end when means must be avoided (1112b25), then equally it should be rational to abandon an end when other ends prevail. It would be arbitrary to restrict coherence to the former case. Consider a case where there is only one way of fulfilling a goal. While efficiency of means may not be relevant, it nevertheless makes sense to say that the one way available may not be desirable or 'best'. And this may be so not simply on the basis of whim or caprice, but because of reasons that follow from an agent's *other* interests and ends. I may not choose that action or may change my mind about doing it, if other considerations based on other ends and interests overrule its prima facie desirability. My choice is conditional upon these further considerations, and coherence with them is part of rationally assessing the initial end. So, it is a hot day and I am desperately thirsty. The only remedy in sight is to drink from a water supply I know to have a high lead content. I rule this out as overall not best. Here, apparently, the criterion of bestness is relative not merely to the desire voiced in the major premise, but to other occurrent, though implicit desires, beliefs and ends with which my action must be consistent and by which it may be overridden. There are thus peripheral considerations, not voiced in the major premiss, which typically guide and constrain rational action.

Now it would be surprising to think Aristotle would not want to include this sort of reasoning within his account of choice, especially if choices are to reflect the overall ends of character. As he himself says, practical reason is not with regard to the separate parts of living, but with regard to good living 'as a whole' (*holōs*, 1140a28). To accommodate this, we might posit another sort of 'bestness' not explicitly in the text, but which emerges from the above considerations. A choice can be 'best' in the narrow sense of an efficient or optimal solution to some *single* objective. But it can also be 'best' in the more inclusive sense of best, all things considered, given an agent's *overall* objectives and beliefs. This latter will include the reasoning of the first sort, but will go beyond it, including decisions about how and whether to satisfy ends given their relation and fit to other ends which are part of some overall complex and guiding conception. An end or action that is more rather than less harmonious with (or inclusive of) a number of other ends may on these grounds be given preference. The best choice, according to this more inclusive criterion, requires a global point of view.

It is obvious that such a constraint will guide typical ethical choices. So, in deciding whether or not to resist the enemy who comes to plunder my home, the valued ends which come into play are not only my courage and willingness to confront my fears, but also my loyalty to my family and general responsibility for their welfare. If confrontation should end in my death, how will they fare in my absence? Who will provide? In the light of these concerns, I may decide it best not to resist the enemy, even if provoked, and decide instead to surrender my material goods, and perhaps even my honour. Deliberation will in this way require the relative weighting of different ends.

It might be tempting to think of this as still no more than a principle of efficiency. Now instead of promoting most efficiently a single end, we promote most efficiently a system of ends ranked so that they maximally promote some more ultimate value. However, as I have said, there is no reductive end or good on Aristotle's scheme in terms of which all goods are commensurable. On his view, the overall objectives that comprise a conception of good living are irreducibly diverse and incommensurable. Different ends will typically have varying degrees of importance in a life, but this cannot be assessed by a precise measurement of any common value. There is no such value. The activities of good living are heterogeneous just as the pleasures derived from these activities are.[40] As we saw in the last chapter, Aristotle insists

---

[40] See the problematic remark Aristotle makes at *DA* 434a5-9. But I take this to be anomalous given his general disagreement with the Socrates of the *Protagoras* in *NE* VII. 3 and his remarks about irreducible pleasures in *NE* X.5. The incommensurability thesis is argued convincingly by David Wiggins in 'Weakness

that no science (*epistēmē*)—(such as the hedonistic calculus proposed by Socrates in the *Protagoras*) can replace careful and sensitive judgement. This does not mean that weighing and balancing cannot be rationally performed, or even that notions of the common good are out of place. Aristotle explicitly appeals to the latter (e.g. 1130b26). But any arrangement will lack the exactitude that might result from a measuring common value. Equally, the arrangement of ends will not be constrained by strict priority rules, such as those which require the maximization of certain ends before others can be satisfied. While this sort of constraint does not require commensurability of values, it does require a kind of inflexibility of judgement that Aristotle would find objectionable.

More needs to be said about these alternatives, and what remains once they are rejected. The issue comes to the forefront when we consider the place Aristotle assigns to contemplation in the happy life. How is it a good to be integrated within the happy life? In what sense is it to be given priority? What restrictions does it place on other activities? I shall take up these questions presently. But first we need to round out the discussion of prohairetic choice, and the sort of rational capacities it involves.

5. CHOICE INCLUDES REVISION OF ENDS

Earlier we said that if it is rational to abandon an end when means must be avoided, then equally it should be rational to abandon an end when another end prevails. That is, ends must be promoted in the light of other ends, and in the light of overall fit. This must be part of what it is to arrive at the rational choices that reveal character. But any thoroughgoing notion of integration of ends seems to require, in turn, the

of Will, Commensurability, and the Objects of Deliberation and Desire', in Rorty (ed.), *Essays on Aristotle's Ethics*, and by Martha Nussbaum in 'The Discernment of Perception: An Aristotelian Conception of Private and Public Rationality', in John Cleary (ed.), *Proceedings of the Boston Area Colloquium in Ancient Philosophy*, i (University Press of America, 1985), 151-201, and *Fragility of Goodness*, ch. 10.

revamping of ends as part of the process. It would be irrational to think that the ends remain unaltered once a more global point of view is taken up. To choose in the light of fit is to alter and revise these ends, as experience and reflection require.

Before arguing for some extension of practical reason in this direction, two possible confusions should be cleared up. First, on the Aristotelian view, ends are never deliberatively chosen, if by 'deliberatively chosen' one means that 'an agent justifies ends independent of all prior or concurrent desires'. Aristotelian practical reason is never autonomous in the Kantian sense of 'free from alien desires'. A good or end is an object of desire, and though that object may be refined and transformed by belief and imagination, it is never a good for us unless it appeals to us as empirically constituted human beings. Our reason is essentially human. What is a reason for us does not have to appeal to agents who know no feelings. This means that we revise ends relative to other desired ends, or on the basis of some more general interest or the like. There is no rational choice, for Aristotle, unless one starts with some desired goods. The point I now wish to argue, though, is that these are not fixed. Reason affects them; it transforms our conception of what is good.

Thus, and secondly, reasoning about ends has primarily to do with reconstituting and tailoring ends through action. It is not so much deciding from the beginning that something matters to us, like peace or health or alleviating suffering, but deciding, through successive encounters with the world, in what way it matters, at what cost, when, and towards whom. It is these questions that an agent answers when she acts; and these questions that give content to an end.

This said, let us consider the extent to which Aristotle is hospitable to a notion of revising ends. Evidence against a notion of setting ends through deliberative choice is not hard to find. Aristotle's claim that virtue sets the end and practical wisdom deliberates about how to promote it (1144a8) establishes a division of labour, and this is reinforced by the segregation of virtue and wisdom into the non-rational and rational parts of the soul respectively. His claim that we come to the starting points of virtue through habituation rather than argument (1151a15-19) corroborates the view of the *Eudemian Ethics* that ultimate practical ends are never a concern of reason; they are never attained by inference or reasoning (1227b25-35). Rather, like hypotheses in science, they are laid down, assumed. We have already gone some way towards arguing against this view. To deliberate about what contributes to an end includes specification and qualification of the end. Moreover, as I shall argue in Chapter 5, the claim that we are habituated to virtue does not entail a process devoid of reason or reflection; the non-rational part takes part in reason (*NE* 1102b14), just as capacities of practical reason begin to develop early on. As Aristotle himself says at 1151a17, habituation *teaches*, is an instructor (*didaskalikos*) of right opinion about first principles, which suggests that teaching need not be narrowly construed as a method appropriate only to the purely intellectual part (cf. 1103a15). Acquiring virtue is thus not a mindless process, and setting down its ends is not a matter of being constrained by what has been rigidly fixed. But equally, the inclusion of experience as central to the teaching of practical reason (1103a16) suggests, from the other side, that even in cultivating practical reason much more than a narrowly construed discursive process will be at stake.

There is considerable further evidence in *NE* VI against the alleged division of labour set up in *NE* II. Since the case has been well argued recently,[41] and since I shall return to the issue again, I shall be brief now in summarizing some of the more seminal points.

1. At 1140a28 Aristotle says that practical wisdom is about what contributes to the whole of good living (*to eu zēn holōs*), and not merely its parts. I take this to be explicit evidence that the concerns of deliberation span widely enough to include the overall ends of character.

2. He continues this thought at 1142b30, suggesting that we distinguish between excellence of deliberation in the unqualified sense 'which succeeds with reference to what is the

---

41 See, for example, Sorabji, 'Aristotle on the Role of Intellect in Virtue'; Irwin, 'Aristotle on Reason, Desire and Virtue'; Dahl, *Practical Reason*, to mention just a few.

end in the unqualified sense' (*pros to telos to haplōs*; i.e. the final good or happiness for a human being) and a more qualified excellence which is 'relative to a more limited end' (*pros ti telos*). He then goes on to say that 'if it is the mark of the practically wise to have deliberated well, then excellence of deliberation will be correctness regarding what promotes the end of which practical wisdom is the true apprehension or grasp' (*hupolēpsis*). The meaning of this passage is unclear and has been the focus of considerable commentary. I generally endorse the view that what *phronēsis* is the true grasp of is the end (*to telos*) and not 'what promotes the end' (*to sumpheron*), at least if that is construed narrowly as instrumental means.[42] Given that the end of *phronēsis* is the whole of good living (at 1140a28), presumably that inclusive notion is here too part of the *phronimos*'s apprehension. Moreover, the grasp of the end, as I have been insisting, need not be antecedently fixed before deliberation. Some view of the end must be presupposed to get deliberation off the ground, but any description of the end may itself become less vague as a result of that piece of deliberation or others. That first principles (*archai*) in ethics come to those who have adequate experience (1142a15-19) suggests that part of that experience consists precisely in making deliberative choices. Through such choices, an agent comes to qualify and refine ends as they find their place beside other ends in a life. We saw in the last chapter that this comprehensive understanding is in part the achievement of *nous* or practical insight. The perceptual aspects of *nous* suggest that ends become qualified not only through deliberation, but also through perception and emotional sensitivity—through recognizing the circumstantial signs and knowing how they concretely shape a more general policy. The end becomes refined through noticing occasions for action as well as through deciding just what the end demands here and now. Thus, perception as well as deliberation shapes ends. And to the extent that both concern a comprehensive good, both capacities involve, if you like, a kind of peripheral vision.

[42] Troels Engberg-Pedersen, *Aristotle's Theory of Moral Insight* (Oxford University Press, 1983), 196; cf. Irwin, who argues for a similar position in his commentary to the *Nicomachean Ethics*, 346.

3. At 1140b9 Aristotle says that we think certain individuals are practically wise men, like Pericles, 'because
they can study [*theōrein*] what is good for themselves and
what is good for human beings in general'. He says again
at 1140b13–20 that the practically wise, unlike the base,
recognize and preserve the ends of good living, that is, the
principles (*archai*; 1140b16, 1140b18) for the sake of which
we choose and act. The emphasis on ends is explicit. The use
of *theōrein* at 1140b10 need not detract from the deliberative
mode of their grasp. The word can be rendered 'see' (as in
the revised Oxford translation), but also, as I have preferred
to render it, as 'study', or comparably 'consider' or 'in-
vestigate'.[43] This rendering gives the word an active sense,
and reinforces the notion of deliberation (at 1112b23 and
1142a31 ff.) as inquiry and investigation (*zētēsis*).

4. The above two passages emphasize that practical wisdom has as its object not only one's own good, but what is
good for a human being in general, unconditionally, *qua*
human being. The search is for what is essential to human
beings, if they are to lead human lives, as opposed to say,
the lives of sea urchins or gods. As such, the good which is
its object is not about some limited preference or inclination
one individual happens to have, but about what constitutes
some more constant human good. This of course is the force
of the human function argument in *NE* I. 7. That celebrated
argument need not be read as an attempt to reduce ethics
to a non-normative basis,[44] but as an appeal to our most
considered views (including normative psychological views)
about what the best human life must be like. Among these
views is a belief in human sociality, which I will explore in
the next chapter.

These remarks should help to clarify Aristotle's vaguer
and more misleading formulation that virtue sets the end

[43] Cooper makes a similar point in the context of Aristotle's discussion of friendship in *NE* IX. 9: '. . . as often in Aristotle, even where it [theōrein] implies the
use of the senses, the word carries overtones of concentrated study, of the sort
involved in theoretical knowledge (its other principal meaning in Aristotle)' ('Aristotle on Friendship', in Rorty (ed.), *Essays on Aristotle's Ethics*, 340 n. 25).

[44] I am indebted to Henry Richardson ('Rational Deliberation of Ends', 114)
and David Charles (*Aristotle's Philosophy of Action*, 230 ff.).

and practical wisdom promotes it (e.g. 1144a8). Once we appreciate that full virtue cannot even be possessed without practical wisdom (as the definition of virtue in *NE* II. 6 makes painfully clear (1107a)), and that practical wisdom reciprocally requires virtue (1144a30), we can begin to see that the end which sets a deliberative process in action may itself be considerably transformed by the process.

We can illustrate this general point by sketching some examples. The examples are not meant to be paradigmatic or even mutually exclusive of each other; they are meant merely to illustrate the sort of shaping of character that can be the result of the deliberative process suggested by Aristotle's account.[45] As will be apparent, they are not examples which derive directly from the text, but I think they are consistent with its spirit.

1. The first example involves the removal of false beliefs that ground a specific end.[46] I have been brought up to believe, as a result of my Midwestern, puritan background, that it is intemperate to gamble. It is an entrenched attitude and one which colours my opinion of others. Ironically, I find myself married to a gambler; though my spouse always loved the horses, it is only recently that he has shown an interest in betting. My reasons for thinking gambling is bad are the familiar ones: that it will lead to obsessive gambling, that it will not be restricted to the race tracks, that it is correlated with loss of job, that it encourages an attitude of profligacy and wasteful spending. Through conversation and investigation I gradually discover that my beliefs are ill-founded. The man who plays the horses is not typically the same man who flies to Vegas for the weekend; among those who play the horses seriously, 80 per cent have serious professional lives away from the track and earn a good living from these professional pursuits; betting on the horses can involve cautious and calculated spending, and indeed a pulling in

---

[45] In thinking about these examples I have benefited from reading Daniel Heller's Senior Essay on Charles Stevenson, 'On Resolving Ethical Disputes: A Revivalist [slightly revisionist] Inquiry into Emotivist Ethics', (Yale University, 1987).

[46] Aristotle suggests this sort of point at 1142a20. I am grateful to Ruth Barcan Marcus for discussion of the particular example.

when luck takes a turn for the worse. In looking at these facts and my spouse's particular case, I realize that his sort of gambling really isn't profligate. My naïve view that gambling is intemperate is therefore revamped; alternatively, we can say my specification of the virtue of temperance is revised. Though I may still have residual negative feelings about the horses, I am committed to a self-conscious policy of bringing my beliefs and attitudes into line. As a fortuitous result of this, the conflict I faced between supporting my spouse's endeavours and my abhorrence to gambling is easing.

2. In this next example, a revised specification of virtue requires the removal of inconsistent beliefs that arise when I consider a competing end. I am a parent committed to a policy of love and caring towards my child. In particular, I believe good parenting involves shielding a child from excessive hurt and disappointment. This is manifest in the way I discourage my daughter from making overtures to children (i.e. inviting them to our house, inviting them to parties, etc.) when I am fairly sure they will reject her invitations. I have sometimes thought my attitude too protective, but usually end up endorsing it anyway. What has given me pause, though, is the realization that my view is essentially at odds with another view which I hold more deeply, namely that a child can only gain a stable sense of self-love by applying her own talents and energies to producing some product of her own or to working out some solution for herself. (Aristotle endorses some version of this second belief, e.g. 1162a22 ff.) In taking this latter view seriously, I have since relaxed the reins on her social exploring, making myself available, though, for problems that ensue and that she cannot resolve herself.

3. In the following case attention to the consequences of an attitude I hold persuades me of a need to change my views. I believe that surrogacy contracts are a just form of contract and indeed a legitimate basis for a utility friendship. Moreover, I believe these arrangements express well both the surrogate mother's freedom to choose to use her body in a way she deems fit, and the commissioning parents' reproductive freedom to have a child. As such, I believe the relationship between the parties can be truly one of mutual

advantage, without exploitation. However, with time and greater familiarity with the actual consequences of these arrangements I revise my views about the justice of the contract and the legitimacy of the eugenic partnership. Studies have shown that upon birth of the child a majority of surrogate mothers undergo a deep sense of loss and abandonment that leads to a period of grieving for the 'lost' child. Equally, the child typically goes through a period of traumatic identity confusion upon learning his biological origins, exacerbated by the lack of preparedness on the part of commissioning parents to deal adequately with the psychological complexities. The wisdom of those that have been a party to such contracts is that the psychological and emotional costs of the practice are simply too great.

Other examples can easily be generated. The general point is that the rational pursuit of ends seems to be arbitrarily (and irrationally) restricted if one makes these ends immune to changed beliefs, or immune to reflection about their compatibility with other ends or beliefs one holds. There is no persuasive evidence that Aristotle wants to restrict reason in this way.

With these examples still in mind, I want to reconsider the specific part played by *boulēsis* in this deliberative process. Thus far we have placed a heavy burden on *prohairesis*. Prohairetic capacities discover means and revise ends on the basis of efficiency, the arrangement of ends with other ends, coherence with warranted beliefs, attention to consequences, and the like. How does *boulēsis* enter? Aristotle says a *prohairesis* cannot be generated without a *boulēsis*, and moreover that it is not any *orexis* (desire) which will generate a *prohairesis*, but only a specific kind of desire, restricted to a specfic class of voluntary agents. But, as I have said earlier, a *boulēsis* can be specified by deliberation. This gives rise to the question of how, if a *boulēsis* can be the product as well as the starting-point of a piece of deliberation, bouletic capacities as opposed to prohairetic ones peculiarly characterize the rational agent? In what sense is positing desired ends specifically rational? The short answer is that it is not, apart from the choice-making capacities of *prohairesis*.

The point can be made as follows. To have the capacity for rational desire, *boulēsis*, on Aristotle's view, is in general to be capable of a conception of happiness. More specifically, it is to be capable of setting the sort of end which happiness is, namely an end constrained by the following criterion: that it be most final, complete, worthwhile, and self-sufficient (*NE* I. 7). In specific deliberations, it is to set ends regulated by this sort of higher-order interest in some most final good. I have been arguing that to have *that* desire and to set ends constrained by it is not to set down, in advance, the content of that conception. That is the product rather than the starting point of deliberation. But this suggests that the prohairetic reasoning which issues in more determinate, particular *boulēseis*, and in a more determinate conception of good living overall, must be regarded as essentially continuous with the setting of ends. To set ends with an eye towards happiness is just to be ready to revise them in the light of circumstances and fit with other ends. Bouletic and prohairetic capacities are thus part of the same dialectical process.

It should be apparent from viewing the deliberative process as constrained by the above criteria of happiness that the deliberation of ends will, as we have said, follow a path essentially similar to the theoretical project Aristotle himself embarks upon in the *Nicomachean Ethics*. The process by which we establish the specific content of happiness will start from accepted and adopted views (*ta endoxa*), just as deliberation of ends will begin with what we have thus far accepted as the result of upbringing, education, and experience. In both cases, we ask to what extent these accepted ends are compatible with other ends we take to be necessary for the most worthwhile life, and to what extent they jointly promote self-sufficiency.

6. FITTING CONTEMPLATION IN A LIFE

We have now argued that the prohairetic choices of a character will include the overall arrangement and revision of ends in a life. But we need to say something about the thorny

problem of contemplation and the way in which contemplative activity might find some place in that overall
arrangement. In what sense is the excellence of contemplative activity, *sophia*, compatible with the excellences
of a more political and communal life? Consideration of the
issue should shed light on the general problem of how a
life combines the different, specifically human excellences. I
shall restrict my remarks to the *Nicomachean Ethics*, since it
is in this work that the contemplative and political ideals of
life are so starkly posed as competitors.

As we have said before, Aristotle argues in *NE* I. 7 that
whatever the happy life is for a human being, it must meet
certain formal criteria. Namely, it must be a final or ultimate
end (*teleion*), everything being chosen for it while it is not
chosen for other ends, and self-sufficient, lacking in nothing
and including everything desirable or choice-worthy in a life
(1097a25–b21). As a life for a human being as opposed to say,
a plant, it is assumed to involve not merely the possession
of a state but activity (*energeia*; 1098a6, 1095b32–1096a1,
1098b35 ff.). This activity will be reflective (*kata logon*),
since the rational part of the soul is specific to the function
of a human being (1098a8), and social, since human self-
sufficiency must be relational (1097b12). The best examples
of this activity are from the outset taken to be moral and
political pursuits (i.e. excellent activities of character and
intellect aimed at the common good; 1129b15–1130a15,
1130b20–7),[47] and the architectonic study of happiness, so
conceived, is politics (1094a27–8). While the contemplative
life is posed early on as one of the three major contenders
for the good life (the other two being the apolaustic and
political lives; *NE* I. 5), its candidacy is not pursued again
until the final book of the *Nicomachean Ethics* (X. 6–8).[48]

---

[47] The Urmson translation of 1129b32—'for many men can exercise excellence
in their own affairs, but not in their relation to excellence'—is misleading; the latter
part of the sentence should read 'but not in relation to what concerns others'.

[48] Thus, I am not persuaded by the view that there are already foreshadowings
of this position in the statement of the formal criteria of happiness in *NE* I. 7. For
that to be the case, we would have to read *teleiotatēn* in I. 7 ('most final or most
complete') as implying an exclusive end, singled out above all others. But, with
David Keyt and others, I see no reason for this exclusionary interpretation. It
seems to fit poorly, both with the further gloss on happiness—namely that it be a
self-sufficient good, 'not as one good among others' but as inclusive, 'lacking in

But when it does return, it seems to do so with a vengeance. And Aristotle appears now to endorse it as the premier life, relegating the practical life of ethical virtue and practical reason to a mere second best. But in what sense does he do this? Since the literature on this subject is extensive, I shall be brief in my remarks and not attempt to untangle all the textual difficulties. The issues are complex, and have been the focus of a resurgence of scholarly debate in the past two decades.[49] My interest here will be the more modest one of sketching in rough a plausible way in which contemplation might cohere with the moral activities of a good life.

nothing'—and with the tripartite classification of ends which follows. At 1097a25 ff. Aristotle distinguishes among ends that are 'ultimate' or chosen for their own sake and never for the sake of other things; ends that are 'subservient' or chosen for an end beyond themselves; and ends that are 'subordinate' or chosen for their own sake as well as for some further, more ultimate end (the labels are from Keyt). It is explicit in the discussion that happiness is to be identified with the first (1097a34), and is an ultimate end that subordinates or includes other activities chosen for their own sakes (since if it did not, there would be some further end, which would be more choice-worthy than it by the mere addition of the least of those goods; 1098b15-22, *Rh.* 1363b12-21).

Equally explicit is the classification of intellectual activity (*nous*) in the group of subordinate goods (*NE* 1097b2). This suggests that pure activity of the intellect is viewed early on as merely a component or part of happiness, and not as itself co-extensive with the whole of it. It is also crucial to note that in Aristotle's other references to the rational part of the soul and a life in accordance with it, the rational part is never exclusively thought of as theoretical. In *NE* I. 7 'the practical life of that which has a rational principle' must be practical in the generic sense that includes theoretical activity (as in *Pol.* VII. 3), as well as practical in the more specific sense of political or ethical activity. Similarly, in the two passages outside Book X where Aristotle identifies the self with *nous*, i.e. in IX. 4 (1166a22-3) and IX. 8 (1169a2 ff.), it is practical *nous* that is most clearly in mind; cf. *Pol.* 1333a25-7.

There is an extensive literature on this subject, and I mention only some of the relevant writings: J. L. Ackrill, 'Aristotle on Eudaimonia', *Proceedings of the British Academy*, 60 (1975), 339-59; Cooper, *Reason and Human Good*, Parts II and III, and more recently, for a revision of his earlier views, 'Contemplation and Happiness: A Reconsideration', *Synthese*, 72 (1987), 187-216; David Keyt, 'Intellectualism in Aristotle' in George C. Simmons (ed.), *Paideia*; *Special Aristotle Issue* (State University College at Brockport, 1978), 138-58, repr. in J. P. Anton and A. Preus (eds.), *Essays in Ancient Greek Philosphy*, ii (State University of New York Press, 1983); Thomas Nagel, 'Aristotle on *Eudaimonia*', *Phronesis*, 17 (1972), 252-9, repr. in Rorty (ed.), *Essays on Aristotle's Ethics*; Nussbaum, *The Fragility of Goodness*, 373-7. I discuss the issue also in my review of Anthony Kenny's *The Aristotelian Ethics* (Oxford University Press, 1978) in *Journal of the History of Philosophy*, 19 (1981), 100-4.

[49] My own thinking on the subject has been sharpened by the recent discussions of Keyt and Cooper (cited above) and in conversations with Sarah Waterlow Broadie.

In *NE* X. 7, Aristotle reconsiders the nature of happiness and as part of the inquiry offers an expanded set of criteria. *Eudaimonia* will be activity (as opposed to passivity) of the best part of us and directed towards the best objects; it will be activity that is most continuous, most pleasant, self-sufficient, and leisurely, aiming at no end beyond itself. Contemplative activity, Aristotle now argues, satisfies these criteria best. It is perfect happiness (*hē teleia eudaimonia*), and the life of reason (*ho kata ton noun bios*), in the sense of the theoretical or philosophical life, is the happiest life (1177a12-18, 1178a4-8, 1178b7 ff.). The practical life, Aristotle further implies, will be merely a means to contemplative activity: 'we work in order that we may have leisure and wage war in order that we may have peace' (1177b4-6). These remarks are, needless to say, disturbing and raise serious interpretative questions. They are antithetical to the whole thrust of the *Nicomachean Ethics*, in which the ethical life is defended as the best life (as the life which best exemplifies excellent activity in accordance with reason) and ethical activities are viewed as actions chosen for their own sake (1105a26-b9);[50] they are said by Aristotle to be *praxeis*, whose end, unlike *poiēseis* or productions, is in the doing itself (1140b6-7).

One way to begin to assess the implications of these remarks is to consider Aristotle's claim that the final end must be a leisurely pursuit, chosen for no end beyond itself. The apolaustic life of pleasure (one of three original contenders for the good life) might seem to fit this description well. But in *NE* X. 6 Aristotle ultimately rejects its candidacy, arguing that such a life, conceived essentially as a life of amusement and play (*paidia*), can never really be chosen unconditionally. It is chosen as a relaxation from work, a respite which permits one to replenish one's energies for further toil. Drinking, dance, and music are, in this sense, all forms of play.[51]

---

[50] This is also the point of 1097b4, where Aristotle argues in a preliminary way that virtue is chosen for its own sake *and* as the constitutive element of some final, comprehensive good.

[51] Music, Aristotle argues in *Pol.* VIII. 4 and 5, also has another, more important educative function—a function to which it is well suited because of its natural pleasantness. I discuss this in further detail in Ch. 5. sect. 7.

While some do make such amusements their end, Aristotle argues that these sort of pursuits, connected as they are with pleasures of the lower faculties, cannot achieve the excellence distinctive of the human life (1177a1-11, *Pol.* 1339b20-35). They are more like a child's pastimes,[52] than the cultivated and intellectual pursuits (*diagōgē*) of the mature adult.[53]

The rejection of recreational pleasure as neither true leisure (*scholē*) nor a serious pursuit which exercises our better part paves the way for the contemplative life. It is an end chosen for no further good and an end which cultivates our higher faculties. Measured against these criteria, it fares better than a life of pleasure (conceived of as play), but also better than a life engaged in moral action. For the latter sort of life is, in a crucial way, contingent upon bringing about further ends, such as welfare or peace. Without these ends, there would be no point to munificence or justice. Hence, even if moral action comes to be valued for its own sake, as it must on the Aristotelian view, its value is derivative upon certain external ends, which are themselves worthwhile. These ends are worthwhile, in turn, given the standing conditions of human society. The effort of virtue is thus to safeguard these ends, and to restore them when they come undone. It is the precariousness of these ends, and not virtue itself, that ultimately gives a point to virtue. This is clear with courage: 'For no one chooses to be at war, or provokes war, for the sake of being at war; anyone would seem entirely murderous if he were to make enemies out of his friends in order to bring about battle and slaughter' (1177b9-13). In this sense, virtuous action is unleisurely: it is work that struggles to safeguard and restore certain ends; it is needed to ameliorate the conditions that human beings find themselves in. At bottom, virtuous activity is an impure *praxis*, contingent upon an external end, and related, in a specific way, to a productive activity aimed at this end.[54]

---

[52] Note the etymological connection between child (*pais*) and play (*paidia*).

[53] So in *Pol.* 1338a30 Aristotle distinguishes *paidia* and *diagōgē*, arguing that the latter is itself an end which befits not the child, but the fully developed individual.

[54] I do not try to sort out the difficult ontological question in the case of virtuous actions of whether the making (*poiein*) of external ends and doing (*prattein*) of ends for their own sake require different descriptions for the same entity, or distinct entities that are co-occurrent. The issue is discussed by David Charles in 'Aristotle:

In contrast, contemplative activity does not repair a damage. There is no separate external end which it originally posits, no fragile and vulnerable good which it protects and preserves. As such, it is pure activity, pure leisure, done for nothing beside itself. It provides a reason for choosing a life from, as it were, an outside perspective, a reason for choosing it unconditionally.[55] In this sense it stands apart from a life of ethical virtue which is chosen from *within* a human life, from a life conditioned by hunger, need, hostility, etc., and from a desire to remedy these persistent conditions through human agency. Indeed, in the absence of these conditions, it would be peculiar to think someone would choose the ethical life as in itself most worthwhile and best. And even in the presence of these conditions, to view virtuous action as the only worthwhile end would be in some sense short-sighted and unliberated. It is as if one were too firmly rooted in the concrete world, too immersed in its daily work, to catch a glimpse of the divine. True enough, the political sphere is 'home' for Aristotle, and not a mere cave which we must be compelled to turn to, as it appears to be for Plato's philosopher king. But it is nevertheless a home that must leave some space for the pure intellectual pursuits that Plato so zealously constructed his city around.

Now it is this more liberated perspective, the perspective which tries to capture in the human being what is most akin to the divine, that seems to inform Aristotle's discussion in *NE* X. 6–8. These chapters are a reminder to look up, to unfetter ourselves for a moment, to savour activities that do not require that we do good or make good. They ask us to leave room for something which expresses the best in ourselves, something we would value apart from any contribution to justice and peace:

But that perfect happiness is some contemplative activity would appear from what follows: we assume the gods to be most blessed and happy; but what sort of actions must we assign to them?

Ontology and Moral Reasoning', in Julia Annas (ed.), *Oxford Studies in Philosophy*, iv (Oxford University Press, 1986), 121–43.

[55] On the general issue of contemplation as an unconditional good, I have profited much from Christine Korsgaard's 'Aristotle and Kant on the Final Good', *Ethics* (1986).

Just actions? Would they not appear absurd making contracts and returning deposits, and so on. What of brave acts, standing up to what is frightening and taking risks for the sake of the fine? Or generous actions? To whom would they give? It would be absurd if they had money or anything like it. And what if they were temperate? Would not the praise be vulgar, since they have no bad appetites? If we were to run through them all, would not the circumstances of action appear trifling and unworthy of the gods? Still, everyone supposes them to live and to be active; for they do not spend their lives asleep, like Endymion. Now if you take away from the living practical action and, furthermore, production, what is left except contemplation? So that the activity of god, which surpasses all in blessedness, would be contemplative. And of human activities, that which is most akin to this would be most of the nature of happiness. (1178b8-23)

The force of this passage is not to make light of our human nature, but to remind us that we are capable of a perspective which can occasionally deliver us from it. Thus the laughter which this passage is meant to provoke has to do with the absurdity of the gods rushing about in a political world, not the absurdity of us doing the same. Nor is the fact that we have to do it regrettable; it is just that we can do other things too which perfect and cultivate our capacities. We can do things which have no apparent ameliorative, social effect. And this, in a way, is news, given the overall thrust of the *Nicomachean Ethics* thus far, and the tone of the final chapter which follows, as Aristotle returns again to the political reality of becoming good.

But what are we to make of the claim that contemplation is perfect happiness, that contemplative activity is what is best? If it is the perfect and best way to spend time, then why should we not maximize it in a life, and make it an end which all other ends subserve? Why not promote morality as merely a condition of contemplation—something valued when it allows the life of contemplation to flourish, something to be shunned when it interferes with the time and means for pure philosophical thought? Aristotle gives us the material for an answer. Because, as he suggests, what is divine in us, namely the life according to reason (here understood narrowly as theoretical reason, though significantly, elsewhere in the *Nicomachean Ethics* understood more broadly to include both practical and theoretical reason (cf. 1166a16, 1166a22-3, 1168a35 ff.), is not the whole of us. 'This reason', he says, 'is what is *most of all*, or what is *especially* [*malista*] a human being' (1178a8). But, as David Keyt pointedly notes, 'To be most of all man is to be less than, and nonidentical with, man'.[56] The force of *malista* is thus to suggest that the identification of self with theoretical reason is at best qualified.[57] It is not exclusively us, nor its activity exclusively our happiness. There are other parts with which we are to be identified which are not co-extensive with contemplative reason. These other goods, e.g. practical reason and moral virtue, are indeed parts of us, and not merely necessary conditions of our existence as humans. The human perspective unconditioned by historical circumstances is not the only standpoint we must take, though it may be the one which, when we do take it (in a life which includes other perspectives), allows for a most perfect form of happiness and self-perfection. Thus, happiness does not consist exclusively of contemplation, though contemplation may be the part of a life that accounts for a superior kind of happiness.

The interest in combining contemplative excellence with the moral virtues is heard again in Aristotle's appeal: '*as far as it is possible*, we must make ourselves immortal and do everything in life in accord with what is best in us' (1177b34). The implication here is that there are constraints on how contemplative activity must be pursued: not as a god would, but as a human would, within the boundaries defined by our social and moral lives. To pursue contemplation 'as far as possible' means as far as the circumstances of practical action allow. Thus, contemplative reason may be what is most authoritative and best in a human being (1178a1-3), but it is neither, in virtue of that, the *only* human end, everything else subserving it, nor (what, practically speaking, comes to much the same) the end, among other final ends, that always has pre-emptive status.

Conversely it would be much too simple to think that the

---

[56] Keyt, 'Intellectualism in Aristotle'.

[57] Note the similar use of *malista* in the two other passages (1166a22-3 and 1169a2) in which Aristotle identifies self with reason.

view Aristotle ultimately embraces gives to moral activity just that sort of pre-emptive priority. Moral action does not always take precedence; indeed what would it mean for it to do so? When would our moral service ever be finished? When would all the fires be put out? If it is not stringent prohibitions that are at the centre of Aristotelian good living, but positive virtues, then there must always be leeway and judgement as to when and at what cost they are to be exercised. To speak of straining every nerve for the sake of the fine (1169a8) does not say how often, towards whom, and in what circumstances, such expenditure is warranted. As we have said before, that cannot be specified exhaustively in advance. In some instances, to omit generous actions in order to safeguard time for leisured study might thus be permissible, and without blame. Given the rival claims and the agent's overall record as regards giving aid to warranted causes, generous action here and now is not required. One's choice is *hōs dei*, or right. But if an agent consistently refuses time or money for such causes, giving the reason that he is in fact committed to such ends, but philosophical pursuits prevail, then the agent seems akratic, and morally blameworthy. It is simply self-deception for him to insist that when the right time comes, he will be moved to help. The record invalidates such a claim. Nor will it do if he overlooks lesser moral actions for one grand display. This policy may maximize leisure time, but it surely seems to indicate an overall lack of the sort of sensitivity and responsiveness requisite for the ideally virtuous agent. Though some have interpreted Aristotle as endorsing this selective detachment from action in his portrait of magnanimity (*NE* IV. 3), and have identified the portrait with that of the contemplator, the picture is clearly at odds with what Aristotle requires of virtue, and indeed of superlative virtue, elsewhere in the ethical treatises.[58]

But the point of this last remark is not to push Aristotle's perfectionism towards a narrowly moral ideal. The moral saint is not necessarily someone for whom Aristotle would

---

[58] I discuss the virtue of magnanimity in my 'Common Sense and Uncommon Virtue', *Midwest Studies in Philosophy* (University of Notre Dame Press, 1988).

save his highest praise. Rather, the Aristotelian virtuous agent is well rounded. His virtue extends at both ends beyond a blander (and narrower) notion of morality, conceived principally as benevolence. He cultivates generosity, temperance, and courage, but also the more earthly qualities of wit, humour, and conviviality (*NE* IV. 6–8). He recognizes a moment for laughter, and knows how to make other people see it, without becoming offensive or slavishly dependent upon an audience. He is personable, prizing not merely good action but the qualities of friendliness and emotional candour. To lead a good life is to lead a life in which these non-moral but human pursuits have some ineliminable place. But his human virtue also has something divine in it, to the extent that the virtuous agent possesses the power of theoretical intellect. And this divine activity enhances and perfects the sort of happiness and pleasure of which he is capable. Thus, I believe Aristotle can still say at *NE* X. 8 that the overall thrust of the full constellation of virtues is towards just and decent living in a political sphere. Fine action retains its moral force. But within the best example of a good life is the recognition of an activity of superior worth and pleasure that is not itself the exercise of moral virtue or intellect in its practical aspect. The life which cultivates this excellence, jointly with other human virtues, is the happiest life. The life devoted exclusively to morality, which finds no leisure for the speculative pursuits of the mind, will only be second best. It will lack something.

Admittedly, this is to leave the matter of adjudication vague, and to offer no procedural rules for how to assess the actual choices which attempt to balance these diverse goods. But I am not sure we can do better than Aristotle here. His by now familiar view is that it would be a foolish precision to attempt to establish principles that resist either the detail or the convictions of a particular case. The very point of his ethical theory, based upon the virtues as opposed to principles or rules, is just that. The result is not to make ethical assessment a matter of mere preference. But where the boundaries fall in specific cases will be a matter of judgement, and perhaps disagreement.

Two further points need to be pursued briefly. First, it

might be objected that the sort of perfectionism Aristotle endorses is, in the end, simply too inclusive, and subjects too much of our lives to the sort of correct judgement (*orthos logos*) implicit in virtue. If you like, practical wisdom rules over too much, at the cost of spontaneity and a more free-wheeling spirit. What we need, the objection goes, is to exempt certain parts of our lives from the pursuit of excellence and harmony. Not everything we do must be subject to rational scrutiny and the demands of hitting the mean. To round out an agent by making all activities subject to the requirements of excellence in a unified life is hardly more attractive than making only the narrowly moral life subject to such scrutiny.

The objection is a difficult one which I cannot pursue in depth here. It raises the question of the competing merits of different theories of virtue, such as Kant's and Aristotle's; and that is a subject for another work. Some brief reply can be offered, however. It is true that the rational pursuit of happiness is overdone if it requires *all* activity to fit together into some comprehensive whole. Sunning on the beach may simply be intrinsically enjoyable, without being viewed either as respite from toil or as enrichment for other sorts of activities. It requires wisdom both to know when to subject activities to evaluation and to know when to exclude them from such judgement. This said, the Aristotelian view nevertheless seems to capture certain intuitions we have about judging people's moral standing by their overall goodness— by the kinds of leisure activities they pursue, by the sort of people they keep company with, by the jokes they find funny. We expect there to be some spill-over—some resistance to racist jokes if racism is viewed as an evil, some disfavour towards spending one's free time drunk if temperance is valued, some interest in choosing virtuous friends if virtue is valued. On Aristotle's behalf, it does seem that this sort of unity in a life is deemed significant and a part of how we assess goodness.

The second point that needs to be addressed is the place of conflict in such a life. I shall be brief on this subject, since it has been given careful and extensive attention by others.[59] The Aristotelian doctrine of the unity of the virtues requires that the virtues be in principle consistent and, moreover, reciprocal: that is, if an individual (genuinely) has one virtue constitutive of goodness, then he has them all (1144b30–1145a2). To possess virtue of this sort is distinct from having the natural virtues. An individual who is by nature generous or temperate may lack courage. But if he has the sort of virtue acquired through proper habituation and practical wisdom, then possession of one virtue implies possession of the full complement. This, no doubt, seems unduly stringent when we include in the list of virtues, as we have above, those which may not be within the reach of many ordinary human beings, such as contemplative excellence. It seems equally stringent when we reflect that certain moral virtues, such as the grand scale virtues of magnificence and magnanimity, may require resources and opportunities of a considerably greater magnitude than those requisite for the cultivation of more ordinary moral virtue.[60] In this sense, the overall fit of the virtues may be more strained than Aristotle allows. Certain virtues may be much more exclusive and inaccessible than others and the fact that an individual does not possess these virtues need not tell against the individual's overall goodness.

This problem notwithstanding, Aristotle's claim that the virtues are in principle consistent needs to be distinguished from the claim that the virtuous life is conflict-free. The fact that the virtues 'may be' in principle consistent does not preclude the possibility of contingent conflicts. Although Aristotle says little explicitly on this subject, it would be peculiar to think that a theorist as sensitive as he is to the limits of rational control over fortune (*NE* I. 8–11) would fail to appreciate that the specific requirements of one virtue

[59] See especially Nussbaum, *The Fragility of Goodness*, chs. 1, 2, 3 and interlude 2, and T. H. Irwin, 'The Unity of Aristotelian Virtue' in Julia Annas (ed.) *Oxford Studies in Ancient Philosophy*, vi (Oxford University Press, 1988). For the general issue of moral conflict, see Ruth Barcan Marcus, 'Moral Dilemmas and Consistency', *Journal of Philosophy*, 77 (1980), 121–36; Bernard Williams, 'Moral Luck', in *Moral Luck: Philosophical Papers, 1973–1980* (Cambridge University Press, 1981).

[60] See ch. 2, sect. 5.

can, in certain instances, conflict with those of another. Such circumstances present an impediment to virtuous action (and to happiness) no less than loss of money or health. Avenging a brother's death may stand in the way of loyalty to a king, honouring a father in the way of love for a mother. Such is the stuff of tragedy, where moral dilemmas cannot be resolved without loss and residue. Aristotle is well aware of this when he defines tragedy in the *Poetics* as 'an imitation not of persons, but of action and life' (1450a15 ff.). What makes for a tragic plot is not character, but the deliberate actions of a character in pursuit of goals, and the reversals of fortune that take place in trying to realize these goals. As with his theory of happiness, so too in his theory of tragedy, it is human agency, not passivity, that is at the core; and with it goes the recognition of the conflicts and impediments that can frustrate otherwise successful action.[61]

7. GOOD AND BAD CHARACTERS

We have been arguing for the role of prohairetic choice in the living of a reflective, well-planned, and coherent life. In the opening pages of the *Eudemian Ethics*, Aristotle is unequivocal about this role:

. . . everybody capable of living according to his own *prohairesis* must set some mark for noble living to aim at, either honour or reputation or wealth or education, which fixing his eyes on he performs all his actions—since not to arrange one's life with respect to some end is a sign of great foolishness. . . (1214b7; cf. 1226b31)

The passage is not uncontroversial in its suggestion (which I have just disputed) that character will be marked by a single dominant end. But I want to focus now on a more restricted point.

Aristotle says that to fail to arrange one's life with regard

---

[61] The relation of Aristotle's theory of happiness to his theory of tragedy is a subject of enormous interest, and one I regret I cannot explore within the confines of this book. The topic has been treated recently with much insight and clarity by Stephen Halliwell in *Aristotle's Poetics* (Duckworth and University of North Carolina Press, 1986).

to ends is a sign of foolishness. The word for foolishness is telling. It is *aphrosunē*—lacking in reason; it suggests a contrast with *sōphrosunē*—literally, preserving reason or soundness of mind (though more commonly, temperance).[62] The term is used by ancient writers to convey an overall sense of self, and in Plato's *Charmides* it is explicitly linked with *aidōs* or a sense of shame. Aristotle may be relying on the contrast here, suggesting that if living without *prohairesis* is foolishness, then living with *prohairesis* comes from a sense of self and purpose.

But could living with *prohairesis* mean more than this? Could it imply not merely having *a* character, but having *character*, that is a *good* character, a character that exhibits the right sort of ends and has a sense of self-grounded not merely in coherent projects but in truly fine ones?[63] Indeed, could not it not turn out that coherence and fineness are more intimately linked so that only certain sorts of ends, namely fine ones, can be pursued in an enduring and progressive fashion? As I have interpreted it so far, *prohairesis* assesses particular actions relative to some arrangement of overall ends. But these ends can be good or bad, and the character whose ends they are, a good or bad character. *Prohairesis* (as well as *boulēsis*) is thus far a neutral capacity open to the virtuous and vicious alike. The choices of each kind of agent will be prohairetic, even though those of the virtuous will hit the mean, while those of the vicious will be in ignorance of what is in fact good (*NE* 1145a5, 1145a20, 1110b30-1).

Aristotle argues this way most of the time. To formulate bouletic wishes requires not that one's character be good, but simply that one be guided by certain ends which one

---

[62] Although in an earlier period and in the early writings of Plato *sōphrosunē* was associated with practical reason and soundness of mind, through the influence of the *Republic* and its discussion of the appetites it came to be associated more narrowly with self-control and temperance. Aristotle uses *sōphrosunē* most often in this later sense (cf. NE 1147b26 ff., 1151b31), though he would have been aware of its earlier meaning and explicitly recalls it at 1140b12. On the history of the term *sōphrosunē*, see Helen North, *Sōphrosunē* (Cornell University Press, 1966), esp. chs. 5 and 6.

[63] I am grateful to John Fischer and John Van Lonkhuyzen for urging me to clarify this distinction.

takes to be constitutive of happiness. A wish must minimally be for an apparent practical good (1113a24): 'No one wishes for what he thinks to be bad' (*EE*1223b8, 1223b33), even though what he wishes and aims at may in fact bring him great evil' (*NE* 1142b19). *Prohairesis* is a capacity which is expressive of *ethical* character, of which both virtue and vice are subspecies.

But it is not at all clear that this is Aristotle's final word on the matter. As I shall go on to suggest, he gives indications that the sort of planning and rationality that exhibit character (and are implicit in prohairetic choice) may not be entirely within the reach of all base persons, in particular those motivated by a prevailing policy of pursuing the ends of appetite. On these grounds, such an individual's claim to full *prohairesis* may have to be qualified.

A related point emerges if we consider that the practical reason associated with virtue is not something separable from virtue but is, as we have said, an intrinsic part of having virtuous states of character (1107a1). It is *phronēsis*, practical wisdom, and an agent cannot be practically wise without being virtuous (1145a1-5). While the non-virtuous will share elements of the virtuous person's practical reason—namely, the deliberative capacities which Aristotle broadly classifies as cleverness (1144a24)—Aristotle seems now to suggest that there may be a greater fit between a rich conception of practical reason and virtuous ends than between the former and vice. This is not to argue that the vicious cannot in principle exercise robust powers of reasoning. The claim is the weaker one, that their ends in fact run counter to the full authority and scope of reason. Stronger rationality constraints are available to the base agent, but typically they fail to motivate.

We can begin by considering the prohairetic capacities of the *akolastos*. This individual, on Aristotle's view, typically sets ends that indulge the appetites. His end, says Aristotle, is 'always to satisfy the present pleasure' (1146b24). While this end sets a policy, taken literally it is a policy that necessarily fails to take into account the future and the interests of a future self. For on this extreme *akolastos*'s view, present desires always outweigh future desires simply in virtue of their being satisfiable *now*. The sort of zero-time preference necessary for prudential planning is missing in this life.[64] As such, the goals of this life seem to compromise what is minimally necessary for character coherence. In this vein, although Aristotle says the *akolastos* acts prohairetically and 'with conviction', the fact that he 'chooses' (*prohairoumenos*) the bestial 'life of dumb grazing' suggests that prohairetic capacities will inevitably be affected by the very content of the end chosen.[65] The ability to plan, schedule, and integrate will be pointless in a life devoted to the cravings of the moment; if and when these appetites no longer satisfy, the capacity to forbear and plan may no longer be easily within reach (1114a3–22). Through neglect and profligacy, reason may atrophy, or at least be robbed of authority—'For [the pursuit of] what is pleasant and [avoidance of] what is painful does not destroy and pervert every judgement . . . but judgements concerning action' (1140b12–19; cf. 1179b26, 1180a5–12).

Profligacy may also destroy the collaborative spirit essential for ethical perception and choice. We considered the social dimension of practical reason in the last chapter and shall pursue it more fully in the next. Without delving into those arguments here, we can say that the rational pursuit of ends includes, for Aristotle, a common or social conception of the good. This entails a jointly articulated end, as well as collaborative efforts in the promotion of it. In an important way rational agency and its objects are extended. What is within our power and perceptual gaze extends beyond the first person. Simply to make the informed choice and to see what is relevant often requires the resources of others (cf. 1143a1–35, 1112b10–11, 1112b27–8). To seclude reason from dialogue is to erect an artificial barrier. But an agent moved by extreme indulgence will most likely be cut off from this extended deliberative perspective. He may be unable to secure the trust required for co-operation with

---

[64] Henry Sidgwick is quite clear on this requirement: the principle of prudence affirms 'that the mere difference of priority and posteriority in time is not a reasonable ground for having more regard to the consciousness of one moment than to that of another' (*The Methods of Ethics*, 7th edn. (Macmillan, 1907; repr. 1963), 381)).

[65] NE 1095b20; cf 1150a20, 1151a6–7, 1151a11 and 1151a13.

others. Indeed even the more limited Aristotelian friendships, based on common pleasures and exchange of services,
will require, if they are to be friendships at all, a certain
amount of goodwill and mutual care.[66] Yet this sort of
other-regard may not be available to the extreme profligate.
An overweening appetite for more than one's own share
may simply interfere with the conditions of friendship. It is
perhaps for this reason that Aristotle claims we are released
from our obligations towards friends whose characters de-
teriorate and take a turn for the worse (1165b13). Such persons can no longer be counted on to act as friends. It may
thus be that neither minimal rationality constraints nor the
constraints generated by a collaborative form of reason will
be met by the extreme profligate.

Of course the case I have in mind is extreme, and it hardly
follows from it that all or most persons who set pleasure as
their predominant end will be unable to accommodate future
desires or collaborate with others in pursuit of that end. To
be sure, there are hedonists, and base ones at that, who, not
riveted to the pleasures of the moment, scrupulously achieve
their ends with forbearance and prudence. They are not
brutish but indeed quite rational and controlled. They are
aware of future desires and may plan now for their eventual
satisfaction. They may enlist like-minded others in their
pursuits. But even so, we might say that there is something
in the single-mindedness of their pursuits that distinguishes
their reasoning from that of the virtuous agent. For even if
the hedonist is moved by goods other than pleasures (e.g. by
friendship or generosity), in the true hedonist these are in a
sense ultimately valued only in so far as they are productive
of extrinsic pleasure (1130b1-5). If they fail to produce
pleasure they are given up. Reason is primarily instrumental;
there is a single value and reason serves it. The role of
rationality is, in this sense, considerably restricted.

---

[66] That even the lesser friendships of *NE* VIII and IX will require the non-
instrumental reciprocation of goodwill is argued convincingly by John M. Cooper
in his influential 'Aristotle on the Forms of Friendship', *Review of Metaphysics*, 30
(1977), 619-48. Together with 'Friendship and the Good in Aristotle', *Philosophical
Review*, 86 (1977), 290-315, repr. as 'Aristotle on Friendship', in Rorty (ed.), *Essays
on Aristotle's Ethics*, 301-40.

But what of the vicious character who seems to give a great value to reason as an intrinsic good? Here we might think of the individual who seeks rational self-reliance in a life and aims to achieve it through asceticism. Towards this end he minimizes his needs and avoids entanglement with others; where he cannot do without the help of others, he secures their help not through trust, but through threats and fear. In keeping his needs minimal, he avoids the sorts of risks and sacrifices that typically come with involvement in the social world. He is niggardly and pusillanimous, staying clear of circumstances which might lead to painful loss or confrontation with fears. He has a sour demeanour which keeps him safe from friendship and more casual social engagement. Like the solitary contemplator of Book X of the *Nicomachean Ethics*, he recognizes that this may be a life open to only a special few. But, he can argue on its behalf, it is a life which yields the satisfaction of self-reliance and the reward of knowing one has used one's own ingenuity to achieve ends. It is a life which does not despise the exercise of practical reason, but enjoys and values it.[67]

The impracticability of this life notwithstanding, Aristotle would still have to conclude that its activities arbitrarily restrict the range, depth, and resources of practical reason. Practical reason that is not political or social is necessarily impoverished (see *NE* VI. 8). It is never adequately cultivated without reliance on others, and has only the narrowest sphere of practice when an agent studiously avoids the sort of circumstances in which others matter. Even contemplation, Aristotle points out in *NE* X. 7, is more likely to make advances if it is pursued in concert with others (1177b1; cf. 1169b17–1170b18). But it is not just *other persons* who enrich one's rational life. So too do circumstances, in which one is forced to confront the sorts of fears, however narrow or global, that hamper mastery. The swimmer who never ventures in the ocean because of fear of the undertow cuts himself off both from one of nature's greatest pleasures and from the chance of greater mastery. More generally, the

[67] I am grateful to Norman Dahl for urging me to take more seriously this challenge and in general for his critical comments on an earlier draft of this section.

person who fears what may happen if he fails deprives himself of countless ways in which he can succeed. This is not to deny that it takes considerable ingenuity to make oneself invulnerable to risks, social or otherwise; but it still seems unlikely that the challenges of doing so will match those stimulated by a rich engagement in the external world, such as virtue requires.

But let us push the comparison of the virtuous and vicious further. Consider the claim that what most crucially distinguishes rational capacities is the ability to revise ends. Let us concede, then, that a sophisticated vicious agent might pursue ends collaboratively, with an eye to other ends and with an eye to the future. And let us even grant that such an agent might welcome challenges, seeking a wide range of subjects on which to employ his reasoning capacities. But what he lacks, the claim goes, is the ability to revise his ends. He is unwilling to revise, and in a way unable to.

On a certain reading of the evidence, Aristotle seems sceptical about the capacity of the vicious to revise ends. In *NE* VII. 8 he describes the base individual as incurable, as having a permanent disability like dropsy. Such an individual acts without repentance, and without full awareness of his vice (*kakia lanthanei*, 1150b29–35). In III. 5, he says that although the unjust and vicious person was once able to revise ends, now such reform is no longer within his power (1114a14–24). The thought is repeated again at VI. 5:

For the principles of action are what actions aim at; but if pleasure or pain has ruined an individual, then the principle will not appear to him [*ou phainetai*], nor will it be apparent that this must be the end and cause of all his choice and action; for vice corrupts the principle. (1140b17–20)

The use of *phainetai* is revealing. What vice has destroyed is the ability *to see* the proper goals of action; thus, it is not merely ends that have been corrupted but, more significantly, one's access to them through perception and reason. Equally, a few lines above, Aristotle says practical wisdom preserves *judgement* about action (*hupolēpsis*) while vice destroys such judgement (1140b13-16). What the vicious lack, as Aristotle says again in this same passage, is the ability to study and see (*theōrein*) the human good (1140b10). It is for this reason, Aristotle suggests in X. 9, that the base must be treated like 'beasts of burden', 'for passion seems to yield not to reason, but to force' (1180a11-12). Such a person 'does not listen to arguments that dissuade him, nor understand them if he does' (1179b26; cf. 1180a5). The vicious, then, may not be able to engage in the process of revising ends. It is not just that they have different ends from the virtuous, but that their rational capacities are more limited as a result.

But these remarks seem to apply once again to the bestial character. We want to know something about the clever scoundrel who seems to use and enjoy his reason well enough, but simply for the wrong ends. He does not give up his ends, because like the virtuous he does not think he should—though when they conflict with other ends or beliefs, he is willing to modify and revise. Thus, the fact that he does not *reform* does not mean that he does not *revise*. In this sense, his capacity to revise seems to be on a par with that of the virtuous. The organized crime leader, moved ultimately by family honour as well as the desire for wealth, may revise his conception of each when they begin to conflict. He may be willing to abandon loyalty to some family members when a huge profit is at stake, while in other instances keeping the whole family intact may mean more to him than money. What each value represents and how each is viewed relative to other ends is not immune to reflection.

Even so, I think Aristotle does have a line of reply—and one that rests on a deep insight. Moreover, it can be sustained against the sort of counter-examples we have been raising in which the vicious person's rational agency seems to know no limits or bounds in achieving its ends. The answer rests on Aristotle's conception of fine activity and the sense in which it involves an internalization of external ends. Let me explain. Virtuous activity, Aristotle tells us, is fine in so far as it is praiseworthy and constitutes its own end. To act for the sake of the fine (*to kalon*; 1115b12,

1116a12, 1120a23) is thus contrasted with acting for the sake of either expedience or extrinsic pleasure.[68] It is the end of virtue, but an immanent end—not some additional value posited over and above the value of virtuous action itself.[69] In this sense, virtuous action is not a production (a *poiēsis* or making of some independent end), but a *praxis* (an action that is its own end). This claim has, with good reason, generated considerable puzzlement, since, as has already been pointed out, virtuous activities are related, in an important way, to external ends or objects, and would be without value unless these ends were themselves valued. There would be no point in acting bravely without wanting to rout the enemy, no point in risking my life unless I wanted to pull the child out of the wreckage. To act virtuously is to desire to bring about some external effect, and one's deliberation would be pointless if it were not tied to a concrete event or object in this way. In the truly virtuous agent, however, what comes to have primary value is not the particular state of affairs to be brought about, but the *action* which has this object and the character state of the agent who brings it about.[70]

Thus, when action is fine what is commended is how one acts towards an end, how one constitutes the action—in short, one's choice of what is *hōs dei*, or appropriate. The focus moves from the external end to the agency. But in so doing, the original end does not become devalued. The courageous still want victory, but only victory constituted by certain sorts of actions; so that even where there is

---

[68] See *Rh.* 1366a33 for a definition of the fine. The general account there (e.g. 1367a1-5) tends, however, toward an ethic of self-sacrifice not apparent in the *Nicomachean Ethics*. For the distinction between acting for the sake of the fine and acting for external ends, the following passage from the *Eudemian Ethics* is representative: '. . . all virtue involves choice, and what we mean by this was said earlier, that virtue makes an individual choose everything for the sake of something, and this end is the fine, so it is clear that courage, being a specific virtue, will make an individual endure what is fearful for the sake of some end, so that he does it neither through ignorance (for, rather, it makes him judge correctly), nor through pleasure, but because it is fine . . . (1230a27-33).

[69] This seems to be the mistaken view of Engberg-Pedersen, *Aristotle's Theory of Moral Insight*, 46, as I argue in my review in *Ethics*, 95 (1984), pp. 175-6.

[70] On this see Eugene Garver,'Aristotle's Genealogy of Morals', *Philosophy and Phenomenological Research*, 44 (1984), 471-92.

defeat, the agent's action is no less fine. It still achieves its internalized end.

Put this way, Aristotle's point is distinct from the one propounded by rule utilitarianism: that an action's worth rests on its general tendency to produce certain effects. For while action that is fine has as its object certain external effects, the action cannot be reduced to a capacity to produce these effects. In this sense the *Rhetoric* definition of the fine oversimplifies. Here virtue is said to be a *dunamis euergetikē*, a 'capacity for beneficence' (1366b4); it is fine in so far as it 'is a capacity . . . to benefit others in many and great ways' (1366a36-8). A substantive connection between what is fine and a specific external end (namely general welfare) is clear enough, but the value is placed on the product rather than on a life lived in such a way that the means towards that end have themselves come to be prized. (It oversimplifies in other ways too. As we noted earlier in the chapter, while the overall thrust of virtue is equitable and decent dealings with others, it cannot be taken to exclude either self-regarding traits, e.g. temperance or a proper sense of pride, or non-moral excellences, e.g. wit, humour, or philosophical wisdom.) The *Nicomachean Ethics* seems to capture the relation between agent and external end better. Justice, in the sense of overall or complete virtue, aims at the social good, at preserving the happiness of the *polis* (1129b25-35, 1130a4-14); but justice is fine never simply as a productive capacity (*dunamis*), but rather as a way of acting or living (*hexis*), where action directed at that external end is itself worthwhile.[71]

This brings us to the nub of our problem with vice. Vicious actions do not seem to constitute their own ends

---

[71] We might now see additional force in the criteria discussed in *NE* III. 3, where Aristotle says prohairetic action chooses what is best and most efficient. The word we have rendered as 'best' is *kallista*, the superlative form of *kalon*. It may be more precisely rendered as 'most finely'. (Contrast *EE* 1226b12 ff., where the more neutral *beltion* is used.) The present suggestion is that prohairetic action may be constrained not merely by the need for coherence with an end or configuration of ends, but by the desire that the actions which realize a particular end or ends should come to constitute an end in themselves. Typically, this will coincide with a moral constraint, cf. 1142b23-5. In *NE* III. 3, therefore Aristotle may in fact be suggesting that *prohairesis* will often involve this moral constraint.

in the same way. Their point and focus seem to remain on the external end—power, gain, deceit, avoidance of risk or fear. Promotion of these external ends are what counts. We can grant, as our above examples attest, that there are those who make an 'art form' of vice—those who savour the manner and style of profiteering. And the means are valued more highly the more ingenious and resourceful they are in achieving their ends. But it is hard to conceive that such individuals would find value in their pursuits if their machinations did not ultimately yield the external ends sought. In contrast, at least on Aristotle's view, the virtuous would still feel their lives had a point and would find intrinsic pleasure in their actions. There would still be a point to one's pursuits if courageous action did not end in victory, or the temperate life ultimately did not protect against disease (1099a12-20, 1117a33-1117b8). The failure would not mean that the life was misspent, even if, ultimately, we could not call it happy.

There is something here we tend to agree with. Frustrated virtue is not a waste of talent and effort in the way that brilliant scheming on a foiled corruption plot is. The point is not the moralistic one—that the vicious have wasted their energies on a bad end. That would beg the question. Rather, it is that for the vicious, the means are not worthwhile without the external end. The action, brilliant as it is, hangs tenuously on the outcome. In this sense, the base view their rational agency quite differently from the way the virtuous view theirs. Indeed if it turns out that the base person typically enjoys her scheming, independent of how successful she is, then it seems we question just how 'real' her viciousness is after all.

For these kinds of reasons, then, I think Aristotle has something interesting to say about the difference between the sort of rational agency that characterizes the virtuous and the base. The externality of the vicious person's ends limits the value and authority of rational agency. It limits the value placed on the action itself. It may be in this sense that vicious activities fail to exemplify the *ergon* or characteristic activity of a human being to live a life of reason. In the next chapter we shall explore in some detail the social dimensions of that life and the extent to which human perfection requires the goods of friendship.[72]

[72] An earlier version of this chapter appeared in the *Review of Metaphysics* as 'Character, Planning and Choice in Aristotle' (1985), part of which was read at the Pacific Division of the American Philosophical Association meetings in spring 1984. I am most grateful to Charles Young for his public comments during that session. I also wish to thank several others who read this chapter at various stages and who offered generous comments along the way: Michael Bratman, John Fischer, Harry Frankfurt, Martha Nussbaum, and Amelie Rorty. In writing the final draft, I have especially tried to meet the incisive criticisms offered by Norman Dahl and Richard Kraut.

4

THE SHARED LIFE

'To delight in doing things because our fathers did them is good if it shuts out nothing better; it enlarges the range of affection—and affection is the broadest basis of good life.' 'Do you think so?' said Gwendolen with a little surprise. 'I should have thought you cared most about ideas, knowledge, wisdom, and all that.' 'But to care about *them* is a sort of affection,' said Deronda smiling at her sudden naïveté. 'Call it attachment, interest, willingness to bear a great deal for the sake of being with them and saving them from injury. Of course it makes a difference if the objects of interest are human beings; but generally, in all deep affections, the objects are a mixture—half persons and half ideas . . .'

Daniel Deronda (Penguin), 470–1.

HAVING examined the roles of practical reason and perception in the shaping of a good life, I now turn to the role of friendship. On Aristotle's view, the specific ends in a life are sustained and given their finest expression through friendship. Ends that are valued become more highly prized as a result of being shared; actions that are fine become finer when friends are the beneficiaries. Nowhere is the collaborative nature of good living more pronounced; nowhere is the dependency of the good life upon what is external more pervasive. Before beginning, however, I wish to set Aristotle's position in broad relief by contrasting it with the Kantian view. The issue is of current interest given recent challenges to impartialist ethics to take more seriously a person's commitments and attachments.[1] I shall be entering

---

[1] Recent challenges come from Lawrence Blum, *Friendship, Altruism, and Morality* (Routledge and Kegan Paul, 1980); Bernard Williams, 'Persons, Character and Morality', in *Moral Luck: Philosophical Papers, 1973–1980* (Cambridge University Press, 1981), 1–19; John Cottingham, 'Ethics and Impartiality', *Philosophical Studies*, 43 (1983), 84–99; and Andrew Oldenquist, 'Loyalties', *Journal of Philosophy*,

that debate in only the most restricted way, though, by strengthening the challenge found in Aristotle's systematic defence of friendship and the shared life.

After setting out that contrast, I shall consider the way in which friendship is an external good which shapes and structures the self-sufficient life; in a significant way, happiness thus comes to include the happiness of others. This will entail the rational capacity for jointly promoting common ends as well as the capacity to identify with and coordinate separate ends. In this regard, I suggest that Aristotle's notion of a friend as 'another self' is compatible with the distinctive ways in which each individual realizes virtue within a shared life. Next I turn to what Aristotle calls the friendship between child and parent. My aim is to isolate specific conditions of attachment required, on Aristotle's view, for friendship in general, as well as to indicate the privileged place of the family in moral education.

I. ARISTOTLE AND KANT

Before setting out Aristotle's view, it is worth anticipating a reply on his part to the Kantian position on friendship as it has been articulated recently by Stephen Darwall and Barbara Herman.[2] The reply will bring into focus aspects of Aristotle's ethical theory that I presuppose in my account. According to Darwall, reasons for an agent to act based on friendly motives are constrained by reasons based on principles of right. This deontological constraint on friendship is developed by Herman. Her claim is that the impartial

79 (1982), 173-93. The impartialist claims that we treat self and our own commitments and attachments as one among others, giving the interests of others the same weight as we give our own. The opponent argues that the commitments and attachments of a person deserve special treatment, and without them life lacks value and meaning. The debate has stirred Kantians and utilitarians alike to find positions within their theories that are friendlier to the goods of friendship. Stephen Darwall explores the utilitarian and Kantian reply in 'Impartialist Ethics and Personal Relationship' (unpublished). Barbara Herman articulates the Kantian position in 'Rules, Motives and Helping Actions', *Philosophical Studies*, 45 (1984), 369-77. Cf. her 'Mutual Aid and Respect for Persons', *Ethics*, 94 (1984), 577-602, and 'Integrity and Impartiality', *The Monist*, 66 (1983), 233-50.

[2] Darwall, 'Impartialist Ethics'; Herman, 'Rules, Motives and Helping Actions'.

point of view of the Categorical Imperative is required both to set the conditions of permissibility for acting out of friendly motives and to impose obligatory ends which then might best be fulfilled by friendship.[3] Herman thus speaks of a double acknowledgement, such that in acting from friendship we recognize that in addition to having that motive, our action either satisfies a positive duty (such as beneficence) or is within permissible constraints set by other duties.

Herman and Darwall's defence of friendship is of a piece with the general Kantian tenet that the pursuit of happiness (of which friendship is a part) is framed by a moral motive, which is lexically prior to other motives and which has its source not in the sentiments but in principles of practical reason.[4] Thus, while we do not have a duty to pursue happiness, the pursuit of happiness (and *a fortiori* of friendship) is constrained by moral considerations. This is consistent with allowing that motives of friendship are often instrumental to acting from a moral motive (in that they provide the supporting conditions for its inculcation and flourishing).[5] But in so far as such motives are based on emotions, they lack intrinsic *moral* worth of their own (even

---

[3] 'What is required is that agents who act from emotion also act permissibly. And where there is an obligation to help, we are required to acknowedge this moral claim, even though we may give help out of compassion, etc.' (Herman, 'Rules, Motives and Helping Actions', 376).

[4] So Kant says: 'And since none the less reason has been imparted to us as a practical power—that is, as one which is to have influence on the *will*; its true function must be to produce a *will* which is good . . . Such a will need not on this purpose be the sole and complete good, but it must be the highest good and the condition of all the rest, even of all our demands for happiness. In that case we can easily reconcile with the wisdom of nature our observation that the cultivation of reason which is required for the first and unconditioned purpose may in many ways, at least in this life, restrict the attainment of the second purpose—namely, happiness—which is always conditioned' (*Groundwork of the Metaphysics of Morals*, tr. H. J. Paton (Harper and Row, 1956), 64).

[5] I believe the point is well illustrated in John Rawls's notion of a Well Ordered Society (developed in *A Theory of Justice* (Harvard University Press, 1971)), in which family and social relations play an essential role in the nurture and maintenance of the moral powers constitutive of free and equal persons. A criticism of friendship as merely instrumental seems to be at the heart of Carol Gilligan's criticisms of Lawrence Kohlberg's *Theory of Moral Development*. Cf. Carol Gilligan, *In a Different Voice* (Harvard University Press, 1982).

though they may have intrinsic value).[6] If they do come to acquire derivative moral worth, it may be in the sense that in some cases acting from friendship is an especially appropriate way of fulfilling a duty required by morality.[7] But here it is the recognition that duty requires that I help, and not simply the fact that I want to help, that gives ultimate moral worth to the action. And that recognition is based on an understanding of what is required of persons (ourselves and others) conceived essentially as rational beings who rationally determine their own ends. It is in virtue of that capacity that others can make a claim on us, and we in turn can make claims on them. This is the (positive) force of Kant's notion of the person as an end in itself. We have a positive duty to promote each other's rationality.

All this is, admittedly, very abbreviated. But my remarks here are intended only as background rather than detailed exposition. The point is to set in context Aristotle's account, not to engage the two thinkers in full confrontation. That is a project for another time and place.

It should be clear that Aristotle's position will be quite different from Kant's on many counts. One central disagreement is this: for Aristotle, the ethical sphere (literally, that which refers to character—*ēthos*) is considerably broader than what falls under the Kantian conception of the moral.[8] As already seen, it will include traits of humour and

---

[6] Kant appears to refer to the class of non-moral qualities of intrinsic worth when he says: 'Moderation in affections and passions, self-control, and sober reflexion are not only good in many respects: they may even seem to constitute part of the inner worth of a person' (*Groundwork*, 61).

[7] I am grateful to Geoffrey Sayre-McCord and Richard Kraut for clarification of this point. In *The Doctrine of Virtue* (tr. Mary Gregor (University of Pennsylvania Press, 1964)), Kant argues for something even stronger than this. There he argues that friendship itself is a positive duty of end (140–5). What he has in mind, more precisely, are friendships in which mutual respect conditions intimacy; such friendships, he says, we have a duty to promote. Yet even here, Kant is deeply sceptical about the practical possibility of such intimacy (how will we know what the other really thinks, how will we know that she will not reveal our confidences or hold us in contempt for our faults), and openly urges a principle of respect 'that requires [friends] to keep each other at a proper distance' (141).

[8] For the claim that Aristotle none the less does have a moral theory, see T. H. Irwin's 'Aristotle's Conception of Morality', in John Cleary (ed.), *Proceedings of the Boston Area Colloquium in Ancient Philosophy*, i (University Press of America, 1985), 115–50.

wit, as well as motives of friendship and, more generally, friendliness. Attachments and sentiments, while excluded from a Kantian view of the moral, will thus be among Aristotle's motives for ethical action. Granted, Aristotle's distinction between the fine and the advantageous (e.g. 1104b32, *EE* 1230a27–33) will bear some resemblance to the distinction between the moral and the non-moral; to act for the sake of the fine is, as we have said, to value as eminently worthwhile the exercise of virtues directed at the common good. And virtue in its most general sense is a kind of justice towards others (*NE* V. 1–2).[9] But there is no clear sense in Aristotle of a specific class of considerations having pre-emptive status over others. The fine is not a regulative notion which sets, from outside, the limits of happiness. Rather, activity for the sake of the fine constitutes the best sort of happiness. Even a pursuit such as contemplative activity, which Aristotle suggests in some places may be the best sort of activity, is not thereby given pre-emptive value over other activities.

Accordingly, the fact that we can be blinded by friendship, or because of it act with too parochial an interest, does not, for Aristotle, thereby remove it from the ethical sphere of valuation. Rather, that fact merely opens it to adjudication with other claims, and to judgements about its appropriateness in the light of those other considerations which must be given their due. Aristotle thus includes motives of attachment within the ethical sphere, while still acknowledging constraints on their permissibility. So in general, Aristotle says, friends are to be preferred in the assignment of our help and aid (1155a7–9, 1160a1–8), but not always and not at all costs. It would, for example, be wrong to help a friend before returning benefits due to others, or to give a loan to friends before repaying a creditor, 'except when helping a friend is especially fine or necessary' (1164b25–1165a4). Similarly, partiality is inappropriate in specific contexts, such as in the case of a public official where the fair adjudication of claims is part of the description of

---

[9] See the concluding part of ch. 3, sect. 7.

that office (1134a33-1135b1).[10] But on Aristotle's view, this is just to say that the expression of virtue through friendship must be harmonized with other ends in the good life. And this is a consequence of his more general view that particular choices must be attentive to the ethically relevant particularities of one's situation. Accordingly, as we have said, a choice is appropriate (or hits the mean) only if it gives due consideration in this holistic way.

Moreover, constraints on the permissibility of an action, in so far as they arise from the expression of other virtues, do not appeal to principles while excluding sentiments from consideration. In making an all-considered judgement of what is best in a particular situation, an agent appeals both to the passional dispositions (*hexeis*) and to the rational judgement (*logos*) of the *phronimos*, or person of practical wisdom. To the extent that the *phronimos* represents the point of view of experience and reflective judgement removed from irrelevant biases (1109b1-9), we might say there is something like an appeal to an impartial point of view in the assessment of action. For Aristotle, however (unlike Kant), the point of view is not that of a rational agent *in general*, but of *human excellence*, constituted as it is by emotional as well as rational capacities. The considerations of friendship are within, rather than outside, this point of view. Reciprocally, the legitimate claims others make on us are not solely in virtue of their rational capacities, and what is needed for their promotion, but more generally in virtue of what is needed for their well-being, understood more broadly. The Aristotelian agent who has the best sort of happiness will also, of course, be capable of a more divine theoretical reason, which he shares (in a limited way) with other rational

---

10 In a similar vein, in *NE* IX. 9 Aristotle distinguishes between an objectionable and unobjectionable partiality toward self. In the first case an individual is partial to himself in the sense that he takes more than his fair share of certain 'fought for' or scarce (*perimachēta*) goods. We rightly censure this individual, for his actions involve a violation of justice; they are a case of *pleonexia*, taking for oneself what others have a legitimate claim to. In the second case an individual is partial in the sense that he desires to make his own character virtuous and to make himself the seat of virtue. This individual is not guilty of a criticizable self-interest, for in wanting virtue for *himself*, he does not violate the claims of others. The implication is that virtue is not a scarce resource divided up by principles of distributive justice. Cf. 1168b15-16, 1169a32, *MM* 1212b8-23.

beings, namely gods (*NE* X. 7–8). But it is not this aspect of reason which guides practical action or grounds the decisions of the *phronimos*.

As a result of the above process of adjudication, it may turn out that the claims of those more distant limit the claims of friendship. But these claims, of wider generosity, justice, or the like, do not have a privileged position in the good life. They do not always trump other virtues, nor are they constituted any less by passional dispositions. Moreover, these passional dispositions are neither blind nor irrational forces, but rationally informed and guided intentional states.

The Kantian and Aristotelian will differ, then, on the value of friendship, given its relation to reason and the passions, and on the method of arbitrating between its claims and those of more distant beneficiaries. While the Aristotelian will agree that partiality and emotion often need to be constrained, this does not detract from their place within the good life. Unlike the Kantian, Aristotle does not merely permit attachment within a theory of morality constituted primarily by impartiality. Rather, he makes attachment essential to the expression of virtue, and living with friends a structural feature of good living—or so I shall argue shortly.

2. FRIENDS AS EXTERNAL GOODS

To begin with, we must set down some definitional points. Friendship (*philia*), Aristotle stipulates, is the mutually acknowledged and reciprocal exchange of goodwill and affection that exists among individuals who share an interest in each other on the basis of virtue, pleasure, or utility (*NE* VIII. 2). In addition to voluntary associations of this sort, Aristotle also includes among friendships the non-chosen relations of affection and care that exist among family members and fellow citizens (cf. *NE* VIII. 9, VIII 12, IX. 6). The term is thus used quite broadly, though Aristotle's primary focus, and mine as well, is on the paradigmatic case of virtue friendship (or what I shall sometimes call, following Cooper, 'character friendship', in order to remind us that such friendships need not be of *perfectly* virtuous agents).[11] To the degree to which the friendship of parent and child cultivates the capacities for character friendship, it too will be of interest in my account.

This said, let us try to understand the way in which friends figure in Aristotle's general scheme of goods. In *NE* I. 8 Aristotle argues that virtue, as a good, is alone insufficient for happiness, and requires in addition certain external goods. The argument is roughly this: happiness, conceived of as doing well and living well (1098b21), requires not merely ethical (and intellectual) virtues, but activities which manifest these excellences. With regard to ethical virtue, ends of character must be realized and implemented in action (1099a1-6). But for this, the proper resources and opportunities must be at hand. Among these resources or external goods are friends:

Yet evidently, as we said, happiness requires in addition external goods; for it is impossible or not easy to act finely without resources. For an individual performs many actions through the use of instruments, through friends, wealth, and political office. And the lack of other goods spoils one's happiness, such as fine birth, good children, and beauty. For one would hardly be happy if one were thoroughly ugly, or born of low birth, or solitary and childless; and perhaps even less so, if one's children or friends were thoroughly bad, or if they were good but died. (1099a31-b6)

This passage suggests that friends will not only be instrumental to happiness (as enabling conditions of action), but also intrinsic parts of it. Aristotle thus seems to have in mind two classes of external goods (which he recapitulates at 1099b27): those which are instruments of happiness, i.e. those things which are by nature co-operative and useful as tools (1099b27), and those which are not merely instrumental, but which are necessary and intrinsic parts of happiness, i.e. 'belong necessarily' (*huparchein anagkaion*,

---

[11] John Cooper, 'Aristotle on Friendship', in A. O. Rorty (ed.), *Essays on Aristotle's Ethics* (University of California Press, 1980), 307-8; Aristotle himself suggests the term at *NE* 1164a12, 1165b8-9, *EE* 1241a10, 1242b36.

1099b27), and the lack of which mars happiness (1099b2).[12] Friends figure in the lists of both types of external goods. The first class of goods is fairly straight forward. Friends may be instruments and tools in the sense in which money and political connection are. They provide us with the means for the promotion of particular ends. As we have said, we depend upon the aid and support of friends for accomplishing ends we cannot realize on our own (1112b11, b28). More broadly, Aristotle says in his initial survey of *ta endoxa*, we need friends in all circumstances and times of life: in times of prosperity as beneficiaries, in times of hardship as refuge, in our youth as tutors, in our old age for care and support, and in our prime for doing fine actions. Friends thus support our well-being both as co-partners in our agency and as objects of our virtuous actions. They provide us with opportunities for virtuous action and sentiment unavailable to the solitary or childless (1155a5-15; cf. 1169b11-15).[13]

The way in which friends figure in the second class of goods, however, is more difficult to grasp. For while friendship has intrinsic worth (certainly Aristotle takes the love parents show towards children to be an end in its own right (*MM* 1211b1-2), and friendship in general 'choice-worthy for its own sake', whatever other benefits it yields (*NE* 1155a29-32, 1159a27)), it does so not in the sense of having some isolated value, like that of an 'adventitious' pleasure (cf. 1169b25-7), which might be added to happiness as one more separate constituent.[14] For there are all sorts of activities in life which we might find intrinsically enjoyable or valuable, but which we would be willing to sacrifice because they play a limited role in our happiness. Thus, I might find

---

[12] My remarks here are indebted to T. H. Irwin's classification of the two types of external goods in 'Permanent Happiness: Aristotle and Solon' in Julia Annas (ed.), *Oxford Studies in Ancient Philosophy*, iii (Oxford University Press, 1985), 89-124.

[13] For a related discussion of the way in which friends figure as external goods, see John M. Cooper, 'Aristotle on the Goods of Fortune', *Philosophical Review*, 94 (1985), 173-96, and Martha Nussbaum, *The Fragility of Goodness: Luck and Rational Self-Sufficiency in Greek Ethical Thought: The Tragic Poets, Plato, and Aristotle* (Cambridge University Press, 1986), ch. 12.

[14] R. A. Gauthier and J. Y. Jolif imply something like the view I criticize in their account of the second class of external goods: *L' Éthique à Nicomaque*, ii 1 (Publications Universitaires de Louvain, 1970), 71.

backgammon an intrinsically enjoyable activity, but when faced with demands on my time I give it up because I find it insufficiently important or enriching of other activities I value. I can abandon it or replace it without seriously marring my happiness. The intrinsic worth of friendship, in contrast, is of a much more pervasive sort, providing the very form and mode of life within which an agent can best realize her virtue and achieve happiness. To have intimate friends and good children is to have interwoven in one's life, in a ubiquitous way, persons towards whom and with whom one can most fully and continuously express one's goodness. The friendships are not external conditions of those activities, like money or power. Rather, they are the form virtuous activity takes when it is especially fine and praiseworthy (1155a9, 1159a28–31).

We might say living amongst friends is a general, though substantive, way of specifying the formal criterion of happiness as a mode of activity (*energeia*, 1098a8, 1098a16).[15] Just as it would be absurd to call a person happy who slept away his life (1099a1–6), so too it would be absurd to think that the person who lacked friends could be happy (1155a5–6, 1169b8–10, 1169b16–17). These *endoxa* seem to be deeply rooted in our nature, and not unrelated to each other, as Aristotle goes on to argue. For if sustained excellent activity is a basic aspect of our happiness, then a most basic way of sustaining and making more continuous our activity is through a life in companionship with others (1170a5–9; cf. 1177a22). Even when the activity is contemplation, the pursuit is better sustained when it is a co-operative enterprise (1177a34).

In what follows I want to pursue this notion of friendship as structuring the good life and suggest that it is because of this role that Aristotle calls friends the 'greatest' and 'most necessary' of external goods (*NE* 1169b10, 1154a4), without whom we would not choose to live 'even if we had all other goods' (1155a5–6, cf. 1169b16–17). As suggested, friendship creates a context or arena for the expression of virtue, and

---

[15] Aristotle also suggests (at 1097b7–12) that it is a substantive way of interpreting the self-sufficiency criterion of *NE* I. 7. I discuss this further below.

ultimately for happiness. More strongly, it extends and re-defines the boundaries of the good life in such a way that my happiness or complete good comes to include the happiness of significant others. Happiness or good living is thus ascribable to me, not as an isolated individual, but as a self extended, so to speak, by friends.

3. HAPPINESS AS INCLUDING THE HAPPINESS OF OTHERS

The kernel of this is in Aristotle's remarks in *NE* I. 7 regarding the self-sufficiency of good living. Self-sufficiency is a criterion of the good life entailing that a life is 'lacking in nothing', there being no other good which when added to it would make that life more desirable (1097b15–22). But since friends are among the goods which make a life self-sufficient, self-sufficiency is relational and the good life a life dependent upon and interwoven with others:

> By self-sufficient we do not mean for a solitary individual, for one living a life alone, but for parents, children, and wife, and in general for all friends and fellow citizens since a human being is by nature political and social. (1097b9–11; cf. 1169b18–19)

For human beings, then, the self-sufficient life is a life larger than that of one individual. So, the *Magna Moralia* reminds us, 'we are not investigating the self-sufficiency of a god, but of human beings' (1218a8), and the *Eudemian Ethics* explains, 'for our well-being is relational [*kath' heteron*], whereas in the case of a god, he is himself his own well-being' (1245b18–19).

The historical import of Aristotle's position cannot be underestimated. The ideal of an ascetic life was close at hand in Plato's writings and represented the major alternative conception of the self-sufficient good. In *NE* X. 7–8, Aristotle himself is of course attracted to this conception, apparently arguing there that a life cannot be perfectly happy if it fully ignores a more divine, contemplative ideal. But on the interpretation presented in the last chapter, Aristotle's claim is not that happiness is to be *identified* with the ascetic life. Rather, it is the more modest claim that happiness must *include* the leisure for contemplation, and that the good person must find time for its incomparable rewards. Contemplative excellence does not supplant the more worldly virtues nor take precedence. It must be conjoined with them in a life which remains essentially political and communal. This differs considerably from the stark portrait of the *Phaedo*. There needy states which require satisfaction from without—such as appetites and affections—are seen as making happiness vulnerable, for they expose it to conditions outside the agent's control. They are prison houses of the soul from which one must be liberated as best one can, if happiness is to be secured against constant lack and deficiency. Though the *Phaedo* does not single out friendship, it is easy to see how it poses such a threat. Friendships, in so far as they depend upon mutual interests and affections, easily dissolve as these interests and affections shift. To form a friendship is in part to expose oneself to this risk. Even if we try to counteract this vulnerability by making constancy a condition of the best sort of friendship (as Aristotle seems to do in the case of virtue friendship, where the constancy of the friendship derives from the stable interest and disposition of each party towards virtue), still constancy can do little to prevent the permanent dissolution of a friendship through death. [16] If anything, the stability of the friendship leaves us least protected against that contingency. For it is when we have lost a lifelong friend or loved one that we truly feel we have lost a part of ourselves and a substantial part of our happiness. Friendship thus makes us vulnerable, and even if constancy is a feature of that friendship, our self-sufficiency remains at best fragile. (In this regard, although Plato requires in the Diotema passage of the *Symposium* that the ascent to the ideal form of life be accompanied by interaction with others, these relations are essentially to be supplanted by a more secure and self-sufficient good whose beauty and goodness can in no way be diminished.)

[16] Aristotle's worry about these problems structures the very way in which he presents the material on friendship. Within the threefold classification of friendship, into friendship based on pleasure, utility, and good character, the former two are *kata sumbebēkos*, accidental, and inferior primarily because they are more transient and less enduring sorts of friendships than those based on the mutual pursuit of virtue (1156a18–1156b24).

That Aristotle chooses friendship as a defining feature of
the self-sufficient life reflects not only his break with the
ascetic goal but his view of happiness as essentially subject
to fortune. The fundamental belief in the sociality of human
beings is an *endoxa* which cannot be compromised in the
specification of happiness.

In *NE* IX. 9 and *EE* VII. 12 Aristotle again takes up the
relation of friendship to self-sufficiency. In *NE* IX. 9 he
reports the view held by some that the self-sufficient person
does not require friends, 'for the things that are good belong
to him, and being self-sufficient, he requires nothing further'
(1169b5-7). Aristotle's disagreement (1169b22-8 and *EE*
1244b6 ff.) centres on the interpretation of self-sufficiency
and, correspondingly, the characterization of friendship. The
solitary contemplator might have minimal requirements for
material goods, and so only minimal need for the sorts of
friends that can provide such services. But, Aristotle argues,
without friends such an agent could never be self-sufficient
with regard to fine activity. The problem with those who
claim otherwise is that they fail to conceive of friendship as
based on something more than utility or transient pleasures,
and self-sufficiency as something correspondingly broader:

What then does the first party mean, and in what way is it true? Is
it that the many identify friends with those who are useful? Of
those sorts of friends, indeed the happy person will have no need,
since the good things already belong to him; nor will he need
friends for pleasure, or only minimally so (for since his life is
pleasant, it requires nothing of adventitious pleasure). And having
no need for these sorts of friends, he is thought not to need friends.
But this is surely not true. (1169b22-8)

The *Eudemian Ethics* amplifies this conclusion: 'This makes
it all the clearer that the only real friend is loved not for
the sake of utility or benefit, but on account of his virtue'
(1244b15).

The upshot of these passages, then, is that while the self-
sufficient solitary may not need others as means or instruments for material living (or only minimally so), he will still
need others to create jointly a life of virtue. The *Eudemian
Ethics* again speaks to this: 'For when we are not in need

of something, then we all seek others to share our enjoyment ... and most of all, we then seek friends who are worthy of living together with us' (1244b18–22). Thus the best sort of friendship provides us with companions with whom we can share goods and interests in a jointly pursued life. This sort of shared happiness constitutes the truly self-sufficient life.

There is considerable further evidence for the claim that friendship entails a weaving of lives together into some shared conception of happiness. Aristotle pursues these issues with some insight in the *Eudemian Ethics*. At 1236b3–6, he argues that the best sort of friendship among relatively virtuous adults (i.e. character friendship) displays not only the acknowledged reciprocation of affection and goodwill, but the acknowledged reciprocation of a choice of one another:

It is apparent from these things that the primary sort of friendship, that among good persons, requires mutual affection [*antiphilia*] and mutual choice [*antiprohairesis*] with regard to one another ... This friendship thus only occurs among humans, for they alone are conscious of reasoned choices [*prohaireseis*].

Again, at EE 1237a30 ff., he makes a similar point:

If the activity of friendship is a reciprocal choice, accompanied by pleasure, of the acquaintance of one another, it is clear that friendship of the primary kind is in general a reciprocal choice [*antiprohairesis*] of the things that are without qualification good and pleasant, because they are good and pleasant.

The significance of the claim rests on Aristotle's technical term, *prohairesis*. As I argued in the last chapter,[17] a *prohairesis* is a reasoned choice that is expressive of a character and the overall ends of that character. The choice of a friend exposes this capacity of practical reason in a perspicuous way. For in choosing a character friend, we select 'another self' (*NE* 1170b6–7), who shares a sense of our commitments and ends, and a sense of what we take to be ultimately 'good and pleasant' in living. We choose another

---

[17] And in my 'Character, Planning and Choice in Aristotle', *Review of Metaphysics*, 34 (1985), 83–106.

to be a partner in the joint pursuit of these ends. In so doing, we choose to arrange our lives around a loyalty to another, and around a willingness to choose ends and pursuits within the context of this loyalty.[18] The choice of such a companion, Aristotle indicates, is not one that is made quickly or easily. It reflects a stable judgement of another (*to kekrimenon bebaion*, *EE* 1237b11, *krisin orthēn*, 1237b12), and this takes time and trust (1237b13–18). As he says, 'those who become friends without the test of time are not real friends but only wish to be friends' (1237b17–18).

Indeed, since for Aristotle the real test (*peiran*) of friendship comes in spending time together (*suzēsai*, 1237b35–7), the specific choices that are constitutive of the friendship are not so much the initial overtures as those that indicate a capacity to share and co-ordinate activities over an extended period of time. These are the choices that indicate two lives can be interwoven together into some coherent pattern of good living.

Significantly, Aristotle does discuss these sorts of choices under the notion of *homonoia*, literally sameness of mind, or, more idiomatically, consensus between friends. *Homonoia*, he argues in the *Eudemian Ethics*, is arriving at the 'same choice' about practical matters (*hē autē prohairesis*), as in the case of civic friendship, where fellow citizens agree about who should rule and who should be ruled (1241a31–3; cf. *NE* IX. 6). In the case of intimate friendships, the consensus is not about who should rule, but about how and what sort of life to live together:

Some have thought friendship to be unanimity of feeling and those who have such a consensus to be friends. But friendship is not a consensus concerning everything, but a consensus concerning practical matters for the parties involved and concerning those things that contribute to living together [*hosa eis to suzēn suntenei*]. (*EE* 1241a16–18)

The notion of consensus (*homonoia*) can be seen as an extension of Aristotle's notion of reciprocal choice (*anti-prohairesis*). In choosing a friend, one chooses to make that

[18] See *EE* 1214b7 on *prohairesis* as a capacity to arrange life with regard to certain ends.

person a part of one's life and to arrange one's life with that person's flourishing (as well as one's own) in mind. One takes on, if you like, the project of a shared conception of *eudaimonia*. Through mutual decisions about practical matters, friends continue to affirm that commitment. Consensus between friends can take various forms. So, for example, two friends come to a mutual decision about how to act fairly and honourably towards another who has wronged them, or about how best to assist a fellow citizen who has come upon hard times. Any happiness or disappointment that follows from these actions belongs to both persons, for the decision so to act was joint and the responsibility is thus shared. This notion of joint deliberation may help us to interpret Aristotle's rather compressed remark that character friends live together, not in the way cattle do, by grazing the same pasture, but 'by sharing in argument and thought' (*koinōnein logōn kai dianoias*, *NE* 1170b11-12).

Equally, consensus may express only a looser agreement about general ends. Two friends may share the conviction that temperance in their personal lives is of the utmost importance, yet each realize that end in a different style and manner. One does it through a scrupulous diet, the other by refusing to take part in frivolous gossip. Their shared commitment is to an end rather than to a specific way of achieving it.

There may nevertheless be a particularly characteristic sort of consensus in friendship. In true friendship, we might say, friends realize shared ends which develop through the friendship and which come to be constitutive of it. Specific common interests are thus a product rather than a precondition of the relationship. Together my friend and I develop a love of Georgian houses, having had no real interest in them earlier. Aristotle's emphasis on developing friendships over time and through a shared history of mutual activity suggests this notion of a common good.[19] But a caveat is in order here. While specific and shared ways of being virtuous will be the product of a friendship, the acquisition of virtuous states of character must, more or less, pre-exist

[19] I am grateful to Gregory Trianosky for urging me to develop this point.

any friendship based on virtue. That is, the agents must choose each other on the basis of a firm and stable character. This is not to deny that through the particular friendship, the commitments of character will deepen and express themselves in ways peculiar to and conditioned by that friendship. So Aristotle insists that the virtuous agent continues to grow, and that friendship itself is the most congenial context for such moral growth (*NE* 1170a11, 1172a10–15, *EE* 1245a15–20; cf. *NE* 1180a1–4); in this way, the notion of a 'firm and stable character' (*NE* 1105a34) does not imply a character that rigidly resists change. Even so, a well-cultivated sense of virtue must be in place from the start, in a way in which the love of Georgian houses need not be.

Friendship may also involve the interweaving of two lives in quite a different way. This can be seen as follows: within a given individual's life, choices (*prohaireseis*) articulate the ends of character in some unified and comprehensive way over time. As we have said, deliberation reflects a sense of planning, and an ability to make choices that best promote not a single end, but a coherent system of ends. Choices of action are made with regard not merely to the parts of good living, but with regard to the whole, and the unity of ends that entails (*NE* 1140a26–8, 1145a1–2).

This model of planning is extended to the shared life of friends. Ends are co-ordinated not merely within lives, but between lives. Thus, just as a particular choice I make is constrained by my wider system of objectives and ends, so too is it constrained by the ends of my friend. So, for example, if a contemplated action of mine precludes a friend from realizing an important goal of hers, then that consideration will figure in my judgement of what is overall best. It may not be an easy matter to determine whose interests should prevail, and as with any decision of the mean, deciding what is right will require giving due consideration to all relevant concerns. But whatever the nature of the solution, the point to be stressed is that what is relevant to the decision goes beyond the *eudaimonia* of a single, isolated individual. The ends of my friend must be taken into account, just as mine must, in the the overall assessment of what is to be done. Indeed, the survival of the friendship depends upon our willingness to exhibit loyalty in this way.

These various ways of forming a consensus within friendship fill out Aristotle's more elliptical remarks in the *Eudemian Ethics*, where he says that friends 'wish to share with each other in a joint life [*suzēn*] the end which they are capable of attaining' (1245b8); they pursue together, to the degree to which they can, the best good (*to ariston*) (1245a20-2). This involves not merely sharing space, or even casual discourse (1245a13-15), but sharing activity (*sunergein*, 1245b3) generated through joint study and deliberation. This is the sort of partnership which above all else (*malista*) is included in the final good (1245b4).

We have been focusing on shared happiness as requiring the sharing of general or specific ends, as well as the co-ordination of ends between lives. But there are other non-deliberative aspects of sharing happiness. Simply put, when a friend does well, I feel happy too. Aristotle explains this sort of 'singleness of mind' (*mia psuchē*, EE 1240b2, 1240b9-10) through the notions of sympathy and empathy, and argues that these sentiments are heightened the more intimate the friendship. At *NE* IX. 10, he says that the more exclusive the attachment to a friend, the better able I am to minister to that friend's needs and to identify with her joys and sorrows (1171a6 ff.). It may be because of my intimate knowledge of her that I can imagine how *she* feels in a particular situation; or knowing how *I* would feel (or have felt) in that sort of situation, and knowing she is similar to me in certain ways, I can imagine she must feel that way. In the *Eudemian Ethics* Aristotle indicates that friends wish to express not merely sharing of grief (*ou monon sullupeisthai*), but empathy, 'feeling the same pain [*alla kai tēn autēn lupēn*] (for example, when he is thirsty, sharing his thirst), if this were possible, and if not, what is closest to it' (1240a36-9). The qualification suggests that though Hume-like empathy, i.e. coming to feel the same affect, may itself be implausible, something like it is none the less desirable, and perhaps the hallmark (or at least, necessary condition) of friendship.[20]

---

[20] It was Geoffrey Sayre-McCord who helped me to gain this insight into Aristotle's remarks.

That is, in true friendship we want to understand 'from the friend's point of view' what she is going through and how things look to her. Imagining how she must feel ultimately aims at coming to see things from *her* point of view. Thus, it is not that I bypass my imagination, but that it ultimately transport me to her feelings.[21]

There is a related way in which we experience a friend's happiness or sorrow as our own. Accomplishments and failures which are not explicitly our own are none the less, through an extension of self, sources of pride and shame. So Aristotle says in *Rh.* II. 6: 'And individuals feel shame whenever they have acts or deeds credited to them which bring some disrespect, whether the acts be their own, or those of their ancestors, or those of other persons to whom they bear some close relation' (1385a1-3). Thus, when our children do well, we feel pride in their achievements, and when they do poorly, shame, as if we ourselves had fallen short. It is not that we are responsible for their errors (though as parents we may be), but that through the sense of belonging and attachment we identify with their good. Aristotle thus seems to be suggesting that feelings of shame need not be traced back to actions for which one is oneself responsible: so, for example, I may feel shame for the criminal actions of my sister just in virtue of our relationship, and not because I bear responsibility for her actions or attribute her failings to character traits I share. Whether such feelings of shame are in fact warranted may be a controversial matter, and not one that Aristotle explores carefully.[22]

4. FRIENDSHIP AND WIDER ALTRUISM

I have argued that through friendship an individual's happiness becomes extended to include the happiness of others.

---

[21] The response to tragedy through pity and fear seems to require something much weaker, namely that we imagine what it would be like for *us*, in our *own* circumstances, to suffer a similar fate (*peri to homoion*). See *Poet.* 1453a4-6, *Rh.* 1385b13-14.

[22] Though Aristotle's distinction between shame felt for 'conventional' and 'genuine' faults (*ta pros ton nomon, ta pros alētheian, Rh.* 1384b25) may be of some help. I am grateful here again to Geoffrey Sayre-McCord.

To have a friend as 'another self' thus entails a conception of good living that is in some significant way shared. I shall examine shortly the way in which this common pursuit does not jeopardize the separateness of individuals. But first I want to contrast friendship with a wider sense of altruism. Altruistic sentiments such as goodwill (*eunoia*), kindness (*charis*), and pity (*eleos*) are constitutive of various virtues in Aristotle's scheme, e.g. generosity (*eleutheriotēs*), magnificence (*megaloprepeia*), and magnanimity (*megalopsuchia*). The definition of kindness in *Rh.* II. 7 is useful for our purposes. It is there defined as a willingness to give 'assistance [*hupourgia*] towards someone in need' (1385a18), and 'is great if it is shown towards someone in great need, or in need of what is important or what is difficult to get, or someone who has need in a crisis, or if the helper is the only one or first one or the most important one' (1385a19-21). Accordingly, in acting out of kindness, our sympathy goes out to an individual because of the circumstances, and not because of *who* the individual happens to be. The situation is different in friendship, when we act out of a specific concern for a *particular* person; because it is *that* person who is in need (and not another), what we can do and are willing to do, and what others count on us to do, is often greater (cf. *NE* 1169a18-34).

These remarks might suggest the following objection: that when we act out of kindness rather than friendship, we somehow *overlook* the person who is the object of our goodwill and consider her merely as an occasion for the exercise of our virtue. We might even seem, in a priggish way, to care more for our virtue than for the particular person towards whom it is being expressed.[23] But on Aristotle's view, I act for the sake of the beneficiary, whether or not I have an enduring or prior attachment to her. Even though in wider cases of altruism the beneficiary is in a sense intersubstitutable with others, this does not diminish my concern for *this person now*. Aristotle makes the point as follows: to

---

[23] The objection might be answered if we say that I act not for the sake of my virtue, but for the sake of this person *because* of my virtue. That is, my virtue explains why I am motivated to make this person the object of my concern. Cf. Herman, 'Rules, Motives and Helping Actions', 370-1.

be a friend is to wish another well and desire good things for her, 'for her sake and not for your own' (*Rh.* 1380b37; cf. 1381b37). Equally, kindness outside of friendship depends upon offering assistance 'not in return for something, nor for some advantange to the helper himself, but for that of the one helped' (*Rh.* 1385a18–19).[24] Thus both friendship and goodwill require the non-instrumentality of our beneficence. But friendship goes further in so far as its objects are not easily substituted by others. I may have a well-cultivated sense of altruism or even be a friendly sort of person who treats others with warmth and affection, but the exercise of these virtuous states does not itself secure for me the good of friendship. For that, I have to become attached to a particular person, and another person to me, in a way that displays mutual regard and affection (*NE* 1155b28–1156a5), and commitment to joint activity. Moreover, while virtuous states of character depend upon external conditions for their exercise, the absence of favourable conditions does not necessarily destroy them. But this is not so in the case of friendship. For friendship is more an activity than a state of character, and a virtuous activity, unlike other virtuous activities, that depends upon a specific person as its external condition.[25] In the absence of that person, there is no friendship.

5. A FRIEND AS ANOTHER BUT SEPARATE SELF

As we said earlier, a virtue friend is 'another self' (*allos autos*), 'another me' (*allos egō*) as Aristotle strikingly puts it in the *Magna Moralia* (1213a13, 1213a24, *NE* 1170b7, *EE*

---

[24] The difference for Aristotle between the two cases is not that I treat a friend more for his own sake than I do a stranger, but that when I fail to help a freind, I commit a deeper wrong and show a greater failing of character. As Aristotle says, 'a wrong becomes intensified in being exhibited towards those that are more fully friends, so that it will be a more terrible thing to defraud a friend than a fellow citizen, and more terrible not to help a brother than a stranger, and more terrible to wound a father than anyone else' (*NE* 1160a4–6).

[25] Aristotle does not explicitly say this, leaving it open at 1155a4 as to whether friendship is a virtue or something (e.g. activity) accompanied by virtue. It is also noteworthy that at 1105b22 Aristotle lists *philia* as a passion, but here he seems to have in mind friendly feeling as opposed to friendship.

1245a30). To some modern ears, the notion has a paternalistic ring to it, and suggests a lack of boundaries that adequately delimit the autonomous self. While a Kantian notion of autonomy is clearly alien to Aristotle, I want to suggest, none the less, that the relationship between virtue friends exhibits some mindfulness both of the differences between friends and of their separateness. This entails that such friends promote each other's good in a privileged way (as only another self can), but in a way that is still respectful of the mature rational agency of each. Given the similarity of virtue friends and the exclusiveness of the relationship, each is in a position to know how best to help the other, and how to help in a way that most reassures and pleases. In those cases where decisions are not joint, intimate knowledge of each other's abiding interests puts each in a position to offer counsel and support over the sort of choices that give real shape to each other's lives. Yet within this extended and interwoven life, the individuals none the less retain their separateness. In this regard, there may be some significance in Aristotle's choice of words at *EE* 1245a35, where he says that a friend is 'a separate self' (*autos diairetos*). But we need to consider further evidence.

Aristotle's notion of self-sacrifice, and what an agent can legitimately forfeit to another, is of some help here. On Aristotle's view, friendship is marked by a level of practical concern and willingness to help that is otherwise uncommon. One comes to count on an intimate friend in a way one cannot count on a stranger or mere acquaintance (*NE* VIII. 9). Aid is given without even having to ask (*Rh.* 1381b35), and often without a return expected. But what is sacrificed, as Aristotle clearly indicates in *NE* IX. 8 (and *MM* II. 13), are external goods, such as money, power, and opportunity (*NE* 1168b15 ff, 1169a20–30); in short, they are the sort of distributable (and scarce) goods one can give away, while still securing for oneself, through that choice, the intrinsic good of fine action. Indeed, what is especially valuable to a self, and the basis for a proper conception of self-love, namely the capacities of practical reason (1168b28–1169a3), are exhibited in the action, so that even when the sacrifice involves dying for a friend, the action will express what is fine.[26] In this sense, Aristotle says, the good man 'seems to assign to himself the greater share in what is fine' (1169b1). The point is not that his desire to help is voided when he himself cannot be the agent (see 1169a33-4); that sort of priggish sense of self is not part of his notion of self-love. Rather, it is that when his agency *is* required, and he acts, his action secures for him the finest sort of good. Even when the choice literally ends in the death of reason, the sacrifice will not compromise his sense of self.

Implicit in this regard for one's own rational agency is a reciprocal regard for the friend. In so far as a friend is another self, in helping a friend an individual cannot pre-empt that friend's rational agency, or desire to make choices that will violate his agency. For it is just because that other individual values virtue and practical reason that he has been chosen as a friend and someone with whom a life can be spent. They are virtue friends, in part, because they are capable of living in relation to one another in a way that does not make one the slave of the other.[27] The result is that such individuals promote each other's interests only in certain ways—not by directly making choices for each other (unless these are jointly deliberated choices or *homonoia*), but by giving each greater opportunities for choice, and greater means for the realization of ends. These means may include scarce (*perimachēta*) material resources, as Aristotle suggests here, but they may also include sought for psychological goods, such as support and esteem and confidence in our endeavours. Aristotle remarks in the *Rhetoric* that it is characteristic of friends 'to praise the good qualities we possess, and especially those which we fear might not in fact belong to us' (1381a35-b1, 1381b10-14). We give friends support and confidence in these ways, without minimizing their separateness.

There is further evidence for the separateness of selves

---

[26] For the proper qualifications of Aristotle's claim that the self is to be identified with reason, see ch. 3, sect. 6, and nn. 48 and 57. On the sacrifice of life for the sake of the fine, see 1117b1-20.

[27] Here I draw on the implication of Aristotle's remarks at 1124b31 that the magnanimous person 'cannot live in relation to another, except a friend. For that would be slavish.' I have profited from T. H. Irwin's notes on this passage; see his translation of the *Nicomachean Ethics* (Hackett, 1985), 327.

within character friendship. We can take up the issue by considering the possibility of virtuous characters having a diversity of ideals. On Aristotle's view, having a virtuous character implies possessing all the virtues, or complete virtue (*NE* 1145a1–2, 1098a17–18).[28] For the virtues imply one another and are inseparable. The pattern of unified virtues might, however, be different in different persons. So one individual might be especially honest, this virtue seeming to gain pre-eminence over others, while another individual might be particularly generous, her interactions being marked, above all, by a sense of bounty. Each individual has all the other virtues, and exercises them appropriately, as external conditions allow. But as a result of nature, development, and resources, certain virtues have gained greater expression and prominence in each individual's life. I believe this is consistent with Aristotle's notion of the unity of the virtues. My claim is not that the honest person *overlooks* the requirements of the other virtues (even though she *is* selective); it is rather that if we were to characterize her decency or goodness, her honesty would deserve special mention. It mediates her goodness in a special way.[29]

Now individuals that come together as character friends might be similar yet different in the above sense that while they share virtue as an overall end, they often express it in ways that are distinct yet complementary. They are not mere look-alikes of one another. Aristotle suggests this thought at *EE* VII. 12. In assessing the truth of the claim that a friend is another self, he comments:

... but the characteristics of a particular individual may be scattered, and it is difficult for all to be realized in one individual.

[28] Aristotle's remarks can be understood as claiming that the virtues are in principle consistent, or, more strongly, that in actual cases of action, they can never contingently conflict. I understand him to be making the first, weaker claim. For further discussion, see the concluding remarks of sect. 6 of the preceding chapter, along with n. 58.

[29] Aristotle's remarks at *Pol.* 1329a9 ff., in which he suggests that different character traits gain pre-eminence at different times in an individual's life, might give limited support here. For a discussion of the sort of character who does *overlook* the more complete requirements of virtue, see my remarks on magnanimity in 'Common Sense and Uncommon Virtue', in *Midwest Studies in Philosophy*, 13 (University of Notre Dame Press, 1988).

For although by nature a friend is what is most similar, one individual may resemble his friend in body, one in character [*psuchē*], or one in one part of the body or character, and another in another. (1245a30-4)

Here Aristotle implies that friends bear varying degrees of similarity to each other. And this may in fact be important to the self-realization of each within the friendship. For if my friend has virtue A to a higher degree than I do, then I should want to strive to perfect that virtue to a greater degree in myself. I should want to emulate the good qualities he has and come to realize them in myself. In Aristotle's concluding remarks on friendship in *NE* IX he alludes to precisely these differences and their role in adult ethical development:

The friendship of good persons is good, being increased by their companionship; and they are thought to become better too by their activities and by improving each other; for from each other they take the mould of characteristics they approve. (1172a10-15)

The supposition is that character friends will realize to a different degree (and in a different manner) particular virtues. Each is inspired to develop himself more completely as he sees admirable qualities, not fully realized in himself, manifest in another whom he esteems. Remarks Aristotle makes about the notion of emulation in the *Rhetoric* are pertinent here. Emulation, he says, is felt most intensely 'before those whose nature is like our own and who have good things that are highly valued and are possible for us to achieve' (1388a31-2). Character friends, as extended yet different selves, are eminently suited as models to be emulated.

There are also implications for Aristotle's pivotal claim that through character friendships the parties gain in self-knowledge. In *NE* IX. 9, *EE* VII. 12, and *MM* II. 15, Aristotle argues that a fundamental reason for including friendship within the happy life is that it enhances one's own awareness and understanding of one's agency and activities. The arguments in these texts are notoriously difficult (especially those in the *Nicomachean Ethics*), but the essential idea is something like this:[30] the good life requires excellent activity (1098a8), but since perception or understanding is a defining characteristic of human life (1170a16), to live that life in the fullest sense (*kuriōs*) requires self-perception of that activity (1170a17–19). Moreover, the pleasure that is intrinsic to that excellent activity (and essential for the good life) is enhanced through the pleasure and good of an awareness of it (1170b1–3). Friends are part of such a life in so far as through an awareness of their activities we see, in the striking words of the *Magna Moralia*, 'another me' (*heteros egō*) reflected, as it were, through 'a mirror' (1213a22–4). We learn about ourselves by having another self before us whose similar actions and traits we can study from a more detached and objective point of view: 'We can study a neighbour better than ourselves and his actions better than our own' (*NE* 1169b33–5). For in our own case, passion or favour at times blind our judgement (*MM* 1213a16–20). Through another just like us, yet numerically distinct, we can see ourselves from a point of view outside ourselves, and so at a distance.

But if another self need not be exactly similar, then self-knowledge might involve contrasting oneself with another, and considering how another would have felt or acted in the same circumstances given that individual's different point of view. This sort of transport of the imagination must, as we said earlier, be a part of friendship. Aristotle's introductory remarks in the *Metaphysics* have application here. Aristotle repeats in that celebrated passage the thought of *NE* IX. 9, that what characterizes human beings is their love of perception and knowledge. But here the emphasis is different:

All human beings desire to know by nature, and a sign of this is the delight we take in our senses . . . and above all else, the sense of sight . . . For this more than the other senses enables us to know and brings to light many distinctions between things. (980a22–8)

---

[30] The argument in these passages, esp. *NE* IX. 9 (1169b30–1170b14), is tortuous. However, Irwin's simplification of the argument in his translation is of enormous help. Cooper's analysis of the contribution of friendship to self-knowledge ('Aristotle on Friendship') remains the best I know. Since I am in basic agreement with both their analyses of the argument, I refer the reader to their works.

Self-knowledge, as a sub species of knowledge, requires the discrimination of what is peculiarly one's own. To overlook differences is ultimately to obscure an awareness of self.

6. CONDITIONS FOR ATTACHMENT

Up to this point we have been considering the chosen friendships of adults, and in particular virtuous adults. I now wish to turn to natural *philia* or the relationship of care and affection between parent and child. In these relationships, unlike those we have just discussed, the child is in a significant way not yet separate.[31] Lacking in mature rational capacities, the child relies upon the parent's reason. A parent makes choices (*prohaireseis*) for a child and promotes his good in a way that would be inappropriate within an adult friendship. However, as we shall see in the next chapter, the absence of fully-fledged prohairetic capacities does not entail that the child lacks *all* rational capacities; the cultivation of cognitive and perceptual capacities must be part of the child's early moral training, just as the cultivation of attachment must be. At present, it is the latter issue which concerns me. The primary texts here are *NE* VIII. 12 and *Pol.* II. 1.

Aristotle's views on filial attachment are in a fundamental way a reaction to Plato. Whereas Plato in the *Republic* urges the removal of the earliest signs of intimacy in the hope of permanently eradicating such tendencies, Aristotle encourages these first displays, believing that attachment early on will permanently fix the place of friendship in that life. For if, as Aristotle argues against Plato, the self-sufficient and complete life is a life lived with others, then the patterns of shared living must be established from the start. The social

---

[31] This is explicit in the following remark from the *Magna Moralia*: 'For there does not seem to be any justice between a son and his father, or a servant and his master—any more than one can speak of justice between my foot and me, or my hand or any of my other limbs. For a son is, as it were, a part of his father [*hōsper gar meros ti*], and remains so until he takes the rank of manhood and is separated [*chōristhēi*] from him, and becomes then an equal and a peer with his father' (1194b11-17). On the child's undeveloped rational capacities, see *NE* 1111b8-9, 1144b8-12, *EE* 1240b31-3, *Pol.* 1260a11-14. For further discussion of these texts, and the claim that the child lacks mature rational capacities, see ch. 5, esp. n. 3.

and relational good must be nurtured in the practices of the family.

We can begin to consider the conditions for attachment in rather broad outline by contrasting Aristotle's views with the teachings of Diotima in the *Symposium*. The ascent of *erōs*, according to Diotima, requires that the love of a particular individual be transformed into a more noble love of the repeatable and universal qualities of that individual as they are found in other persons as well as in impersonal embodiments, such as institutions and sciences. The claim is that the reinstantiation of these features in other individuals suffices to make these new individuals objects of love.

Aristotle's argument, as we shall see, implies that a notion of friendship based on Diotima's model violates certain psychological features of attachment. It violates the strong sense of friendship as self-referential, i.e. a friend is *my* friend and is treated as she is because she stands in a particular relation to *me*. On Diotima's model, there is no clear sense that the reduplicated objects retain that strong and special relation of 'being mine' characteristic, presumably, of the initial attachment. The sense of belonging has been diluted, Aristotle will suggest, by there being just too many individuals with whom I can reasonably expect to develop an intimate relationship. The psychological feature of exclusiveness, that is characteristic of friendship, is absent.

Let us consider these points more closely in the context of Aristotle's remarks in *Pol.* II. 1.[32] Here Aristotle makes these points in arguing against Plato's radical claim in *Rep.* V that political harmony and unity require the abolition of the nuclear family. In its place will be established a communistic family in which the children of the city become the common children of the older generation. Plato describes it as follows:

For no matter whom he meets, he will feel that he is meeting a brother, a sister, a father, a mother, a son, a daughter, or the offspring or forebears of each. (*Rep.* 463c)

---

[32] The importance of these texts was brought to my attention by Martha Nussbaum, in 'Shame, Separateness, and Political Unity: Aristotle's Criticism of Plato', in Rorty (ed.), *Essays on Aristotle's Ethics*, 295–435.

That city, then, is best ordered in which the greatest number use
the expression 'mine' and 'not mine' of the same things in the same
way . . . (*Rep.* 462c)

Now Aristotle's view is that a notion of *philia* which requires
this extended use of 'my mother', 'my son', etc., cannot be
sustained. For when 'mine' is used as in the *Republic*, 'each
of two thousand or ten thousand applying it to the same
thing' (*Pol.* 1262a8), 'the expressions "my son" or "my
father" become less frequent' (*hēkista legein ton emon ē huion
patera ē patera huion, Pol.* 1262b17). The notion of standing
in a special relation to an individual becomes weakened, on
the one hand by common ownership (for a son becomes only
fractionally one's own, *Pol.* 1262a2–6), and on the other by
having too many sons between whom to spread one's love.

   Aristotle formulates this more precisely in terms of two
closely related psychological principles: 'There are two
things above all that make persons love and care: they are a
sense that something is one's very own or proper to oneself
[*to idion*] and a sense that one must be content with it [*to
agapēton*]' (*Pol.* 1262b22–3). Some comment about the
meaning of *agapēton* is in order here before proceeding.[33]
On a reading weaker than the one I have offered, the word
might be rendered 'is worthy of love'; but this seems too flat
to convey Aristotle's intense disagreement with Plato about
the exclusiveness of friendship. A stronger reading might
have the sense 'that the object is *all* one has'. But this seems
too strong, since not all parental love for children will be for
only children, nor do children love only one parent. Equally,
Aristotle intends his remarks to apply to sibling love, where
several siblings can have the same sort of relationship with
each other. What is wanted is thus some notion of *weak*
exclusivity which puts some limit on the number of others
with whom one can feel intense and intimate love, but which
does not restrict that number to *one*. This is all Aristotle
needs to contrast his view of natural *philia* with the more
diluted (literally 'watery' (*hudarē*), *Pol.* 1262b16) attachments of *Rep.* V. I hope the translation of *to agapēton* as

---

[33] I am grateful to Richard Kraut for urging me to clarify this.

'what we must be content with' conveys this intermediate position.

Both the above principles, *to idion* and *to agapēton*, express, then, a form of exclusiveness. The first suggests that the whole of an object is one's own, i.e. it is not collectively owned or collectively taken care of. The second suggests that there are few others with whom one stands in the same relation; that is, the object of attachment cannot be easily substituted for. In the extended family of the *Republic*, Aristotle argues, both principles are violated. He illustrates the violation of the first (*to idion*) by the following analogy: as with a household that is neglected when it is taken care of by too many servants, so too children are neglected when they are the common responsibility of many individuals. For each parent passes responsibility on to someone else, with the result that the children are in the end inadequately cared for (*Pol.* 1261b33–8). The children, in turn, lacking a sense that they belong exclusively to a particular individual (*hōs hekastou*—instead of, as they do, to any one of many—*tou tuchontos*), fail to develop the intensity of feeling characteristic of the parent-child relationship (*Pol.* 1261b39–1262a2). The inability to form attachments is explained by the absence of a sense of *to agapēton*—the sense that a given parent cannot be readily exchanged for any other. The implication, then, is that although parents and children of the *Republic* refer to one another as 'mine', the sense of belonging requisite for attachment cannot be sustained in the absence of a greater degree of exclusiveness.

It is worth noting that Aristotle's remarks are compatible with the sort of division of labour he himself would have advocated for the household (*NE* 1162a20–9, *Pol.* I. 5). For on his view each parent, as well as the various slaves, should have different roles in the management of the family. The division increases, rather than impedes, efficient care. The crux of his argument in *Pol.* II is that Plato, in requiring that the many parents of a child all fill the same function, rules out the possibility of an effective system of shared care. Aristotle's two psychological principles can thus be seen as reinforcing a notion of division of labour, so long as he stipulates that it is a specific aspect of the care of a child that is primarily one's own (*to idion*), and that the child in turn depends upon that role being consistently filled by one particular individual (*to agapēton*).

Although Aristotle dwells on the case of natural *philia*, his remarks about exclusiveness have more general application, as suggested by the discussion in *NE* IX. 10. There Aristotle argues that the number of intimate friendships any individual can have is highly limited (1171a10–15; cf. *EE* 1238a9–10, 1245b20–6). Such friendships require a considerable devotion of energy and time, and preclude not only other such friendships, but other loyalties and commitments. They are cultivated and sustained at the cost of other investments of time and interest.³⁴ In the case of having too many friends, he says, one cannot actively identify with the points of view of them all (*sunaisthanesthai*, *EE* 1245b22), or actively show each affection (1238a9). In a sense, too many friends impede rather than sustain one's fine activity.

In the discussion of the family in *NE* VIII. 12, Aristotle continues his account of the conditions for attachment. The requirement that a friend be 'one's own' (*to idion*) is here specified in terms of parents loving children 'as in some way belonging to themselves' (*hōs heautōn ti onta*) and children in turn loving parents 'as in some degree deriving from them' (*hōs ap' ekeinōn ti onta*, (1161b18–19, 1161b27–30). The love between siblings, on Aristotle's view, is initially, at least, a love rooted in this common sense of belonging to parents (1161b30).

Although these remarks make some appeal to biological connections, such connections by no means exhaust what Aristotle takes to be relevant or most central to attachment. The sense of belonging between parent and child is more generally like that of craftsman to product (*poiēma*): in both cases the makers 'are favourably disposed [*eunoi*] to what they themselves make' (*MM* 1211b35–9). Here, belonging

---

³⁴ Larry Thomas explores in principle considerations for restricting friends to a small number (ideally, he argues, to two). His argument is essentially that the sort of face to face disclosure of self requisite for genuine friendship is jeopardized by the possibility of third party reports. *See his Living Morally: A Psychology of Moral Character* (Temple University Press, 1989). Also, pertinent is his 'Love and Morality: The Possibility of Altruism', in James Fetzer (ed.), *Sociobiology and Epistemology*, (Reidel, 1985), 115–29.

is an attachment which results from creating a product. The sense of one's own requires the sense of *making* something as one's own. This seems to be true, on Aristotle's view, even among adult friends. For he suggests that adult friends 'mould' each other (*apomattontai*, *NE* 1172a12), and influence greatly the course of life each follows.

Moreover, in the case of parents, the productive efforts are not merely of bringing children into the world, but of nurturing and raising them: 'For parents are the cause of children's existence and nurture, and from their birth onwards, of their education' (1162a6–7). The parents' production, is thus ongoing and constant, 'guided by memory and hope' (*MM* 1211b38). While it is important to note that Aristotle describes a mother's love as greater than a father's, we should not understand him to be claiming that it is because a mother is more biologically connected with her children. It is simply that 'to give birth to children is more laborious' (*NE* 1168a25–8, 1161b27, *EE* 1241b5 ff.). It is the *activity* and *labour* (*to prattein*) that makes for the greater attachment. Again activity is the source of pleasure. So he generalizes in the *Nicomachean Ethics*: 'Everyone loves more the things they have brought about through effort, for example, those who have worked for their money love it more than those who have inherited it . . . and for these reasons, mothers love their children more than fathers' (1162a22 ff.). This reading seems to be confirmed by Aristotle's biological theory, according to which the mother's body is regarded as merely the accidental matter in which the form, carried by the father's sperm, is instantiated.[35] As such, it is the father, and not the mother, who bears the essential biological relation to the child. Thus, although it is the labour of giving birth that is at issue, it is not necessarily the biological aspect of that labour that Aristotle chooses to emphasize, either through his science or through his analogies.[36] The idea of a

---

[35] For a valuable study of Aristotle's view of women as reflected in his biological studies, see G. E. R. Lloyd, *Science, Folklore and Ideology* (Cambridge University Press, 1983), Part II.

[36] There is greater emphasis on biological attachment in Aristotle's claim that mothers love their children more not only because of their labour but because 'they know better than fathers that the children are their own' (1168a26). Thus, although the mother's matter is accidental to the child, the mother can none the less be

purely gestational mother, who has no genetic relation to the child she bears, might not be such a terribly strange notion to Aristotle!

It is also worth speculating that given Aristotle's view of the mother's primary function in the household, her labour will extend to the nurture and early upbringing of her children. While she herself will lack education, and by her very nature, the full authority and control of rational powers (*Pol.* 1260a14), she will nevertheless be capable of executing orders for running a household in which the children's early education takes place.[37] Her love and intimate knowledge of her children will be important elements in that education, and significant counterparts to the less personalized aspects of public education which Aristotle is eager to offset (*NE* 1180b8–12). We shall be considering some implications of this at the end of the chapter.

The attachment of children to parents, in turn, is not, on Aristotle's view, merely or primarily biological, but an intentional response to the affection and nurture displayed toward them as beloved objects. This emerges from several remarks Aristotle makes. For a start, he says that 'children love their parents only after time has elapsed when they are capable of understanding and discrimination' (*NE* 1161b24–6). Most fundamental in this process is distinguishing their own parents from other adults. So in *Phys.* I. 1, Aristotle explains: 'Children at first call all men "father" and all women "mother", and only later distinguish each of them from other adults' (184b12–14). The implication of these passages is that as children become capable of discriminating their own parents from other adults, they come to recognize their parents' special affection for them. They perceive

certain of her own contribution, and certain that she is the biological mother, in a way the father cannot.

[37] On the role of women in ancient society, see Averil Cameron and Amelie Kuhrt (eds.), *Images of Women in Antiquity* (Croom Helm, 1983), esp. Mary Lefkowitz, 'Influential Women'; Susan Walker, 'Women and Housing in Classical Greece: the Archaeological Evidence'; and Riet Van Bremen, 'Women and Wealth'. Cf. also the helpful source book by Mary Lefkowitz and Maureen Fant, *Women's Life in Greece and Rome* (Duckworth, 1982); W. K. Lacey, *The Family in Classical Greece* (Cornell University Press, 1968); and Sarah Pomeroy, *Goddesses, Whores, Wives, and Slaves* (Schocken Books, 1975).

themselves 'as' (*hōs*, *NE* 1168b18) belonging in a special and exclusive way. In addition they perceive their parents' love as unfailing and abundant. So Aristotle says, 'Of all the kinds of friendship we have discussed, it is in the friendships between kin that love is present in the greatest degree [*malista*], and especially so in the relation of parent to child' (*MM* 1211b18-20). It is given from the start as soon as a child is born (*NE* 1161b25), and is given non-instrumentally, for its own sake (*MM* 1211b27-35), without debts incurred for benefits conferred (*MM* 1211b22-7, *EE* 1239a18). The child's attachment is a response to these perceptions of love.[38]

7. VIRTUOUS PARENTS AND VIRTUOUS CHILDREN (OR SONS)

They teach and admonish them from early childhood and throughout their lives. And when the child understands more quickly the things which he is told, trainer and mother, and moral tutor and even father himself all vie with each other to make the child as good as possible, instructing him through each thing he says and does, pointing out that this is right and this wrong, this thing fine and that thing ignoble, this holy and that impious, do this and don't do that . . . (*Protag.* 325c-326a)

In this section we shall be considering the family as a privileged sphere in which early ethical education takes place. Aristotle's reinstatement of the family at the centre of early training marks, as we said earlier, a clear break from Plato's more radical notions. It also marks a break from the intellectualist tradition (spearheaded by Socrates and the Sophists) in which ethical education becomes more the responsibility of the professional expert than of the loving parent in the home. The corruption of the family by the new intellectualists is satirized by Aristophanes in *The Clouds*.

---

[38] My remarks have benefited from John Rawls' discussion of the family in *A Theory of Justice* (Harvard University Press, 1971), sect. 70-2; Jean Piaget, *The Moral Judgment of the Child* (Kegan Paul, 1932; repr. The Free Press, 1965); and Jerome Kagan, 'The Concept of Identification', *Psychological Review*, 65 (1958).

In this play Strepsiades, having sent his son to the new rhetoricians to learn the verbal skills for outsmarting creditors, ends up childless, for his son is lost to a new morality which teaches irreverence for the family as well as the skills of argumentation to rationalize it.[39] Aristotle's break with both Socratic intellectualism and Platonic radicalism coincides with a return to the sort of traditionalism Protagoras outlines above in the Great Speech of the dialogue that bears his name. But on Aristotle's telling of that story, it is not merely that parents are privileged transmitters of virtue—the claim Socrates challenges Protagoras and other Sophists to demonstrate as proof of virtue's teachability—but that they are so in virtue of a kind of relationship that itself has intrinsic value for the ethical life. This is just as we should expect given the essential character of the Aristotelian good life as shared.

The stable attachment between parents and child facilitates the parents' role as educator in several ways. The pre-eminence of parents in the child's life makes them ready-to-hand models for emulation, as well as attentive judges of the child's specific needs and requirements. The child's acknowledgement of the parents' love and trust engenders a willingness to learn from them and a readiness to comply: 'For just as in cities, the customs and types of characters have force [*enischuei*], so too in families, the reasons and examples of the father have sway, and even more so on account of the kinship and the benefits he confers' (1180b3–7). For these sorts of reasons, Aristotle continues, a scheme of education which includes *paideia* within the family has clear advantages over an exclusively public education (1180b7–12).[40]

But it would be a mistake to think of the child's love and trust of his parents as primarily establishing the child's

---

[39] I examine this play at length in Chapter 1 of my Ph.D. thesis 'Aristotle's Theory of Moral Education' (Harvard University, 1982); see also Martha Nussbaum's 'Aristophanes and Socrates on Learning Practical Wisdom' in Jeffrey Henderson (ed.), *Aristophanes: Essays in Interpretation* (Cambridge University Press, 1980).

[40] There are additional texts relevant to the issue of the role of parents in *paideia*. Most helpful are the remarks on the acquisition of shame in *Rh.* II. 6, esp. 1384a33–b25, and the discussion of emulation at *Rh.* 1388a30 ff.

compliance to rules and precepts. Rather, what Aristotle points to in the above passage is a view of parents informing certain ideals of character, through reason and example (*logoi kai ethē*), that influence (*enischuei*) the child's own sense of virtue. The nature of parental authority in the unequal filial relation thus has more to do with the power and force of a particular model of character than with a demand for conformity to rules. Habituation requires, as we shall see in the next chapter, not rote memory of rules, but the exercise of judgement and reason as a part of practice.

There are, however, problems with the notion of placing the family back at the heart of moral education. One has to do with the suitability of the mother as a character model. Given the relative absence of the father in the private sphere and yet his presumed superior virtue over the mother, how qualified is the mother to play a primary role in the transmission process?[41] More generally, what happens in families when parents (and extended parents, in the sense of trainers, tutors, and nurses) are inadequate models for emulation; in other words, how does civic education counteract the lottery of who one's parents happen to be? And even in families where the parents are exemplary, how does education encourage something more than blind conformity? I shall turn to the first question now. The second question I treat briefly in the next section. The third question is the focus of the following chapter.

The notion of transmitting character ideals through the filial relation raises the glaring problem of who is to be the exemplary model within the family. Aristotle's reinstatement of the family dismantled by Plato appears to reinstate the traditional social roles of contemporary Athens.[42] Unlike the women in Plato's guardian class, Aristotle's woman is effectively excluded from the public and civic roles of the citizen and relegated into the home. Her management extends primarily to the household, where she

---

[41] Note the *Protagoras* passage quoted at the beginning of this section in which it is reported that the 'father himself' (*kai autos ho patēr*) vies to care for the child (325a7).

[42] See, for example, Susan Moller Okin, *Women in Western Political Thought* (Princeton University Press, 1979), Parts I and II.

is ultimately subordinate to her husband's authority. In the house, she becomes, alongside other trainers and domestic slaves, a custodian and ethical tutor of her children. Indeed, in a programme of education in which the actual and pervasive presence of adult figures counts for a lot, and the relationships which adults have with children count for even more, it would appear that the mother becomes a central figure in the ethical education of her young. For she, more than the father, has special feelings for the child (1161b27). The relationship she forms with the child thus becomes a model of what it is to become psychologically and emotionally vulnerable to others. In addition to a capacity for attachment, she teaches a sense of reliance on others, a sense of loyalty and intimacy, and a sense of co-operation and care which the virtuous person will need for forming friendships as well as for acting virtuously in general. Given her proximity to the children, it is her interactions with them, her clues about what to notice as ethically salient, her instructions about the appropriateness of emotional response and action that are formative. *De facto*, her instructions count for a lot, particularly in a theory which stresses both early development and the special benefits of learning from those whom one loves and trusts.

Yet all this sits in uneasy tension with the unsuitability of women as ethical exemplars. Women, on Aristotle's view, are rationally defective. Lacking control of their passions, their deliberative capacities are without authority (*akuron*, *Pol.* 1261a14). Although Aristotle acknowledges that women have a kind of virtue (*NE* 1162a22, *Pol.* 1260b10–20), their virtue remains essentially inferior. In a sense, it is like natural virtue, defective in the resources and experience requisite for practical insight (*NE* VI. 13). As such, women are permanently unable to assess questions from all sides, or bring to bear the sort of empirical knowledge that good decision-making requires. This lack of practical reason further entails that whatever virtues a woman may have, they will be disjointed, and will fail to support any overall conception of good living. It is not simply that women lack the deliberative skills requisite for the political arena; more generally, they lack what is needed for full virtue and wisdom at home.

While such a view is not formally inconsistent, it nevertheless implies a kind of early tutor who will be ill-qualified for the sorts of roles Aristotle himself argues for.[43] As we shall see in the next chapter, early training requires critical practice and a tutor who can guide in this practice. Such practice will involve the development of practical intellect and perception in so far as these cognitive capacities are necessary for properly directed emotions, desires and choices. If women are unable to guide in this process— unable to see circumstances in their proper perspective, unable to assess if an injury was warranted, unable to react with the sort of knowledge which ensures a correct choice—then they will be deficient even as educators in the home. I believe this remains a problem for Aristotle.

Still, there is a brighter side to Aristotle's view worth fastening on. And that is that while women may be excluded from full virtue, none the less what we think of as a traditional preserve of women—namely intimate attachment and affection—is on Aristotle's view open to men. Its principal expression for men will not be within the family or even towards women in heterosexual relationships,[44] but towards other men with whom an enduring interest in virtue is shared. We may deeply regret that these richest virtue friendships were not open to women, and that, conversely, intimacies within the family were less attractive to men. But to Aristotle's lasting credit, we must remember that he above all recognized the permanent value of personal attachment— however restricted the different spheres might have been— and recognized that men, as the model of human potential, must accord it a central place in their lives. This, it may be argued, is more than most moral theory has done.

8. THE LIMITATIONS OF PRIVATE EDUCATION

The inadequacy of the woman to fulfil the tutoring role raises the more general problem of contingencies which affect the

---

[43] I am grateful to Anthony Brueckner for urging me to clarify my position here.

[44] Although Aristotle allows that marital relations may, if the parties are virtuous, constitute a *kind* of virtue friendship (1162a22), given the sort of virtue of which

educational process. If virtue is to be acquired, then it requires favourable circumstances for acquisition—a good family, good birth, reasonable opportunities, and means for emotion and action. Aristotle often assumes that conditions will be favourable, and that in the normal course of events children will acquire virtue through the family. But this is optimistic. Optimal conditions will be within the reach of only those of a certain class, and even there the possibility remains open that those in the extended domestic family will be less than exemplary models of virtue. Even if we leave aside the issue of the mother's inferior nature, the father, though by nature capable of genuine virtue, may for a myriad of reasons fall short of full virtue. What then of the children's fate, given the influential role of parents in their lives?

It might be argued here that this is an intrinsic disadvantage of a system of private education. As Aristotle himself remarks against Plato, one's own parents must themselves *suffice* as objects of love and honour (*Pol.* 1262a8). But what if one could do better by having within reach other models? What if other people's parents could provide more exemplary models? Aristotle is well aware of this problem and thus insists that the private educational process must be part of a broader civic education. One purpose of this civic education is to expand the learner's horizons, to bring him into contact with the exemplary characters of his culture and tradition. In this connection, the mimetic education of *mousikē* (poetry and drama) will be important, and we shall be saying something about this in the next chapter. But first we need to examine more basic assumptions about moral habituation.[45]

women are capable, such friendships will be in principle inferior to homosexual friendships of character.

[45] Versions of this chapter were read to audiences at Brown University, the University of North Carolina at Chapel Hill, and Wesleyan University. In addition to helpful comments from these audiences, I am especially grateful to Larry Blum, Barbara Herman, Thomas Hill, R. I. G. Hughes, Richard Kraut, Martha Nussbaum, and Geoffrey Sayre-McCord for their criticisms and interest at various stages.

5

THE HABITUATION OF CHARACTER

ARISTOTLE'S remarks on the habituation of character have been accepted for the most part as an uncontroversial part of his ethical theory. What seems certain on any reading is that character states are acquired through practice of corresponding actions. Under traditional interpretations, however, practice is seen primarily as a non-rational training of desires towards appropriate objects. Habituation is thus viewed as essentially separate from and antecedent to the development of rational and reflective capacities.

A well-known commentator has made the following remarks about the second book of the *Nicomachean Ethics*:

> We need only compare the theory of virtue in this book with the discussions in the *Meno* of Plato, to see how immensely moral philosophy has gained in definiteness in the meantime. While becoming definite and systematic, however, it had also to some extent become scholastic and mechanical . . . A mechanical theory is here given both of the intellect and the moral character, as if the one could be *acquired* by teaching, the other by a course of habits.[1]

To be sure, the commentator, namely Alexander Grant, is critical of this mechanical theory; but he none the less takes it to be Aristotle's view—Aristotle's alternative to Socratic intellectualism, and the equation of ethical virtue with knowledge (*epistēmē*). Socrates' mistake, Aristotle himself says, is that 'he used to inquire what virtue is, but not how and from what sources it arises' (*EE* 1216b10-11; cf. 1216b19-22).

[1] A. Grant, *The Ethics of Aristotle* (Longmans, Green, 1885), 482-3; cf. 486, 241-2. J. A. Stewart concurs with Grant's view; see his *Notes on the Nicomachean Ethics of Aristotle*, i and ii (Oxford University Press, 1892; repr. Arno Press, 1973), 171.

But Aristotle's inquiry into these questions, indeed his transformation of ethical theory into a theory, like Plato's, about *how* to be good, does not issue in a mechanical theory of habituation, or so I shall argue in this chapter. Similar claims have been made by others in recent years, most notably by Burnyeat and Sorabji.[2] If my argument is distinctive, it is because it brings to bear a broader range of texts which show just how thoroughgoing Aristotle's conception of critical habituation is. In particular, I hope to show how the various capacities we have been discussing in previous chapters—perceptual, affective, and deliberative, are cultivated within such an education.

My motive in taking a serious look at the process of moral education is the belief that the mechanical theory of habituation ultimately makes mysterious the transition between childhood and moral maturity. It leaves unexplained how the child with merely 'habituated' virtue can ever develop the capacities requisite for practical reason and inseparable from full virtue. As I have maintained throughout this book, full virtue is not simply the excellence of the non-rational part, but itself combines the excellences of character and of practical reason. This is the unmistakable force of the definition of virtue in *NE* II. 6 as a character state concerning choice as determined by the reasoning of the *phronimos*. It is the point of the claim made in Book VI that one cannot be good without practical wisdom nor wise without virtue (1144b30-3).

Now it is true that no one would seriously hold that rationality emerges in an instant. To say 'Now a boy becomes a man' (at whatever age—thirteen, eighteen, or twenty-one) is to create an artifice for law, not to explain

---

[2] Myles Burnyeat, 'Aristotle on Learning to be Good', in A. O. Rorty (ed.), *Essays on Aristotle's Ethics* (University of California Press, 1980), 69-92, esp. 73-4, and Richard Sorabji, 'Aristotle on the Role of Intellect in Virtue', *Proceedings of the Aristotelian Society*, 74 (1973-4), 107-29, repr. in Rorty, 201-19. I have benefited greatly from both these articles. For a comprehensive general history of Greek education, see Henri Marrou, *Histoire de l' éducation dans l' antiquité* (Editions du Seuil, 1948). I also found of interest, in thinking about general issues in ethical education, Joel Kupperman's *The Foundations of Morality* (George Allen and Unwin, 1983), ch. 12, and his 'Character and Education', *Midwest Studies in Philosophy*, 13 (Notre Dame University Press, 1988).

when and how.[3] But the mechanical theory does not offer such an explanation, nor allow us plausibly to infer any. It gives us no indication of the way capacities are cultivated for their eventual maturity. A reasonable account need not require that such capacities develop perfectly continuously, nor at an even pace. A more plausible alternative is that there is an uneven rate of growth, with starts and stops in the development of particular capacities. Aristotle might accept something like this picture: there might be an early period in which affective capacities are cultivated, followed by the more active development of rational (and deliberative) capacities, and then eventually the emergence of full rationality.[4] This recognizes the general fact that there are conditions of internal readiness as well as environmental factors that affect the rate of progress. Growth will be marked by spurts and impasses. Thus, the extremely young child, on his view, may not engage in the reasoning process in a very extensive way. It is true, his perceptual and discriminatory capacities will awaken early on, as Aristotle indicates in various places (1161b28, 184b14, 1448b7–10), and he will enjoy the power of discriminating differences. As the child becomes older, the cultivation of these cognitive capacities will become an essential element in the development of the affections. But he will not yet, in a substantive way, cultivate the more deliberative skills that enter into complex choice-making. That comes later.

I shall argue for something like this conception in the pages that follow. My overall claim is that if full virtue is to meet certain conditions, then this must be reflected in the educational process. The child must be seen as being educated towards that end. This will require a developmental

---

[3] Indeed, Aristotle too speaks of the boy arriving at manhood. So at *MM* 1194b15 ff. he says: 'For a son is, as it were, a part of his father, until he attains the rank [*taxin*] of manhood and is separated from him. Then he is in a relationship of equality and parity with the father.' And again at *EE* 1224a26–30 he speaks of the arrival at a 'certain age [*hēlikiai*] to which we ascribe action [*to prattein*]'; cf. *Problems* 955b22 ff., *NE* 1143b8–10. My general argument is that while such notions are a convenient way of marking maturity, they are not especially helpful in detailing moral growth.

[4] I am grateful to Richard Kraut for urging me to take more seriously this last alternative.

conception of cognitive and affective capacities, as well as a conception of habituation as in varying degrees reflective and critical.

The chapter, then, will proceed roughly in this way: after introductory remarks about the plausibility of ascribing to Aristotle a developmental model of the child's ethical growth, I shall examine the non-rational part of the soul and consider the sort of rationality it none the less includes. This will lead us to Aristotle's intentional theory of the emotions, and to a broad sketch of how we refine the discriminatory capacities included in the emotions. With this as background, we shall be in a position to assess Aristotle's remarks about the habituation of character and to consider the way in which it allows for the critical practice necessary for developing fine discrimination. Central to the account will be Aristotle's view that practice yields pleasure to the extent to which it exhibits increasingly fine powers of discernment. Finally, I shall argue that the general conception of habituation as reflective and critical coheres with Aristotle's view of experience as training practical reason through trial and error as well as inquiry.

1. THE VIABILITY OF A DEVELOPMENTAL MODEL

Before proceeding, then, we need to assess the viability of ascribing to Aristotle a developmental conception of the child's ethical growth. Some hesitation about this point seems well grounded, given Aristotle's general tendency to lump the child, together with the animal, as constituting a single contrast case to the ethically mature adult. The single grouping implies that the child's defects are in some way permanent (at least for the duration of childhood), and that the acquisition of certain abilities and states is an all or nothing matter. So Aristotle tells us that along with the animal, the child lacks the deliberative capacities for choice (*prohairesis*) and action (*praxis*) characteristic of the adult (1111a25-6, 1111b8-9, 1144b8, *EE* 1224a26-30 and 1240b31-4). Both pursue pleasures which are not un-qualifiedly good (*NE* 1152b19-20, 1153a28-31, 1176b28-

30, *EE* 1236a2–7, 1228b19–22, 1238a32–4) and lack the sort of judgement (*hupolēpsis*) that can oppose (and control) desires (*NE* 1147b5, *EE* 1224a25–7); thus they can be neither akratic nor enkratic (continent or controlled). Like the slave, the child requires external reason for guidance (*Pol.* 1260a34, 1260b3–8). The picture, on the whole, is derogatory and static: 'No one would choose to live through his life with the mind of a child, however much he were to enjoy the things that children enjoy' (*NE* 1174a1–4); 'No sensible person could endure to go back to it again' (*EE* 1215b22–5).

But we should not be misled by what Aristotle says. First, it is immediately obvious that any grouping of child and animal is undercut by an argument for species differences of the sort that Aristotle emphasizes elsewhere, and that form the basis of his doctrine of a peculiar human function (*ergon*) and excellence.[5] Second, the grouping obscures the notion of maturation which Aristotle himself deploys in other contexts, and which is crucial for a more accurate characterization of the child and of education. Thus, in Book I of the *Politics* Aristotle says that the child has a deliberative part (*to bouleutikon*), 'but in an undeveloped form' (*atelēs*, 1260a13–14). And he continues: 'Since the child is undeveloped [*atelēs*], it is clear that his virtue is not relative to himself, but relative to the fully developed individual, and the one who is in authority over him' (1260a32–3). These remarks openly invite a developmental model in which the child is viewed not statically, but as in progress toward full humanity, on his way towards some end. Deficiencies of reasoning are regarded not as fixed, but as merely temporary phenomena within a complex, and differentially paced, process of growth. To lack deliberative skills at a certain stage does not imply the absence of other cognitive capacities specific to ethical response.

---

[5] Cf. *NE* I. 7, *Meta.* I. 1, *DA* III. 3, 9–11, *MA* 6–11. Very roughly, there is an 'explanation of motion' common to all creatures, for both humans and animals are moved by critical and desiderative faculties. In the case of animals, however, critical faculties are limited to perception, memory, and perceptual imagination. Human capacities include these, but in addition belief, thought, the manipulation of belief through syllogism and deliberation, and choice.

An important caveat needs to be made here: this model will apply primarily to the male child. As we said in the last chapter, the female, Aristotle contends, has rational capacities that are permanently deficient, and that permanently limit the sort of virtue she can attain (*Pol.* 1260a12–30). In a sense she *is* and will remain forever a child, her limited opportunities designed to reflect her limited abilities. At full maturity, she will still lack rational authority and will be capable only of a subordinate sort of virtue and happiness.[6] It can be argued, as I have, that even within her restricted domestic sphere the woman demonstrates considerably more virtue than Aristotle's official doctrine allows. But for the time being, the contrast between the male and female child underlines the merely transient nature of the boy's rational defects.

2. THE RATIONALITY OF THE NON-RATIONAL PART

Part of the impetus for viewing the habituation process as essentially non-cognitive comes from Aristotle's remarks at the end of Book I and beginning of Book II of the *Nicomachean Ethics* that virtuous character is acquired through habituation (*ex' ethous*) of the non-rational part (*to alogon*) of the soul. This is distinguished from the virtue or excellence of the rational or intellectual part (*to logon*), acquired for the most part through systematic teaching and exposition (*ek didaskalias*). But the separation of these parts of the soul (and their training) requires, as Aristotle himself recognizes, considerable qualification. After adopting the Platonic division into rational and non-rational parts 'as adequate' for his own purposes (1102a26–8), Aristotle thus proceeds for the rest of *NE* I. 13 to clarify and refine the distinction: the desiderative part of the non-rational soul (*to orektikon*, i.e. appetites, emotions, and in general feelings— *pathē*) does not engage in reasoning but can listen to reason,

---

[6] Her deliberative part is *akuron*, or lacking in authority (*Pol.* 1260a13). Cf. W. W. Fortenbaugh, 'Aristotle on Slaves and Women', and a reply by Elizabeth V. Spelman, 'Aristotle and the Politicization of the Soul', in S. Harding and M. B. Hintikka (eds.), *Discovering Reality*, (Reidel, 1983), 17–30.

and thus partake of reason in a certain way (1102b14, 1102b26-1103a3; cf. 1098a4). It can be controlled, persuaded, and shaped by the rational part.

In the *De Anima* Aristotle is openly cautious about the practice of dividing the soul into parts, warning that any division will always be relative to a particular pursuit or inquiry, and that consequently parts can be proliferated or diminished, carved up in this way or that, to suit an inquiry. In certain schemes, particular capacities will thus resist easy pigeon-holing. So the perceptual capacity is not easily classifiable as exclusively desiderative or rational, nor is imagination. In a more custom-tailored scheme, these capacities might be assigned to distinct parts (*DA* 432a30). But equally, Aristotle argues, desire (*orexis*) is considerably more complex than the division of the soul into rational and non-rational parts suggests. There is, as we have said before, a kind of desire—rational wish or *boulēsis*—which is distinctive to the rational part and which is intimately connected with the capacities of reflection and revision. Even appetites and emotions, which Aristotle is never tempted to assign to the rational part, will have cognitively specifiable constituents.

We must bear in mind these clarifications as we go on to examine the process of habituation. In particular, we will want to have them in mind in assessing Aristotle's claim that the rationality of desire is a kind of obedience, a way of listening to and obeying (*katēkoon, peitharchikon*) the authority of a separate and higher part (*NE* 1102b12-1103a4). The analogy Aristotle adopts in Book I of the *Nicomachean Ethics* is of the child's relation to the parent: desire obeys the reason of the rationally authoritative part as a child listens to his father (*hōsper to patros akoustikon ti*, 1102b31-1103a3). The analogy informs the claim made in the *Eudemian Ethics* that 'character [*ēthos*] is a quality of the part of the soul that is non-rational, but capable of following reason [*dunamenē akolouthein*], in accordance with a prescriptive principle' (1220b6-8; cf. 1220a5-13).

The analogy of a child compliant to the exhortations of a rational adult might seem to reinforce the image of desire borrowing reason exclusively from outside, being guided

primarily by exogenous controls.[7] But as a picture either of
the child or of the tutoring of desire it oversimplifies and
misrepresents more interesting things Aristotle has to say
about both. First, as we shall see, though the child's reasons
will be borrowed in varying degrees from outside, they will
also be generated internally by the child's own perceptions,
beliefs, and feelings. These, in dialogue with the beliefs of
an experienced adult, will shape desire. Second, leaving
aside the source of reasons and reasoning, the notion of
desire co-operating with reason is at best vague, and needs
to be filled in by a more precise account of exactly how
cognitive elements inform desires, and how habituation is
involved in this process. Without some answers to these
questions, we can hardly begin to understand the process
of educating character.

3. THE INAPPROPRIATENESS OF HARSH SANCTIONS

We shall be filling out the picture, but first it is worth
making some negative remarks that will delimit the account.
The educational process does not seem to be, on Aristotle's
account, one that is particularly harsh or coercive. This is
not to deny that the threat of punishment will have a place,
just as will the use of external rewards and positive
reinforcement. These will be present, most obviously in the
form of praise and blame, and in the reactive attitudes of
parents. Rather, the intention is to distinguish such gentle
methods of external sanction from those which are excessively coercive or severe and which bypass altogether
the engagement of reason. The latter, too, will have a place
in the city, as methods of deterrence and reform for likely
and actual offenders. But they will be restricted to those
who are insensitive to reason, who because of a life pursuant
of brutish pleasures require brutish methods of constraint
(1179b27-9, 1179b23, 1180a12). The child is excluded from
this camp, not only on the grounds that he is not yet fully
responsible and hence fully culpable, but on the grounds

---

[7] Cf. *Rep.* IX, 590d.

that his reason, though undeveloped, is not corrupted or incapable of response. He is educable, and if properly brought up, can be moved by argument:

And argument and teaching surely do not influence everyone, but rather the soul of the listener must be cultivated beforehand by means of habits for loving and hating finely, just like earth that is to nourish the seed. For the individual whose life is governed by passion will not even listen to an argument that dissuades him nor even understand it; for how can we ever persuade such an individual to change his ways? And in general, passion seems to yield not to argument, but to force. (1179b24–31; tr. Irwin)

The key is thus early training. As such, the picture is as it should be, forward-looking—of a child who will some day more fully understand and reason; of an education that, as Aristotle says in the *Politics*, is 'with a view towards the next stages'[8] and 'which allows us to pursue through it many other kinds of learning' (1338a39–41); of a life that can be spoken of as happy, on the expectation (*dia tēn elpida*) that the child will some day have both the intrinsic and the extrinsic goods necessary for happiness (*NE* 1100a1–4).

In this regard, though Aristotle says ethical immaturity can occur at any chronological age (1095a5), he must view as significantly different the way we treat such immaturity in the young and in those in their prime. For those who have already been corrupted by a life of pleasure and immoderate feeling, rational persuasion and dialogue are no longer viable means of effecting reform. For the young, though they naturally veer toward excess and immoderation, the aim of education is to ensure that reason and argument have sway.

4. THE INTENTIONALITY OF EMOTIONS

A comprehensive account of the acquisition of Aristotelian virtue would require going through the full range of virtues

---

[8] *Pol.* 1336b37 ff; cf. 1340b35–9. On this first passage, see the helpful discussion of Carnes Lord, in *Education and Culture in the Political Thought of Aristotle* (Cornell University Press, 1982), 44–8.

implicit in goodness, and saying something about what the subconstituents of each virtue are and how they might be acquired, e.g. for courage, how fear must be felt but confronted, the sorts of circumstances and beliefs appropriate to the right response, exposure to which might cultivate that response. Different passions will be involved in different virtues, and different circumstances will be appropriate for the exercise of each. The opportunities and resources for cultivating one virtue need not coincide with the opportunities for cultivating another. Some passions might be more resistant to reform than others, and some vices more blameworthy (1119a22–32). Though Aristotle himself undertakes this sort of extensive accounting of the virtues, I cannot go through it in detail. Rather, what I wish to do is to consider virtue in a general way as a complex of capacities—perceptual, affective, and deliberative—and suggest how these capacities are cultivated.

I shall begin with the training of the affective capacities. Virtue, on Aristotle's view, is a mode of affect and conduct. To be generous is to choose to give assistance to those who merit it without undue internal noise or resistant inclination. Both correct judgement and correct feeling are required. Though Aristotle does not insist, as some have, that the child's initial stance to the world is egoistic (indeed a child may be endowed with considerable 'natural' virtue, 1144b3–5), he does hold the uncontroversial view that virtue without wisdom can be blind (1144b10), just as unbridled passion can interfere with the pursuit of chosen ends. Kindness towards the wrong persons can be harmful, just as uncontrolled fear can stand in the way of facing the challenges and risks necessary for pursuing desired ends. There is a certain urgency about moderating desires and directing them towards the right objects: 'Hence we ought to have been brought up, from our very youth, as Plato says, to find pleasure and pain as it is appropriate. For this is right education' (1104b11–13; cf. 1105a6–7).

But to appreciate the urgency of reforming desires is not to say how or in what way to effect the change. I want to argue that Aristotle's explicit theory of emotion as intentional or cognitive provides us with a clue: emotions will be educated, in part, through their constitutive beliefs and perceptions. Cultivating the dispositional capacities to feel fear, anger, goodwill, compassion, or pity appropriately will be bound up with learning how to discern the circumstances that warrant these responses. Hitting the mean in our affective response, i.e. getting right the degree and nuance of the reaction, and in general its inflection, would be inconceivable apart from some critical judgement which informed it.

Granted, appropriately directed emotion may still lack the univocal and unconflicting voice that Aristotle requires of mature virtue. My pity for the homeless may betray a certain arrogance about my own good fortune, and my good-will may have to fight to conquer less noble desires. To the extent that I struggle against what I view to be recalcitrant desires, my virtue is still only a kind of control or continence (*egkrateia*) and falls short of the more thoroughgoing harmony that the *sōphrōn* or truly temperate person exhibits. This is a reminder of what a tall order Aristotelian virtue may be. But it does not compromise the claim that the training towards that end is none the less a process in which desire is informed through the formation of belief.

We can take as background to this claim Aristotle's insistence, in various key places, on the central human desire to perceive and discriminate difference. This is explicit in the opening remarks of the *Metaphysics*:

All human beings desire to know [*eidenai*] by nature. And evidence of this is the pleasure that we take in our senses; for even apart from their usefulness they are enjoyed for their own sake, and above all others, the sense of eyesight . . . For this more than the other senses enables us to know [*gnōrizein*] and brings to light many distinctions. (980a20–7)

These remarks, conjoined with parallel remarks in *Poet.* IV, make it explicit that critical activity and its enjoyment characterize all stages of development. At the early stages,[9] discriminatory activity will often take the form of *mimēsis*. The latter is roughly understood to mean our notions of

---

[9] On other early signs of the child's capacity to discriminate, cf. *Ph.* 184b11–12 and *NE* 1161a25.

imitation and representation and implies here a way of coming to identify actual objects and events through familiarity with representations and enactments of them:

> It seems in general that the origin of poetry has two causes, and that these have to do with human nature. For imitating is natural to humankind from childhood up and human beings differ from animals in this, that they are the most imitative of creatures and learn first through imitation. And it is also a part of human nature that they all delight in imitative work [of others]. And a sign of this is what happens in actual practice. For though objects themselves may be painful to see, we enjoy seeing the most detailed representations of them, for example, forms of the least distinguished of animals and of corpses. And the reason for this delight is that learning [*manthanein*] is the greatest of pleasures, not only for philosophers, but also for all others as well, to whatever extent they may share in the capacity. And it is for this reason that they delight in seeing representations. For it turns out that in seeing they learn and figure out [*sullogizesthai*] what each thing is, for example, that this is a that ... (*Poet.* 1448b4–17; cf. *Rh.* 1371b4–10)

Intellectual delight, here, seems to hang on making a discovery, on coming to understand or actively puzzle out (*sullogizesthai*) what is not yet familiar in terms of what is. 'This is a that' is, within the mimetic mode, a classification of actual characters, ways of acting and feeling, features of circumstances, etc., through familiarity with some represented form. Within the ethical sphere, 'to figure out that this is a that' is again a matter of broadening one's inductive base, of the learner sizing up situations in terms of past experience plus some imaginative and affective feel for how it is related to what is at hand. It is significant that Aristotle describes this process as *sullogizesthai*. It is itself a kind of critical activity which, in the case of action, precedes the practical inference (*sullogismos* or deliberation) about what to do. As we have described it in earlier chapters, it involves a discerning of the particulars, a reading of the situation in terms of salient considerations. As such it is a reasoning that is non-procedural; it is a 'figuring out' by 'improvising' (1106b15), by remaining close to and affected by the concrete details.

The discrimination of ethical relevance will ground affective responses. By tutoring the child's vision of the world, by instructing him to attend to these features rather than those, desires become focused and controlled in specific ways.

These remarks rely heavily on the account of the emotions in the *Rhetoric*. As I have hinted, what Aristotle outlines there is an intentional theory in which passions are viewed not as blind promptings and urgings that merely happen to us, but rather as selective responses to articulated features of our environment. This same sort of selectivity characterizes, on Aristotle's view, the appetites of both humans and animals. The agent moved by thirst or hunger responds cognitively to those features of the environment which can satisfy that need. Moreover, the need itself comes to be more specific and particular as it focuses on some apparent good. In this way, then, desires 'are prepared' by cognition.[10] They display an intentional character in so far as they are directed at features of situations which an agent regards in a certain light.

The intentional theory of emotion in the *Rhetoric* falls within the general aim of that book, which is to familiarize the orator with the sorts of beliefs that typically accompany the different emotions. The claim is that the orator will be effective in arousing emotions if he can bring his listeners to the appropriate beliefs. To this end, he will need to know the dispositions associated with the different emotions (*pōs diakemenoi*), their typical objects (*tisin*), and the sorts of circumstances and occasions in which they are typically manifest (*epi poiois*, 1378a22–4). So, for example, if anger is to be aroused against an opponent in court, the orator must persuade his hearer that his client has suffered gratuitously at the hands of that party. By manipulating belief and perception in this way, the rhetorician hopes to provoke a specific emotional response against a specific individual.

Within Aristotle's analysis, however, beliefs, perceptions,

---

[10] *MA* 702a18. Cf. Martha Nussbaum on a discussion of this passage in Essay 3 of her *Aristotle's De Motu Animalium* (Princeton University Press, 1978), 154 ff.

and *phantasiai* or imaginings[11] are not merely causes of emotion, but partial constituents. The definition of anger illustrates this. 'Anger is a desire [*orexis*] accompanied by pain towards the revenge of what one regards as a slight [*phainomenēn oligorian*] towards oneself or one's friends that is unwarranted' (*Rh.* 1378a30–2). Here it is clear that while emotions are expressed as feelings involving pleasure or pain,[12] these feelings are not identifiable independent of their relation to specific evaluations or beliefs constitutive of the emotion.

In addition to reactive beliefs, beliefs (and desires) about acting on an emotion will often figure in the definition and may occasion a distinct set of derivative feelings. Anger will thus include a consequent desire for revenge, the prospect (*phantasia*) of which yields pleasure (*Rh.* 1378b1–2; cf. 1370b1, 1370b29). Aristotle suggests that it is often such constitutive beliefs about goals that demarcate otherwise similar emotional responses. Spite and hubris (*epēreasmos, hubris*), for example, are forms of slighting that fall under the general definition of 'an actively held belief [*energeia doxēs*] about someone who appears to be of little worth' (1378b11); they become distinguished, however, by their goals: spite aims at thwarting another's wishes without specific advantage to oneself (1378b18–20) while hubris aims at enhancing one's self-image by proving oneself, through such slights, to be superior and more powerful (1378b27 ff.).

Emotions thus have cognitive components and are partially shaped and informed by these elements. But it would be a mistake to try to fully untangle these elements. For emotions, as we have said before, are themselves a sensitivity, a mode of discriminating and registering particulars. As such, the evaluative content of emotions may not be purely cognitive or intellectual. To respond compassionately to a loved one who is suffering may not simply be a matter of (intellectually) seeing, and feeling compassion as a result, nor conversely of seeing *because* one

---

[11] For a comprehensive discussion of *phantasia*, see Nussbaum, Essay 5 of *Aristotle's De Motu*, 221–67.

[12] Cf. *Rh.* 1378a20–1, *NE* 1105a21–3, *EE* 1220b12–14.

feels compassion, but of seeing with an intensity and resolution that is itself characterized by compassion. One would not have seen in *that* way unless one had certain feelings. The mode of seeing is distinct. Thus emotions shape and colour how and what we see just as what we see refines and shapes how and what we feel. The capacities and functions are deeply intertwined.

5. LEARNING TO SEE ARIGHT

The above remarks about the relation of discrimination to the emotions have significant consequences for the account of ethical education. Though Aristotle does not fully elaborate upon these in the text, we can allow ourselves to extrapolate in a way that is consistent with its spirit.

We should begin by asking how the perceptions constitutive of emotions, and ultimately of moral responses, become refined. The parent, like the orator, is in the position of persuading. He or she makes prescriptions to the child and the child listens out of a complex set of desires (love of parents, the desire to imitate, fear of punishment, hope of reward, etc.). But the parent aims not simply to affect specific actions or desires; e.g. to thwart greed, to encourage compassion, to temper anger. Rather, part of what the parent tries to do is to bring the child to see the particular circumstances that here and now make certain emotions appropriate. The parent helps the child to compose the scene in the right way. This will involve persuading the child that the situation at hand is to be construed in this way rather than that, that what the child took to be a deliberate assault and cause for anger was really only an accident, that the laughter and smiles which annoy were intended as signs of delight rather than of teasing, that a particular distribution, though painful to endure, is in fact fair—that if one looked at the situation from the point of view of the others involved, one would come to that conclusion.

These examples illustrate that the child is not an empty box in which beliefs are instilled, but an individual who has, to a greater or lesser degree, already formed certain construals and judgements, which become adjusted and revised through interaction with an adult. Education is thus a matter of bringing the child to more critical discriminations. The Aristotelian presupposition is that the ability to discriminate is already there and in evidence, as is an interest and delight in improvement. What is required is a shifting of beliefs and perspectives through the guidance of an outside instructor. Such guidance cannot merely be a matter of bringing the child to see this way now, but of providing some sort of continuous and consistent instruction which will allow for the formation of patterns and trends in what the child notices and sees.

This emphasis on the internal process must be central to education in a way that it remains at best peripheral to rhetoric. Though the educator persuades and exhorts, the goal is not to *manipulate* beliefs and emotions—to influence an outcome here and now—but to prepare the learner for eventually arriving at competent judgements and reactions on his own. Any method which secures rational obedience must at the same time encourage the child's own development. This implies that the child borrows the eyes of wisdom (1144b10-12), 'listens to the words of elders and of the more experienced' (1143b11-13), not passively but in a way that actively engages his own critical capacities. Accordingly, Aristotle would probably object to the practice of the parent who says, 'Do this, don't do that' without further descriptions or explanations. The child can legitimately ask 'why', and some description and explanation will be in order. What is required is some dialogue and verbal exchange about what one sees (and feels) and should see (and feel); in other words, actual descriptions which articulate a way of perceiving the situation and which put into play the relevant concepts, considerations and emotions (see *Pol.* 1253a12). I take something like this to be a part of the sort of reasoned 'admonition' and 'exhortation' by which parents guide children (*NE* I. 13, 1102b33-1103a1).[13]

---

[13] Cf. *Pol.* 1260b6-8, which qualifies this picture and seems to run counter to the spirit of *NE* I. 13.

It seems to be an essential part of how we train sensitive discernment of the particulars. Within this Aristotle can no doubt say, as we do, that there are many proscriptions that the child cannot understand until later and many partial explanations that will have to suffice until then. Nothing I have said would require a claim to the contrary. The point is the much more modest one: that emotions cannot be shaped without some simultaneous cultivation of discriminatory abilities. This is included as a part of habituation. It is a part of coming to have the right pleasures and pains.

Perhaps more than Aristotle suggests, we should not assume that the direction of exchange flows solely from parent to child, for the child's vision may sometimes instruct the adult's. What the child sees so clearly and compellingly may be obfuscated in the adult by more tutored and abstract perceptions. In particular, the child's emotional vulnerability may make him alive to concerns the adult only inadequately or too dispassionately notices. Thus Aristotle himself remarks in the *Rhetoric* that youth often 'prefer to do what is fine over what is advantageous, for they live more by their characters and emotions [*ēthei*] than by reasoning and calculation [*logismōi*]' (1389a32–5).

And so it is often the child who sees through his emotions, and who can attend to others in a way that is intense and empathic.[14] The child's example is an instructive reminder that we as adults may be at peril of losing our emotions, of over-intellectualizing them, of so protecting them that they become robbed of their spontaneity and candour. It suggests that there is something to be preserved in the child's emotional vulnerability, some (natural) virtue in the child's intense emotional responses that efforts at moderation must not eradicate.

There is good reason to believe Aristotle would applaud educational efforts that respected this resource. We have just noted a suggestion from the *Rhetoric* in this direction. In a passage which follows on the one quoted (and which we will discuss at greater length later), the claim is more

---

14 See *Rh.* I. 12 on the emotional intensity (and excess) of children's responses.

direct. Here Aristotle contends that the elderly no longer
live by their emotions, that, hardened by life's misfortunes,
they have made themselves invulnerable: 'And they neither
can love intensely or hate intensely, but as proposed by
Bias, they both love as though they are about to hate, and
hate as though they are about to love' (1389b23-5). This is
clearly not meant as praise, but as a stern warning against
what can happen when we stray too far from more candid,
less protected responses. Virtuous activity falls short if, in
the end, it disregards the passions, if behaviour fails to
evidence the proper feelings and sentiments in addition to
the proper actions and beliefs.

6. LEARNING TO MAKE CHOICES

We have been focusing on the training of desire and the
role of perception and belief in this training. The training
of the non-rational part thus has an essential cognitive
dimension. But in what sense is the rational part itself
cultivated? In what sense do deliberative capacities become
trained? As we said earlier, the child is, on Aristotle's view,
incapable of the sort of reasoned choices, or *prohaireseis*,
that characterize mature virtue. This, however, will not bar
the child from all deliberation. The child is capable of
voluntary choices which may require a certain level of
simple means–end reasoning and specification of ends. Also,
to the extent that realization of an end requires various
steps, the end may set up a certain agenda to be achieved
in time. All this we referred to in Chapter 3 as the simple
model of planning. But what the child is excluded from—
at least the child whose deliberative capacities are still quite
immature—is the sort of 'all things considered' judgement
that comes with prohairetic reasoning. This will include, as
we detailed in Chapter 3, an evaluation of alternative means
as well as an assessment of ends in the light of other ends
which might take priority. It is to judge an action best,
given an agent's *overall* objectives and beliefs. This may
further entail a revamping of acquired ends, in the light of
considerations of fit and specific convictions. Now it seems

eminently reasonable to assume that a child's rational capacities are not yet ready for this level of deliberation. As Aristotle conceives such deliberation, it shares much in common with the dialectical reasoning characteristic of the mature student engaged in justifying an account of good living.[15] Still, if, as I have contended in this chapter, we need to make some sense of a transition to full rationality, then there must be a time when, in the more mature youth, these rational capacities are cultivated.

In a complete scheme, experience in this more complex sort of choice-making will constitute a later stage of development. It will precede the emergence of mature virtue and presuppose the sort of sensitive judgement and emotional response of the person who has been trained to notice the circumstances of moral action. But this is to recognize that even at the more intermediate stages of becoming virtuous, the learner does not simply perform some action-type, as one perhaps does in developing a skill, but *reacts* to the circumstances, and then *decides* how to act. This is itself a part of making voluntary, intentional choices. There is judgement and decision, even if not reflective evaluation (or justification) of the choice. To gain practice in the relevant actions is to come to work out, with appropriate guidance and models, what to do. For the more mature youth whose deliberative capacities are actively developing, the choice will be reflective and subject to rational justification. It will take into account the more complex and competing factors that need to be weighed in the balance, and represent a judgement as to what is best in the light of these varied factors. Practice in action is eventually, at the later stages, practice in choice-making of this sort.

But here it is important to remember that for full virtue, Aristotle requires not merely that actions be 'chosen' in the above sense, but that they be chosen for their own sakes. Thus, in a passage in *NE* II. 4, which we will be returning to again, Aristotle notes that there are three conditions of

---

[15] I defended this line of interpretation in the introductory chapter. It is developed with considerable insight by Henry Richardson in his 'Rational Deliberation of Ends', Ph.D. thesis (Harvard University, 1986).

mature virtue: first, the virtuous agent must act knowingly; second, he must choose virtuous acts and choose them for their own sakes (*prohairoumenos di' auta*); and third, he must act from a firm and unchanging character (1105a30–4). I wish to focus on the second condition. As I have said before, virtuous actions have, in some important sense, external ends. Generosity aims at alleviating need, temperance aims at health, battlefield courage aims at victory and, perhaps ultimately, peace. The actions are ameliorative and aim at certain external conditions which are valued within a human life. But, as Aristotle implies above, to be fully virtuous is not simply to choose actions which will tend to promote those ends. In addition, and perhaps more importantly, it is to find the actions which promote these ends, themselves valuable. Thus, while the actions derive their original value from external ends, in time it is the actions themselves that come to be valued.[16] They come to constitute their own ends. To act for the sake of the fine is just this: to value the actions which express virtue, even if these actions do not ultimately achieve their planned goals. From the point of view of cultivating virtue, the claim is that learning virtue is more than learning balanced deliberation, more than learning how to make certain general ends, such as peace and welfare, one's target. In addition, it is learning to value the actions which realize these ends, and the sort of person who reliably performs them. This, it is Aristotle's claim, cannot be learned apart from actual practice in virtuous action.

7. HABITUATION AS CRITICAL PRACTICE

With these considerations as background, we are now in a position to interpret Aristotle's more explicit and well-known remarks about habituation. Character, on Aristotle's view, is the acquisition of states (*hexeis*) through habituation

---

[16] For an illuminating discussion of this issue, see Eugene Garver, 'Aristotle's Genealogy of Morals', *Philosophy and Phenomenological Research*, 44 (1984), 471–92.

(*ethismos*). The process of habituation involves essentially practice and repetition:

Now character [*ēthos*], as the word itself indicates, is that which is developed from habit [*ethos*]; and anything is habituated which, as a result of guidance which is not innate, through being changed a certain way repeatedly [*pollakis*], is eventually capable of acting in that way (*EE* 1220a39-b3, tr. Woods; cf. *Pol.* 1332b1 ff.)[17]

As Aristotle says more simply in the *Rhetoric*: 'Acts are done from habit because individuals have done them many times before' (1369b6). Through repetition an acquired capacity becomes almost natural, or second nature: 'For as soon as a thing becomes habituated it is virtually natural. For habit is similar to nature. For what happens often is akin to what happens always, natural events happening always, habitual events being frequent and repeated' (*Rh.* 1370a6; cf. *Mem.* 452a27).

Excellence of character or virtue, according to the above picture, is contrasted with abilities (*dunameis*) which are innate, which cannot be changed through habituation (*EE* 1220b4, *NE* 1103a20-3) and which exist prior to rather than consequent upon practice. This obviously does not entail that virtue will be independent of antecedent affective and cognitive capacities (1103a26-32). The point is rather that these are merely indeterminate capacities, not latent *dunameis* for virtue.

Character states thus arise through the sorts of activities that are involved in their exercise. This is the explicit point of a celebrated, though insufficiently analysed, passage from the *Nicomachean Ethics*:

We acquire the virtues by first acting just as we do in the case of acquiring crafts. For we learn a craft by making the products which we must make once we have learned the craft, for example, by building, we become builders, by playing the lyre, lyre players. And so too we become just by doing just actions, and temperate by doing temperate actions and brave by brave actions ... and in a word, states of character are formed out of corresponding acts. (1103a31-b21; cf. 1105a14, *EE* 1220a32)

[17] *Aristotle's Eudemian Ethics*, Books I, II, and VIII, tr. Michael Woods (Oxford University Press, 1982).

But to say that we become just by doing just actions is to abbreviate a whole series of steps. As we have seen, action presupposes the discrimination of a situation as requiring a response, reactive emotions that mark that response, and desires and beliefs about how and for the sake of what ends one should act. We misconstrue Aristotle's notion of action producing character if we isolate the exterior moment of action from the interior cognitive and affective moments which characterize even the beginner's ethical behaviour.

These remarks prepare us for an understanding of the notion of repetition implicit in Aristotle's conception of habituation. Aristotle would clearly agree with the old saw that 'practice makes perfect',[18] that we become better at something by doing it repeatedly and persistently. But what is the real content of this sort of phrase? For one thing, to repeat cannot really mean to do the same action over and over again. Various considerations are pertinent here. First, as we said above, there is no external husk of all just actions that we can isolate and repeatedly practise. Any just action will be contextually defined and will vary considerably, in terms of judgement, emotion, and behaviour, from other just actions. It would be absurd to demand (and certainly run counter to the spirit of Aristotle's inquiry) some extractable piece of behaviour, training in which could form character.

Second, even if we take up the more straightforward case of practising a skill where there is some isolatable sequence of steps, repetition of that sequence cannot involve doing the same action, if by that is meant doing just what one did before. For repeating in that way seems to ensure that one will stay in a rut, do the same thing over and over again (mistakes included), rather than show improvement or progress. Indeed, it seems to make progress impossible.

A more plausible conception of repeating the same action, again within the simplified skill analogy, will involve trying to approximate some ideal action type that has been set as one's goal. Learning through repetition will be then a matter

---

[18] For an illuminating discussion of this old saw which has influenced my remarks, see Vernon A. Howard's *Artistry: The Work of Artists* (Hackett, 1982), 157–88.

of successive trials that vary from one another as they approach this ideal way of acting. In each successive attempt, constant awareness of the goal is crucial, just as measuring how nearly one has reached it or by how much one has fallen short is important for the next trial. The practice is more a refinement of actions through successive trials than a sheer mechancial repetition of any one action.

On this view, then, practice achieves progress to the extent that repetition is critical. Whether the states to be acquired be primarily physical, intellectual, or emotional, and concerning *technē* or character, the rehearsal requisite for acquiring them must involve the employment of critical capacities, such as attending to a goal, recognizing mistakes and learning from them, understanding instructions, following tips and cues, working out how to adapt a model's example to one's own behaviour.

In the case of virtue, the practice of actions will obviously be more complex. Virtuous action, as we have said, will combine a judgement of circumstances, reactive emotions, and some level of decision about how to act. Here too the learner will follow the examples of emulated models, and may have in mind general precepts and rules of thumb. Following models and bringing to mind the appropriate precepts will in itself require cognitive skills. But these alone will be insufficient without the sort of imagination and sensitivity requisite for knowing how a type of action and dispositional response translate to the situation at hand. Becoming sensitive to the circumstances in which action is called for as well as flexible in one's conception of the requirements of a precept is all part of practising virtuous action.

The notion of critical practice is already implicit in Aristotle's discussion of habituation at *NE* II. 1. We learn how to play the lyre, he says, by practising not merely with persistence, but with an eye toward how the expert plays and with attention to how our performance measures against that model. Without the instructions and monitoring of a reliable teacher, a student can just as easily become a bad lyre player as a good one:

Again, just as in the case of the crafts, the same causes and means that produce each virtue also destroy it. For playing the lyre produces both good and bad lyre players. And analogously, this is so for builders and all the rest; for building well makes good builders while building poorly makes bad builders. For if this were not so there would be need of no teacher. (1103b7-12; cf. 1104a27, 1105a14, *EE* 1220a32)

At issue here is how we make determinate more indeterminate capacities and actions. Since the capacities are not latent excellences, a teacher must be on hand to direct the progress. (This falls within Aristotle's general theory of *dunameis* at *Meta.* IX. 2 and 5 in which rational capacities—understood broadly as those which are not physical and as such do not have fixed ends—can produce contrary ends or effects. To produce one effect rather than another, desire or rational choice must guide the exercise of the capacity; *Meta.* 1046b1 ff., 1048a8-12.) In the case of virtue, unlike skill, it is more difficult to speak of a neutral action which is at once the means for virtuous or vicious action. The action cannot be separated from its end in this way.[19] Even so, occasions may be viewed in some sense as neutral, as being opportunities either for the development of a particular virtue or for its ruin, just as more basic abilities or dispositions can. So, Aristotle continues, just as danger is a moment for cowardice or bravery (*NE* 1103b16), so appetites and anger are at once the basis for temperance and gentleness or for indulgence and irascibility. The role of the tutor in helping us to see and respond aright is even more urgent here.

There are further sources of evidence in Aristotle's writing that support a critical conception of practice. The first requires looking again to the example of *technē* and to Aristotle's belief that to have *technē* is to have a skill that its possessor can teach to others. The claim now is not that beginners must have teachers, but that anyone who has

---

[19] This is the point of an otherwise obscure remark Aristotle makes at *NE* 1140b2 ff.: 'And the person who voluntarily errs with respect to *technē* is more desirable than the person who voluntarily errs with respect to practical reason and similarly the virtues.' The idea, I believe, is that whereas it may be desirable to use a particular *technē* for a non-standard end (as when a tennis coach uses his skill to demonstrate how to hit a bad forehand shot), it is less desirable to 'misuse' virtue. Indeed it is unlikely that full virtue *can* be misused.

sufficiently learned a skill must himself be (capable of being) a teacher of it. Thus, Aristotle argues that possessing *technē* differs from the possession of less systematic experience (*Meta.* 981b7–10), just as for Plato it differed from the possession of a mere knack.[20] The capacity to formulate and teach a skill might thus require precisely defined procedural rules, or, what is pedagogically more plausible, a looser set of critical cues and hints as to how to proceed at each stage.[21] Though we would probably want to distance ourselves from Aristotle here and argue that even the latter condition is too strong a requirement for possessing a *technē*, its inclusion is still indirect evidence for the view that practice involves an awareness of what one is doing; for in order to teach others one must be aware of how one achieves certain ends. That awareness is deepened in the novice by attentiveness to the cues and comments of the expert, and in the expert, by the very process of formulating what one understands more implicitly.

Ethical action will not, of course, be procedural (*NE* 1140b22–5; cf. 1105a28–b4). Accordingly, cues and tips will not be expressive of some more systematic, long-hand rules that a teacher can pass on to others. Even so, explicit teaching must take place, as we have argued above; but what is passed on will be ways of reacting, seeing, and understanding which will aim at establishing enduring patterns of action.

Significantly, Aristotle's views about musical education (*Pol.* VIII) support the same general picture of critical practice. Though we cannot address here, in any detail, the complex issues of ancient music or chronicle its time-honoured place in traditional *paideia*,[22] a few brief remarks

---

[20] Cf. *Gorgias* 465a, and *Meta.* 981a25–31: 'And in general it is a sign of the man who knows and of the man who does not know, that the former can teach, and therefore we think craft more truly knowledge than experience is; for craftsmen can teach, and men of experience cannot.'

[21] Cf. Howard's excellent illustration, in *Artistry*, 9–116, of the language of coaching used in teaching singing.

[22] Though *Pol.* VIII is the primary source for Aristotle's views on the place of music in education, additional remarks in *Poet.* 1447a18–b9 enhance the picture. Aristotle says here that *mimēsis* is produced in 'rhythm, speech, and melody, and in these either separately or mixed together . . . flute and lyre playing, for example,

should shed some light on the way in which music figures
in Aristotle's own account. Training in music involves
essentially, for Aristotle as for Plato, a mimetic enactment
of poetry, song, and dance. (Thus the Greek term *mousikē*
is only imprecisely translated by our term 'music'.) The
performance is typically with accompaniment on lyre or
aulos and is set to specific, highly conventionalized musical
modes (*harmoniai*) meant to 'express' the character or mood
of the individuals depicted in the poetic text. Hence the
modes are said by Aristotle to be ethical (i.e. to convey
character). And the learner's mimetic enactment of them
(through performance) is a way of coming to feel from the
inside the relevant qualities of character and emotion. It is
an emulative and empathetic kind of identification. Together
with the positive reinforcement that comes from pleasure
music naturally gives, the mimetic enactment will constitute
an habituation, an *ethismos*:

And since music happens to be a kind of pleasure, and virtue is

using melody and rhythm alone'; dancers use rhythm alone for 'through the
rhythm of the dance figures, they imitate character, emotions, and actions'. On
difficulties in interpreting this passage, see Gerald Else, *Aristotle's Poetics: The
Argument* (Harvard University Press, 1967), 17 ff. As regards the ethical character
of music, the pseudo-Aristotelian remarks in *Problemata* IX. 27 are suggestive:
'And in its rhythm and in its arrangement of high and low sounds, melody has a
similarity to character ... And the motions [of sounds] are connected with
practical action, and actions are signs of character' (919b26-37). For a detailed
study of the place of music in Aristotle's educational curriculum, see Carnes Lord,
Education and Culture.
   On the general subject of ancient music, scholarly study is extensive, and I
shall restrict myself to mentioning only a handful of works that are directly related
to the issues raised above. (A more extensive discussion of the literature, and of
the issues Aristotle himself raises, can be found in my Ph.D. thesis, 'Aristotle's
Theory of Moral Education' (Harvard University, 1982), ch. 4. There I discuss
also the conception of *mimēsis* in tragedy.) First, there are the classic studies of
D. B. Monro, *The Modes of Ancient Greek Music* (Oxford University Press, 1894),
and R. P. Winnington-Ingram, *Mode in Ancient Greek Music* (Cambridge
University Press, 1936). More recent discussions are provided by Donald Jay
Grout, *A History of Western Music* (Norton, 1973), 27-34, and Warren D.
Anderson, *Ethos and Education in Greek Music* (Harvard University Press, 1968).
Most recent is the comprehensive and penetrating study of ancient music
undertaken by Andrew Barker, *Greek Musical Writings*, i. *The Musician and His
Art* (Cambridge University Press, 1984) in which the author systematically
compiles Greek writings on music and musical theory. On the subject of *mimēsis*,
I have learned greatly from Göran Sörbom, *Mimesis and Art: Studies in the Origin
and Early Development of an Aesthetic Vocabulary* (Scandinavian University Books,

concerned with proper enjoyment and loving and hating rightly, it is clear that there is nothing more necessary to learn and to become habituated in [*sunethizesthai*] than judging rightly and delighting in good characters and fine actions. Rhythm and melody provide keen likenesses of anger and gentleness, and also of courage and temperance and of all the opposites of these and of all the other states of character. (This is clear from experience. For in listening to such music, our souls undergo a change.) And becoming habituated to feeling pain and delight in likenesses is close to feeling the same way towards the things that are their models. (*Pol.* 1340a15-28)

The idea, then, is that music provides the child with exemplars of character, and allows the child to feel 'from within' what the emotions and actions of such characters are like. All this is complex and needs a fuller account within a theory of mimetic education. What I wish to stress here is Aristotle's own insistence that mimetic education requires not merely that the child cultivate the mimetic powers of an *audience*, but that the child be trained as a *performer*, as someone who himself must act and practise (*Pol.* VIII. 6, esp. 1340b20-1341b15). And this, Aristotle insists, is precisely that those who are to judge and delight correctly (*krinein kai chairein orthōs*) in fine actions and characters must practise such actions themselves, making the sorts of judgements and coming to have the sorts of emotional responses that are appropriate to the characters. Thus, Aristotle says, 'it is impossible or at least difficult for those who do not themselves perform to be good judges of others' (1340b24-5). His principal point is *not* that they will be bad *aesthetic* critics. That may be true too. What he means, rather, is that they will be inadequately prepared to judge *ethical* character, in literature and in real life. For they will not have learned first hand, through their own critical attempts at *mimēsis*, what sorts of emotions and responses characterize different sorts of states.

1966). Finally, of related interest is Plato's theory of art and poetry; for a lively analysis that also illuminates more general issues about the role of poetry in ancient Greece, see Giovanni Ferrari, 'Plato and Poetry', in *Cambridge History of Literary Criticism*, i (Cambridge University Press, 1987).

8. THE PLEASURE INTRINSIC TO PRACTICE

Additional direct and compelling evidence for the notion
of critical practice comes from Aristotle's remarks about
the relation of practice to the pleasure consequent upon it.
On Aristotle's view, practice would be neither necessary
nor sufficient for acquiring states and abilities if it did not
yield derivative pleasures. For it is the pleasure proper to
a particular activity that impels us to perform that activity
the next time with greater discrimination and precision:

> For the pleasure proper to an activity increases that activity. For
> those who perform their activities with pleasure judge better and
> discern with greater precision each thing, e.g. those finding
> pleasure in geometry become geometers, and understand the
> subject-matter better, and similarly also, lovers of music, lovers
> of building and so on, make progress [*epididoasin*] in their
> appropriate function when they enjoy it. (1175a29–35; cf. 1175a36–
> b24, 1175b13–15, 1105a3–7)

Conversely, the pain derivative upon an activity impedes
progress, just as alien pleasures from other activities distract
from an appreciation of the activity at hand (1175b16–23).

More precisely, upon what does this pleasure depend?
On the interpretation I shall offer, pleasure not only issues
in but arises from discriminatory activity.[23] The model I
ascribe to Aristotle is thus that of a chain of activities which
increase in discriminated complexity as well as in derivative
pleasures. On this model practice yields pleasure to the
extent to which practice itself is critical. And pleasure, in
turn, yields further critical activity.

These claims require further examination of Aristotle's
account of pleasure. According to a unified account of
pleasure in *NE* VII and X, pleasure is the perfect actualization of a state or faculty of the soul in good condition
exercised upon appropriate objects (1174b14–1175a2).[24] It

---

[23] Although David Charles emphasizes only the first half of the process, his
account, I believe, is essentially compatible with mine; cf. *Aristotle's Philosophy
of Action* (Cornell University Press, 1984), 182–3.

[24] This is a highly complex issue which I cannot take up here. Very briefly,
the account is unified if we consider the perfection of activity at 1174b31 not to
be something over and above the activity. In this way the notions of pleasure as
unimpeded activity (*NE* VII) and as perfection of activity (*NE* X) both define

is activity that is unimpeded (1153a15), that is, without the impediments either of a defective nature or of external goods inadequate for the full exercise of a state. Thus, the pleasure of seeing requires both that the natural faculty of eyesight be in good condition and that it be exercised upon the finest perceptible objects (1174b15 ff.). Similarly, the pleasure which arises from virtuous activity (1104b3 ff.) is the pleasure of realizing a virtuous state without either internal impediments (i.e. insufficient or conflicting motivation) or external obstacles. In this way, the pleasure of virtue falls under the general account of the pleasure of excellent activity.

But there is an immediate problem. On this general view, the pleasure derived from a particular activity depends upon the capacities for that activity being well-developed and mature. Pleasure as perfect actualization requires a well-developed nature. But if this is so, then the account makes very puzzling the role of pleasure in learning virtue. For pleasure seems to arise only when a state is fully developed, and not when it is becoming so.

One reply to this objection is that this account of pleasure is consistent with the motivational role of pleasure at 1175a29-b24 in the following restricted way: the progress the geometer makes when he experiences pleasure in his activity involves the realization of an already acquired state or capacity in more precise and complex ways. Genuine development and improvement are involved here, though not the sort involved in initially acquiring a state.[25] Progress in the sense of refinement of an already existent state seems to be what Aristotle has in mind at 1172a12-15 when he says virtuous persons become better (*beltious*) through the company of virtuous friends. Although the virtuous person has already acquired a stable and firm character, that

---

pleasure as a form of activity. On Gosling's view, in particular, pleasure as the perfection of actualization is not additional to the fully actualized state, but its formal cause. J. G. B. Gosling and C. C. W. Taylor, *The Greeks on Pleasure* (Oxford University Press, 1982), 253.

[25] In *DA* II. 1 Aristotle refers to the realization and cultivation of such a state through activity as its second actuality. The first actuality of an organism is the acquired, non-active state, which will itself be the actualization of some more basic potentiality.

character is capable of further development and improvement through the activities of friendship.

But can pleasure attach to a broader notion of development, in particular one which includes the acquisition and habituation of states, such as virtue? If so, pleasure would arise not only from the exercise of developed capacities and states upon appropriate objects, but from the activity or practice which constitutes their development. Such pleasure derivative upon practice would be the pleasure of an imperfect actualization, imperfect not because of external impediments (though these might exist), but because of an imperfect state.

A preliminary answer to the above questions depends upon how we understand imperfect. On Aristotle's view a state or capacity may be defective in several ways. The state or capacity might be impaired temporarily, as in the case of an individual for whom sweet things taste bitter because of a cold; or impaired permanently, either because of some natural shortcoming, as in the case of those whose reason will always lack authority, or because of an irreversible illness, as in the case of those who cannot see in the light because of opthalmia; or impaired because it is not yet fully developed, as in the case of the (male) child. In this last case, although an individual's activities are imperfect, with the right opportunities and objects they can come to approximate the full potentialities of the species. The pleasure of this imperfect actualization is a real pleasure, that is, a pleasure specific to the capacities of a human being, though a pleasure lesser in degree than that of the most perfect actualization.

Aristotle raises the notion of degrees of pleasure in *NE* X. 4:

Hence for each faculty the best activity is the activity of the subject in the best condition in relation to the best object of the faculty. This activity will also be the most complete and the pleasantest. For every faculty of perception, and every sort of thought and study, has its pleasure; the pleasantest activity is the most complete; and the most complete is the activity of the subject in good condition in relation to the most excellent object of the faculty. (1174b18-24; tr. Irwin)

Exercise of the perceptual and critical faculties appears to admit of degrees. The more complete the actualization, the pleasanter the activity. But within that continuum, even the learner gains pleasure from the exercise of his abilities. The point is reminiscent of Aristotle's comment in *Poet.* IV, discussed earlier, that learning is pleasant not only to the philosopher but to all, whatever their capacity for it.

Our earlier problem still seems to remain, however: Aristotle's example at *NE* 1174b20 is of the individual who comes to use his perceptual faculties in more and more discriminating ways. Yet according to 1103a26-31, perceptual capacities, unlike states of virtue, exist antecedent to practice. Consequently, the pleasures derivative upon such activity do not refer to the process of habituation or acquisition, but once again to the process of actualizing an already existent state.

But does Aristotle ever relax the distinction between activities that engender states and activities that actualize states that are already formed? I shall argue that in a limited sense, he does.

At *NE* II. 4, after outlining his doctrine of habituation as the acquisition of states through corresponding actions, Aristotle raises the following puzzle familiar to readers of the *Nicomachean Ethics*: 'The question might be asked, what we mean by saying that we must become just by doing just acts, and temperate by doing temperate acts; for if men do just and temperate acts, they are already just and temperate' (1105a17-20).[26] His solution in Book II is precisely to differentiate habituating actions from actualizations. Both actions will concern the same sorts of circumstances and external requirements (1104a28-b5), but the actions of the novice will lack the full structure of motives and reasons characteristic of the person who already has a stable character (1105a29-35).

But in *Meta.* IX. 8 Aristotle offers a different solution to a related (though distinct) problem. Here he describes a puzzle about the acquisition of craft knowledge:

---

[26] There is of course the related paradox of learning in the *Meno*: in order to inquire about things we do not yet know, we must already know them.

This is why it is thought impossible to be a housebuilder if one has built nothing or a lyre player if one has never played the lyre; for the individual who learns to play the lyre learns to play by playing it, and similarly in the case of all other learners. And so arose the sophistical puzzle, that one who does not possess a knowledge will none the less be producing the object of that knowledge: for he who is learning it does not possess it. But since, of that which is coming to be, some part must have come to be, and, of that which in general is changing, some part must have changed (this will be clear in the case of change) so, equally, the one who is learning must, it would seem, possess some part of the knowledge he is learning. (1049b28–1050a2)

The force of Aristotle's remarks is to show that the learner, even at the very beginning stages of his apprenticeship, is already acquiring some of what the expert has. And to the extent that he is, he will receive the pleasures consequent upon exercising those states. Though no one would seriously hold that the apprentice becomes an expert in an instant, Aristotle goes to some pains here to make explicit the general sort of incremental process that must be involved.

Now the acquisition of craft knowledge, Aristotle insists, is distinct from the acquisition of character, so a solution to one sort of puzzle will not necessarily be a solution to another. Thus, shortly after Aristotle raises the ethical puzzle in *NE* II. 4, he distinguishes the case of the crafts and the virtues. I quote a passage to which we have already referred:

But the case of the crafts and the virtues is not similar. For the products of the crafts have their goodness in themselves, so that it is enough that they should have a certain character when they are produced. But it is not true that if acts in accordance with virtue have themselves a certain character they will be done justly or temperately. The one who does them must also be in the right state of character when he acts. First, he must act knowingly, second, he must choose the acts, choosing them for their own sakes, and third, he must act from a firm and unchanging character. Except for the knowing, these conditions are not required for possessing a craft. But in the case of the virtues, the knowing has little or no weight, while the other two conditions count not for a little, but for everything. (1105a25–b3)

These remarks should serve to remind us once again of the limitations of Aristotle's own analogies between craft and virtue acquisition. The difference, Aristotle suggests here, is that acquiring an art, such as grammar, will be primarily a matter of internalizing certain procedural principles and producing a product that embodies that procedure (or knowledge). Virtue, on the other hand, will be a matter not of learning implicit procedures, but of having reliable motives, expressed in chosen actions which come to have intrinsic value. The actions will not be chosen by procedure, nor will what is brought about valued apart from the actions which realize it.

Now habituating ethical action will not, at least at the early stages, meet these conditions. The learner's temperate actions may be directed at health, but the motive will neither be reliable nor the actions themselves chosen as a valued way of living. In a more dramatic way than in the case of the crafts, there may be qualitative differences between what the learner and the expert possesses; the development may be less smooth or continuous. This seems to be so simply in virtue of the fact that prohairetic capacities develop late. Even so, it can none the less be argued that what the learner does gain through habituating actions is not something externally necessary to full virtue, but itself a *part* (albeit an imperfect or not fully developed part) of what virtue is. To become aware of the circumstances necessary for the specific virtues, and to begin to form the right sorts of emotional responses and decisions for action, is itself a part of having virtue. It is not simply preparation for virtue, but doing something of what virtue requires. It might be in this way that we can make sense of the idea of pleasure which comes with learning virtue: though the habituating action is not itself an exercise of a perfected state, it is none the less an exercise of a part of virtue, and yields pleasure to the extent to which it develops that part. (Perhaps the case of convalescence and its pleasures (1154b14–21, 1152b34 ff.) provides a partial analogy for the pleasure of an imperfect character state. In both cases, some small part of the person continues to exist—i.e. the healthy part or the part that has the potential to develop—the activity of which is the proper focus of the non-accidental pleasure of 'getting better' or 'developing'.[27] In the case of virtue, pleasure increases as the character state develops.)

This notion of degrees of pleasure[28] also offers the most natural reading of Aristotle's general view that moral habituation is the cultivation of fine (or noble) pleasures and pains. As already quoted: 'We need to be brought up, right from early youth, as Plato says, to find enjoyment and pain in the right things' (1104b11-13, cf. 1105a3-8). By this remark, Aristotle might mean no more than that a student comes to enjoy the intrinsic pleasures of virtuous activity through essentially external pleasures and pains; the association of virtue with reward, and vice with reproof and castigation, makes virtue derivatively pleasant and vice, painful. As suggested earlier, this will be a part of Aristotle's account (cf. 1104b16-18). In general, he argues, the difficulty of learning virtue requires that the process be sweetened in various ways. Music serves this instrumental role in early *paideia* because of its natural pleasure and appeal for children (*Pol.* 1340b15-19). In a somewhat more complex way, the special affection children have for their parents makes the family a privileged and effective environment for ethical learning (*NE* VIII. 12; 1180b3-12).

But this conception of external pleasures and pains cannot exhaust Aristotle's notion of correct education. In addition there will be the intrinsic pleasure of approximating to virtue through action and emotion. Without some such notion, the idea of valuing virtuous action for its own sake would be curious indeed.

9. PRACTICE INCLUDES EXPERIENCE

To summarize, then, good character arises through the sorts of judgements, emotions, and actions which approximate to

---

[27] The analogy was suggested to me by David Charles.

[28] Gosling and Taylor detect in Aristotle's writings the notion of a continuum of activity whereby human beings approximate the most perfect activity of divine beings (*The Greeks on Pleasure*, 249). They cite *Meta.* 1072b13-30, *NE* 1154b24-8, 1178b7-28 in support of their case. Yet Aristotle's remarks elsewhere about

the virtuous person's behaviour. Practice takes place not in a vacuum, but in response to the requirements of highly concrete, practical situations. A by-product of this sort of habituation, or what I have dubbed critical practice, is a sense of pleasure which stimulates further growth.

Aristotle's account, it should be obvious by now, is antithetical to any view which regards character as the maturation of internal capacities independent of significant interaction with the environment.[29] While Aristotle has a notion of natural virtues (i.e. the innate proclivity in some towards temperance, justice, courage, etc.), these are isolated capacities, he insists, which do not imply the presence of the other virtues (1144b33-1145a3), and which in the absence of proper habituation and guidance can lead to considerable harm (1144b8-14).

One final way of focusing on the conception of critical practice is by examining Aristotle's notion of experience (*empeiria*). I shall consider it first in relation to notions of inquiry and explanation, and second in relation to the experience of failure and disappointment.

Experience, Aristotle instructs us in *Meta. A* and *Po. An.* II. 19, is connected memory of a number of (perceived) instances of a particular sort of event: 'And in the case of human beings, experience arises from memory. For many memories of the same things make up a single experience' (*Meta.* 980b29-981a2; cf. *Po. An.* 99b35-100a8). The definition is clearly limited, for experience is not merely a way of remembering the past or of forming concepts on the basis of past impressions, but a way of managing the future in the light of the past; that is, it organizes the past (our past feelings, perceptions, and beliefs) in such a way that we gain a familiarity (*sunētheia*) and imaginative feel (*phantasia*) for what may lie ahead. It thus steers us in our future encounters. The remarks that follow make this clear (*Meta.* 981a12-24). For Aristotle goes on to show that experience is displayed in our ability to recognize (*gnōrizein*)

our composite natures and necessarily human function (especially *NE* 1178a8-b8, I. 7) suggest that the point may be less well founded.

[29] This has been taken by some to be Piaget's view. See Susan Isaacs, *Intellectual Growth in Young Children* (Routledge, 1930).

and judge the requirements of particular situations as they arise; through familiarity with individual cases, we can make informed choices.

In the *Metaphysics* and *Posterior Analytics* discussion, it is important to note, experience is a precursor to the possession of craft (*technē*) and science (*epistēmē*); in the *Nicomachean Ethics*, it is a precursor to the possession of character states and practical reason. Thus, courage at *NE* 1116b3 is 'thought to be an *empeiria* with regard to the particulars'; as in the case of soldiers' bravery, it is 'an extensive familiarity and awareness [*malista suneōrakasin houtoi*] of the many empty dangers of war' (1116b6–7).[30] Experience here is deepened not by procedure, but by a continued and fine attuning to the demands of individual cases.

Such exposure requires considerable time and living; it will be a gradual and slow process (1103a16, 1142a16). And different virtues will require familiarity with different circumstances and access to different sorts of resources. Courage will thus require opportunities for endurance of great danger; temperance will require the more ubiquitous conditions of needing to moderate bodily desires. To evince cowardice may, in this sense, be less reproachable than to be intemperate (1119a25). For complete virtue, however, sufficient exposure to the various spheres of experience will be required. And while such experience will be acquired piecemeal, it must eventually be integrated to form larger, more interlocking patterns. This will comprise the practical knowledge essential to possession of the unified virtues (1145a1).

It is important, too, to appreciate that the growth of experience requires not only that beliefs (or memories) be accumulated and consolidated, but that on occasion they be jolted—that certain connections be broken and reassessed in the light of anomalies. For the youth, this involves encounters with exceptions. These often mark a moment of puzzlement about how to proceed or understand, given

---

[30] Cf. 1115b4, 1180b18.

past experience.[31] The child learning virtue regularly encounters exceptions and limitations. Learning how and when to be generous, and under what conditions and with what sorts of means, requires the constant qualification of some less refined grasp of that virtue. So, for example, the child's desire to be generous to a friend might have to be constrained by the reminder that the intended gift has already been promised to another, or perhaps that it is not his own to give in the first place. Or the demands of fairness in playing a game might require that special feelings toward a friend be on this occasion restricted; while partiality is often not inappropriate, here and now it is. Indeed, this sort of recognition of legitimate exceptions characterizes learning virtue, at all stages.

Within Aristotle's conception of experience in *Meta. A*, this would entail that the pattern of memories constitutive of experience of a particular type of event or circumstance has become strained and requires readjustment. Though Aristotle does not explicitly develop this account of the way in which experience is extended, it is clearly consistent with the general view in *Meta. A* that the capacity to discriminate difference is a condition of having experience in the first place. The reorganization of belief in the light of perceived differences is a part of that same capacity to acquire experience.

As suggested, the discrimination of what is aberrant or different typically prompts puzzlement, or inquiry. The learner asks why her past pattern of experience cannot accommodate the present facts. Thus *aporia* leads to questioning, and the discrepancy registered in the question is resolved when some explanation or justification of the relevant difference is cited. The explanation will vary in complexity and depth, depending upon the readiness of the learner. But to what extent does Aristotle recognize this

---

[31] Cf. Isaac's moving and insightful account of a child's sense of puzzlement and curiosity in *Intellectual Growth in Young Children*. Equally moving is Gareth Mathew's account of the child's incipient philosophical temperament, in *The Young Child and Philosophy* (Harvard University Press, 1980), and *Dialogues with Children* (Harvard University Press, 1984).

sense of inquiry in the young learner? We gain some insight from the following considerations.

Aristotle's general methodology requires that in all cases in which we learn the ultimate origins or principles of a discipline we do not begin with these principles, but eventually arrive at them as part of a more advanced study. As he says, we begin with the 'that', and only later move to the 'because'. The learner, for a time, must be satisfied that something is the case, without understanding why it is so. Thus, we do not begin, in the case of the good life, with a defence of virtue, but with a commitment to it. Only later do we deepen our commitment through an understanding of why it is a defensible life:

> For which reason we must be brought up in fine habits if we are to be able to listen adequately to lectures about what is fine and just and about political matters, in general. For the starting point [*archē*] is the 'that' [*hoti*], and if this appears sufficiently clear, we will not need in addition, at this stage, the 'because' [*dioti*]. And the sort of individual who has been trained this way will have or can easily grasp the starting points and principles [*archas*]. (1095b4–8)[32]

But to postpone inquiry into the ultimate origins of a discipline is obviously not to postpone all inquiry relevant to learning the facts. As Aristotle's opening sentence makes clear, the explanation that is at issue here is of the sort that Aristotle's lectures on ethics can yield: namely, some theoretical and general account of the substantive and formal features of good living. Obviously, at the beginning the student is neither ready for this nor requires it. But to

---

[32] Cf. 1098a33 ff.: 'Nor must we demand the cause [*aitian*] in all matters alike; rather it is enough in some cases that "the that" be established well, as in the case, for example, of starting points [*archas*]. For "the that" is the first principle and is the starting point [*prōton kai archē*]. And some starting points are studied through induction, some through perception, some through habituation, and others in other ways.' The use of *archē* in this passage, and at 1095b4–8, esp. 1095b8, is systematically ambiguous. On the one hand, we inductively begin with 'the that' in order to arrive later at *archas*; on the other, 'the that' which is the starting point [*archē*] itself constitutes a first principle [*archē*]. See Grant, *The Ethics of Aristotle*, i. 304; also R. A. Gauthier and J. Y. Jolif, *Aristotle: l'Éthique à Nicomaque*, 2nd edn., ii/1 (Publications Universitaires de Louvain, 1970), 19, who speak of 'le principe-commencement'. For further discussion of *archē*, see chapter 2, n. 53.

be not yet ready for such an account in no way tells against a readiness for less complex explanations. It is no accident, then, that the passage refers back to Plato's dialectic (*Rep.* 511b) and gives a reminder (*mē lanthanetō*), in Aristotle's familiar reformulation, that in the order of learning we do not proceed from principles knowable in themselves but move inductively towards them from principles knowable to us (1095a30–b4).[33] While the person ascending will not yet grasp such ultimate principles, the Platonic model suggests a dialectical progress between having just begun the ascent and having arrived.

Within Aristotle's account, I suggest this progress involves a readiness for more partial and incomplete explanations, either that the student himself offers or that are offered by others along the way. Indeed the point of Aristotle's methodology of proceeding from what is obvious to us to what is more knowable in itself is to indicate a gap between the desire to know and the capacity to grasp an explanation adequate to the subject-matter. That gap does not preclude the utility of giving explanations, but underlines rather that a good explanation must build upon what the learner can understand. What satisfies the child without misleading will be inadequate for the adult, and vice versa.

Thus, nothing Aristotle says precludes the educational path being marked by stages of inquiry and explanation or there being an explanatory dimension to the acquiring of adequate habits. Nor is this precluded by Aristotle's pertinent remarks at *Top.* I. 11:

It is not necessary to examine every problem or thesis, but only that which puzzles [*aporēseien*] someone who requires argument and does not need castigation or lack perception. For those in doubt about whether to respect the gods and love their parents require castigation, while those who question whether snow is white lack perception. (105a3–8)

The sorts of inquiries under consideration fall into neither of these categories. The learner's questions about how to deploy ethical concepts and how to make decisions

[33] See *Phys.* 184a17–21.

appropriate to these judgements typically exhibit neither irreverence toward authority, nor ignorance of the perceptually obvious. This brings home the point that the 'why' of the student of ethics is really more a 'how': how am I to construe these events? how am I to proceed here? how is this different from circumstances I have encountered before? how, ultimately, am I to live? These are not the 'why's' of the moral sceptic, but the demands for explanation of individuals (of all ages) interested in living well.[34]

In a sense, indeed, the question never turns from 'how' to 'why', at least within Aristotle's account. That is, even when one begins to understand *why* moral virtue is a defensible good and *why* a life in which it is featured is to be preferred over other lives, the question is never asked by one who suspends belief or commitment. There is no Thrasymachus in Aristotle's story, no sceptical challenger who has not yet enlisted virtue in his life. In this ethical inquiry at least, the explanations of ultimate principles are not meant to persuade the unconverted. They presuppose and amplify a more preliminary grasp.

Perhaps the more straightforward, if less rich account comes from a related passage from the *Eudemian Ethics*:

So we must not think that the inquiry that makes clear not only the 'that' [*ti*] but also the 'why' or 'how' [*dia ti*] is superfluous even for the student of politics. For this sort of approach is the philosophical method in each discipline. But still, great caution is required here. For, because it appears to be the mark of the philosopher never to speak in an unconsidered fashion, but always with reason, there are some who often go undetected when they produce arguments that are foreign to the inquiry and idle; they do this sometimes because of ignorance, sometimes because of charlatanry; by these are caught even those who are experienced and of practical ability . . . This happens to them through lack of training [*apaideusian*]; for it is lack of training to be unable to distinguish, with regard to each subject, between those arguments which are appropriate to it and those which are foreign. (1216b35 ff.)

The virtue of this passage is that it clearly states that both

34 Cf. Burnyeat, 'Aristotle on Learning to be Good', 81.

the 'that' and the 'why' (or 'how') will be of concern to the student interested in living well, that because idle arguments can mislead even the experienced, first-hand training in the sorts of explanations relevant to ethics will be urgent. Thus if we are to become critical listeners of discourse on ethics, we must first be trained to become critical inquirers. Ethical education must, to some extent, include this training.

There is another aspect of experience which is relevant to the ethical education of the young. This is the experience of disappointment or failure. In *Rh*. II. 12 and 13 Aristotle claims that youth need a certain exposure to disappointment and misfortune in order to knock them out of their naïve trust of others and over-confidence in their abilities. His remarks emerge in the context of a rather sharp and hyperbolized comparison of youth and the elderly:

And youth trust others readily because they have not yet often been cheated; and they are optimistic . . . for they have as of yet met with few disappointments. And they live their lives for the most part in hope; for hope looks to the future and memory to the past, and for youth the future is great, the past brief . . . And they are great-souled, for they have not yet been humbled by life or learned its necessary limitations. (1389a16–31)

In general, the young are over confident about their abilities and about the goodness of others. The elderly, Aristotle goes on, err in the other extreme:

They have lived many years, and have been deceived many times and have made many mistakes . . . And they are cynical [*kakoētheis*], and this cynicism is a matter of seeing everything in the worst light. And furthermore, their experience makes them distrustful, and their distrust makes them suspicious of evil . . . And they lack confidence in the future, because of experience, for most things go wrong or at least turn out for the worse . . . And they feel pity for others, not out of kindness, as youth do, but out of weakness, for they imagine that anything that befalls anyone else might easily happen to them. (1389b13–1390a21)

Aristotle characterizes the experience of disappointment and failure as leading to cynicism. Of such disappointments, the elderly have seen too many, and youth too few. But these are two extremes, and presumably there is some middle ground between the two, such that disappointment in moderate degree has positive pedagogical value. But precisely what sort of value does it have?

In part this depends upon how we view the disappointments. If they are in fact due to outside factors which no amount of foresight or ability could have prevented (e.g. loss of friends through death, a conflict of attachments or duties, a natural disaster, monetary losses due to means fully beyond one's control, etc.), then what is to be learned is simply the natural limits of an agent, and how to come to accept these limits. On the one hand, Aristotle seems to be talking about the lessons learned from this sort of disappointment. The child needs to distinguish what is and what is not within her control, what is due to her own failure and what is due to accident and an uncooperative world. She needs to be humbled by the limits of human agency.[35] But equally Aristotle has in mind failures which, though caused by external conditions, might be avoided in the future by greater familiarity with these conditions. Youth thus have something to learn about whom to trust and whom not to trust, whom to view as good and whom to view as deceitful, which abilities of their own to rely on and which to recognize as unfit for a particular job. Their failures are in part failures of judgement which more living and experience may be able to correct. While Aristotle suggests elsewhere that adults may often be held culpable for such errors,[36] this seems unlikely in the case of children. For it simply may not be reasonable to suppose that at this point they could have known better. What we hope, rather,

[35] Thus while Aristotle optimistically suggests at *Meta.* 981a4 that experience tends to eliminate chance (thus endorsing Polus' remark that experience produces craft, but inexperience produces luck), his more systematic remarks in *Phys.* II. 4–9 rightly point out that experience cannot entirely eliminate the unexpected or unintended. If anything, as the above passage from the *Rhetoric* on youth and elderly argues, experience, in a certain way, prepares us for the unexpected. It is also important to note his remark in *Phys.* II. 6 that chance, as the unintended consequence of deliberated action, cannot be experienced by children in so far as they lack a capacity for (and presumably a conception of) a deliberated act. I shall not argue specifically against this, since the force of my general argument is to show that such an exclusion of children from rational capacities is inconsistent with Aristotle's richer account.

[36] I have in mind the discussion of *harmartēma* at *NE* 1135b17 and *Rh.* 1374b8.

is that children learn from such experience, that they judge more wisely in the future in the light of what they now know and can expect.

It should be clear by now that Aristotle's account of habituation extends well beyond the truism expressed in the phrase that 'we learn by doing'. At issue is *how* we learn by doing, or, as Aristotle himself asks at the outset of the *Eudemian Ethics*, 'how and by what sources does virtue arise?'. This, he says, is the 'most valuable' inquiry (1216b10–22). The inquiry, as conducted by Aristotle, leads to a rich and lasting theory which has at its centre the related beliefs that learning virtue is neither a mindless nor purely intellectual matter, and that the process requires practical reason and desire working in tandem throughout.[37]

[37] I have read versions of this chapter at the Conference on the Theory and Practice of Teaching Ethics, University of San Diego, February 1987, the University of Connecticut, and Lehigh University. I am grateful to Gerasimos Santas for his public comments on the version read in San Diego. I would also like to thank Ronald Polansky for his comments, and especially Richard Kraut, whose insightful criticisms prompted modification and revision of my views.

Index

Index Locorum